WIN-WIN

WIN-WIN

W. Edwards Deming,
the System of Profound Knowledge,
and the Science of Improving Schools

BY JOHN A. DUES
UNITED SCHOOLS NETWORK

GORHAM, MAINE

Copyright © 2023 | Myers Education Press, LLC

Published by Myers Education Press, LLC
P.O. Box 424 Gorham, ME 04038

All rights reserved. No part of this book may be reprinted or reproduced in any form or by any electronic, mechanical, or other means, now known or hereafter invented, including photocopying, recording, and information storage and retrieval, without permission in writing from the publisher.

Myers Education Press is an academic publisher specializing in books, e-books, and digital content in the field of education. All of our books are subjected to a rigorous peer review process and produced in compliance with the standards of the Council on Library and Information Resources.

Library of Congress Cataloging-in-Publication Data available from Library of Congress.

13-digit ISBN 978-1-9755-0581-3 (paperback)
13-digit ISBN 978-1-9755-0582-0 (library networkable e-edition)
13-digit ISBN 978-1-9755-0583-7 (consumer e-edition)

Printed in the United States of America.

All first editions printed on acid-free paper that meets the American National Standards Institute Z39-48 standard.

Books published by Myers Education Press may be purchased at special quantity discount rates for groups, workshops, training organizations, and classroom usage. Please call our customer service department at 1-800-232-0223 for details.

Cover design by Teresa Lagrange

Visit us on the web at **www.myersedpress.com** to browse our complete list of titles.

DEDICATION

For teachers and students everywhere, with you we can build an education system that enables Joy in Work & Learning for everyone.

CONTENTS

Foreword by David Langford	xi
Note from United Schools Network by Andrew Boy	xiii
Introduction: Deming & Profound Knowledge	xv
Chapter 1: System of Profound Knowledge	1
Chapter 2: Transformation from Mythology to the New Philosophy	23
Chapter 3: Principles for Transformation	41
Chapter 4: System Basics	73
Chapter 5: Using Systems Thinking	91
Chapter 6: Understanding Variation	113
Chapter 7: Using Knowledge about Variation	137
Chapter 8: Building Knowledge in Context	159
Chapter 9: Psychology's Role in Improvement	183
Chapter 10: A Win-Win for You	203
Glossary	215
Appendix A: Improvement Process	225
Appendix B: Creating a Process Behavior Chart	227
Acknowledgments	237
About the Author	239
Index	241

FOREWORD

First attending a Dr. W. Edwards Deming Four-Day Seminar in 1986 caused brain strain as Dr. Deming invalidated everything I was taught and had experienced concerning school management and learning. However, instinctively then and now, Deming's thinking is the answer to improving education systems. As an international trainer and consultant applying Deming thinking to improve education, 40 years of experience have proven that Deming was correct. In John Dues' book, *Win-Win*, John explains the same mental transformation he experienced while learning about Dr. Deming. He also relates the journeys of many other leaders living through the process of applying Deming thinking to education.

Moving to a Deming-based approach is a true personal transformation. The neural pathways of thinking about school management and learning facilitation are created and reinforced from childhood. These pathways must be disrupted for new learning to take place. The same failed education management is taught even today and supported by those who work in the education system. John lays out the case for new thinking and describes the components of a Dr. Deming education transformation.

John contacted me to talk about my Deming journey to quality education. Initially impressed with John's understanding of Deming's System of Profound Knowledge, I became convinced that he was committed to learning. We worked to deepen his knowledge over many months through an executive coaching cycle. When John received a continual improvement grant, we worked together to design and implement Continual Improvement Fellowships for staff at John's schools. Meeting every two weeks, we were able to coach teachers and administrators in their journeys to transform learning in their classrooms and schools. The fellowships were a gratifying and successful experience for everyone involved.

There are many pathways to begin learning and transforming education systems. However, John explains what Deming called a discontinuous journey. Over the last 40 years, everyone who seeks knowledge has had a discontinuous journey to understanding the Deming System of Profound

Knowledge application. This discontinuous learning is due to the fact that the learning and applications are so profound and offer such massive improvement potential that the human brain cannot absorb that much change quickly. Therefore, undertaking the Deming learning journey, applying, and changing systems over a long period is a continual effort, and what seems profound today will seem elementary years from now.

Struggling to make sense of Profound Knowledge, exceptionally Understanding Variation, probably means having the same schooling as most of us have experienced. Endeavoring to comprehend it will likely cause pauses while the brain assimilates knowledge and then seeks to apply it. This is what is meant by a discontinuous journey. If you love education and want the systems to survive and thrive, give this book to school board members, parents, administrators, teachers, and students to save our schools from destruction.

David P. Langford
Chief Executive Officer & Superintendent
Langford Learning

NOTE FROM UNITED SCHOOLS NETWORK

BY ANDREW BOY

The founding years at Columbus Collegiate Academy (CCA), the original school in what would become the United Schools Network (USN), were hard. The school launched in 2008 with 57 6th graders and six staff members in the basement of a church in the Weinland Park neighborhood of Columbus, Ohio. Resources were limited. There was no gym or green space or playground area for the students. Busing was inconsistent and unreliable. Every Monday, the classrooms had to be reset because the church we rented space from had Sunday services. These issues made student enrollment challenging as parents were faced with choosing between a promising new school with limited resources and their neighborhood schools. Staff who were already paid significantly less than their peers in nearby school districts had to endure pay cuts in years one and two. And yet, despite the obstacles, we were united around a simple belief: every child, regardless of zip code, deserved an outstanding education, and every child, regardless of background, could achieve outstanding results. Our students and staff proved the power of our model in our first year, gaining national recognition for our academic results.

It was on this foundation that USN has grown from a single school serving those 57 6th graders in 2008 to a network of four schools serving more than 1,000 students in 2022. Our student body mirrors the neighborhoods we serve: 100% of our students are economically disadvantaged, 86% are students of color, and 19% have identified disabilities. However, our students continue to outscore their neighborhood and district peers, proving what's possible in public education. At the heart of our success has always been a talented team of educators—eager to serve, to learn, and to improve.

John has been among the most dedicated and talented of those team members; he has been a trusted colleague, leader, and friend since we launched that first school in 2008. He led CCA as its school director and was recognized as the Ohio Charter School Leader of the Year near the end of his tenure there before transitioning to the Home Office team as we began to grow into a network of schools. No matter what role he has served in, be it teacher, building administrator, or systems leader, John has long been at the leading edge of the network's learning. Over the last several years, this focus has turned to studying W. Edwards Deming's System of Profound Knowledge and applying it to our schools. He has helped us all see the importance of thinking in systems, understanding variation in data over time, designing iterative tests of change to improve processes, and understanding the human side of change. Central to Deming's ideas is the Win-Win philosophy. As John says near the end of the book, "Ultimately, the goal of Win-Win and transformation is the optimization of systems within which we live and work, making it possible to realize the full potential of these systems and everyone working within them."

As schools emerge from the tumult of the last few years, this is a message we need now more than ever. Transformation to something better is possible. John's book helps show us the way.

INTRODUCTION

Deming & Profound Knowledge

The great moral teachers of humanity were, in a way, artistic geniuses in the art of living. [1]

—ALBERT EINSTEIN

O N THE EVENING OF July 13, 1950, W. Edwards Deming had a historic dinner with Ichiro Ishikawa and top officials from the leading Japanese industries at the Industry Club in Tokyo. These officials came by invitation to hear Deming speak and represented 80% of Japan's capital at a time when the country's economy was still reeling from the decimation from World War II. Over the next several decades, Deming would take 27 trips to Japan. What he taught the Japanese, beginning in 1950, combined with what he learned from Japanese quality leaders coalesced into the System of Profound Knowledge near the end of his life. Among the most important lessons he imparted to the Japanese during those initial meetings was the idea of appreciation for a system.

When Deming first arrived, he predicted that it would take five years for Japanese industries to begin to penetrate the world market if they followed his teachings. They bested that prediction and within four years some of Japan's products, such as cars, color TVs, and computer chips, began to make progress on the international stage. By the 1970s, American industry had lost 50% of its market share in sectors such as automobiles, consumer electronics, and medical equipment, among others, as the Japanese produced higher and higher quality products. By the 1980s, American business leaders were screaming about an unlevel playing field, demanding tariffs be placed on Japanese products. All the while, Japan's business sector, led by the Union of Japanese

Scientists and Engineers (JUSE), had instituted a quality revolution with a continual focus on improvement. Beginning in 1951 and annually since then, JUSE has awarded the Deming Prize to individuals who contribute to quality and to companies that achieved certain described standards of quality.[2]

It is this Japanese rise to prominence, and Deming's role in it, that Clare Crawford-Mason captured in the 1980 NBC documentary "If Japan Can, Why Can't We?" While the program was not a hit with the general public, it did send a shockwave through the American business sector. Soon after, these leaders were scrambling to find out more about this little-known 80-year-old statistician who had ushered in the quality revolution in Japan three decades earlier.

As Crawford-Mason's boss, Reuven Frank, had aptly noted when they first started the documentary project, W. Edwards Deming truly was "a prophet ignored in his own homeland." However, this all changed beginning in 1980 and continued until Deming's death on December 20, 1993. I think it is a fair assessment to say that Deming felt compelled to keep working far past a typical retirement age to spread what he had learned throughout the country he loved, now that people were finally taking his message seriously. This legacy continues through The W. Edwards Deming Institute, and through others who have seen the success that results from implementing his methods and the System of Profound Knowledge.

My hope is that I can live up to Deming's lofty ideals for those that have heard his message. Writing *Win-Win* is a first step on my journey to share what I've learned about his continual improvement methods so far. Ultimately, I'd like to play at least a small role in stewarding his message in the education sector for which he cared so deeply.

Defining Improvement

As you begin your own learning journey, I have a challenge for you. Get a piece of paper and a pen, and list examples of successful improvement efforts you've led in your school system before reading any further.

Once you have your list, let me provide you with the definition of improvement that will be foundational to the ideas presented throughout the book. *Improvement* results from fundamental changes you've made to some component of your system that do the following:

- alter how work or activity is done or the make-up of a tool;

INTRODUCTION

xvii

- produce visible, positive differences in results relative to historical norms; and

- have a lasting impact.[3]

Go back to your list and cross out any examples that don't meet all three conditions. If you're left with very few items or perhaps none at all, then this book is for you.

Subject-Matter Knowledge

When we as educational leaders are confronted with a problem, we typically assemble a school or district team to improve the problem. The team relies on the expertise they've acquired across their careers as classroom teachers, building administrators, and district level leaders. Let's call this subject-matter knowledge. It includes skills like classroom management, curriculum design, lesson delivery, and data-driven instruction, among many other activities. Subject-matter knowledge is critical for developing changes that result in improvement. While an obvious necessity, it alone is not sufficient. When serving on school and district leadership teams, I often felt that I was missing an important part of the improvement picture. These are the pieces of the puzzle no amount of subject-matter knowledge provides. These puzzle pieces include:

- seeing and understanding our organizations as complex systems;

- knowing when and how to react to changes in important data;

- understanding how to get potentially good ideas to work in our context; and

- understanding the role psychology plays in improvement work.

Profound Knowledge

W. Edwards Deming proposed a body of knowledge he called a "System of Profound Knowledge." Deming defined the System of Profound Knowledge as the interconnection of the theories of systems, variation, knowledge, and psychology. The ability to improve schools is enhanced when we join together subject-matter knowledge and profound knowledge in innovative ways. This interplay is illustrated in Figure 0.1.

Figure 0.1.
Increased Improvement Capability with Two Types of Knowledge

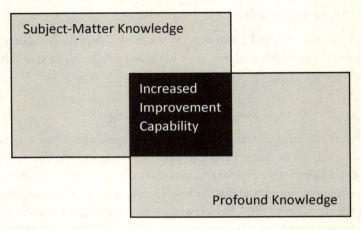

This latter type of knowledge is little known in the education sector, but it has long been utilized in industry and healthcare.[4] The System of Profound Knowledge is a lens, a theory by which to view our organizations differently. Deming described profound knowledge as having four interdependent components:

- Appreciation for a System
- Knowledge about Variation
- Theory of Knowledge
- Psychology

It is a management philosophy that provides the foundation for the methods, techniques, and tools used during improvement projects. It is a way of thinking with some tools attached.

Win-Win is for Systems Leaders

Win-Win is for systems leaders that lead our country's school districts, charter management organizations, and educational nonprofits and government agencies as well as for those that train these system leaders in our graduate schools of education. A leader of improvement does not need to be eminent in the four components of profound knowledge, but they do need to understand the basic theory, their interconnectedness, and why they are necessary

INTRODUCTION   xix

for these efforts. *Win-Win* provides this basic understanding. The aim of the book is to equip you with the knowledge and skills needed to harness the power of the System of Profound Knowledge in your own school improvement efforts.

What to Expect in Win-Win

The first two headings of each chapter include the aim or purpose of the chapter as well as an overview of the key concept. Other sections expand on the ideas from the chapter aim and key concept. What you will learn in each chapter is summarized below.

- **Chapter 1** defines the four components of the System of Profound Knowledge.

- **Chapter 2** defines transformation and describes commonly-held management myths.

- **Chapter 3** describes 14 principles for the transformation from the myths to a new philosophy.

- **Chapter 4** defines a system and describes the basic structure and components of a system.

- **Chapter 5** describes how to use systems thinking to optimize schools.

- **Chapter 6** introduces you to the Theory of Variation.

- **Chapter 7** teaches you how to interpret the variation in your data.

- **Chapter 8** describes how to use the Plan-Do-Study-Act (PDSA) cycle to build knowledge in your context.

- **Chapter 9** outlines several psychological concepts important for improvement efforts.

- **Chapter 10** provides you with guidance on how to get started using profound knowledge.

- **The glossary** defines terms that are important to understanding the science of improvement.

- **Appendix A** outlines a ten-step improvement process including guiding questions for each step.

- **Appendix B** is a step-by-step tutorial on how to create a process behavior chart.

United Schools Network

United Schools Network (USN) is a small, non-profit charter management organization in Columbus, Ohio. It serves as the district office for four public charter schools in the city. The basic design of USN is that one elementary and one middle school serve the east side of Columbus while one elementary and one middle school serve the west side of Columbus. Nearly all of the students that attend USN's schools are economically disadvantaged. I serve as the Chief Learning Officer of the network where one of my primary responsibilities is to lead continual improvement projects. Throughout the book, I use examples from my work at USN in order to make the theoretical concepts of the book more concrete. Table 0.1 serves as an overview of the network that may be helpful to reference when I use the schools in the example scenarios throughout the book.

Table 0.1.

United Schools Network's Organizational Overview

Organization	Grades	Founded	Neighborhood
Columbus Collegiate Academy	6-8	2008	Near East Side
Columbus Collegiate Academy-West	6-8	2012	Franklinton
Home Office (district office)	---	2013	Franklinton
United Preparatory Academy	K-5	2014	Franklinton
United Preparatory Academy-East	K-5	2017	King-Lincoln

Endnotes

1. I first encountered this quote in The Symphony of Profound Knowledge. Edward Martin Baker, *The Symphony of Profound Knowledge: W. Edwards Deming's Score for Leading, Performing, and Living in Concert* (Bloomington, IN: iUniverse, 2017), 3.

2. Peter Scholtes, *The Leader's Handbook: A Guide to Inspiring Your People and Managing the Daily Workflow* (New York: McGraw-Hill, 1998).

3. Gerald J. Langley, Ronald D. Moen, Kevin M. Nolan, Thomas W. Nolan, Clifford L. Norman, and Lloyd P. Provost, *The Improvement Guide: A Practical Approach to Enhancing Organizational Performance*, 2ⁿᵈ ed. (San Francisco: Jossey-Bass, 2009), 16.

4. Ibid.

CHAPTER ONE

System of Profound Knowledge

The System of Profound Knowledge provides a lens. It provides a new map of theory by which to understand and optimize organizations that we work in, and thus to make contributions to the whole country. [1]

—W. EDWARDS DEMING

How MANY OF YOU have pursued the school improvement magic bullet? The magic bullet has taken many forms across my more than two-decade career in education, and I suspect you'll recognize its siren song even if you haven't fallen prey yourself. It may have reared its head as a reading curriculum, an online tutoring platform, a revised organizational structure, or a new five-year strategic plan. You may have dabbled in all four of these areas—curriculum, online programs, human capital planning, and strategic initiatives—among many others. The attraction to these magic bullets doesn't seem to weaken, even when you recognize that there is no such thing.

There is an urgency to improve America's education system for good reason, especially in our nation's most disadvantaged schools post-pandemic. Attendance rates and test scores were low prior to the pandemic shutdowns of 2020, but those outcomes have dropped considerably in many places, even after returning to in-person learning. These schools are often chronically stressed work environments where of course it makes sense that educators are trying to latch on to any number of change ideas.

Unfortunately, these magic bullet school improvement ideas are pursued at tremendous costs in the form of time, money, and energy. Too often in our attempts to improve schools, we go fast, learn slowly, and fail to appreciate what it takes to make some promising idea work in practice. Left in the never-ending wake of good intentions are educators with initiative fatigue. After many cycles of this type of improvement effort in both traditional public and public charter schools with high economic disadvantage rates, the System of Profound Knowledge caught my attention.

Here's why.

A few years ago, I stumbled across a *U.S. News & World Report* cover story from 1991 entitled "History's Hidden Turning Points," which included a list of nine lesser-known but nonetheless world-changing events. The list included the mission of the Apostle Paul to spread Christianity during the first century A.D., Napoleon's conquest of Europe in the early 19th century, and the introduction of "The Pill" as a reliable form of birth control in 1960.[2] Among this list was W. Edwards Deming's guiding of the economic and quality miracle that occurred in Japan beginning in 1950. The full list of these events is captured in Table 1.1 that follows.

Table 1.1.

History's Hidden Turning Points

History's Hidden Turning Points (*U.S. News & World Report* cover story from April 22, 1991)
1. The Mission of the Apostle Paul (1st century, A.D.), which profoundly defined and expanded Christianity worldwide.
2. The Great Black Death Plague of Europe (starting in 1347).
3. The numerous unheralded discoveries of America (including the Phoenicians, c. 600 B.C., and the Norsemen, c. 1000 A.D.), prior to Columbus in 1492.
4. The Japanese total rejection of firearms for over 250 years in favor of the traditional samurai weapons (swords, etc.) from c. 1600 to c. 1850.
5. Napoleon's conquest of Europe (c. 1806).
6. Mark Twain's "Great American Novel," *Huckleberry Finn* (1885), which paved the way for many of the great authors that followed him (e.g. Jack London, F. Scott Fitzgerald, Hemingway, etc.).
7. America's misplaced support (starting in 1927) of China's Generalissimo and Madame Chiang Kai-shek, directly contributing to US involvement in both the Korean and Vietnam wars.
8. The introduction of "The Pill" as a reliable form of birth control (1960).
9. Dr. W. Edwards Deming's leading role in the Japanese quality and business miracle that occurred after World War II.

SYSTEM OF PROFOUND KNOWLEDGE

What was it exactly that put Deming on the list of historical turning points with such rarefied company? What was it that he did to guide the economic and quality miracle in Japan after World War II left the country devastated? These are the questions that drove me deep into the study of Dr. Deming and his System of Profound Knowledge. As an educator, I wanted to know if the System of Profound Knowledge could be applied to school improvement efforts to bring about a similar type of quality miracle. I'm thoroughly convinced that this is possible, so much so that it led me to write *Win-Win*.

Aim of this Chapter

The purpose of this chapter is to provide a foundation for the learning that will occur in the rest of the book. It includes the definition of the System of Profound Knowledge, an overview of each of its four components, and examples for how the theory can be applied in schools. It will make the case that the System of Profound Knowledge is the map of theory systems leaders need to bring about breakthrough improvements in the schools they lead, even if initially there is cognitive dissonance with some of the ideas.

What is the System of Profound Knowledge?

The *System of Profound Knowledge* is a management theory that can be used to guide school improvement efforts and, more broadly, to lead school systems. This theory was developed by W. Edwards Deming during more than six decades of continual improvement work across the globe. Deming gave us a way to view our organizations that was previously unknown; a lens that gives us profound knowledge about these organizations. *Profound knowledge* means a deep understanding of the organization itself or some process that is important to the organization. It is the interaction of the four components of the System of Profound Knowledge— (1) Appreciation for a System, (2) Knowledge about Variation, (3) Theory of Knowledge, and (4) Psychology—that give us the deep knowledge necessary to manage a complex organization such as a school system. When we lack profound knowledge, we are more likely to be enticed by fads of the day, the aforementioned magic bullets. We are also more likely to be swayed by the proverbial squeaky wheel or to overact to emotion. With it, we have a new map of theory by which to understand and optimize the organizations in which we work. It is through this lens that we can systematically make any number of decisions that arrive on our desk daily, be it evaluating the purchase of a new curriculum, deciding on a particular organizational structure, or reviewing a parent complaint.

As indicated by the arrow in Figure 1.1 below, the area in the Venn diagram where the four components intersect is where we gain profound knowledge, where we learn how to continually improve problems facing our organizations, and ultimately where transformation can occur (the concept of transformation will be explored in Chapters 2 and 3).

Figure 1.1.
Deming's System of Profound Knowledge

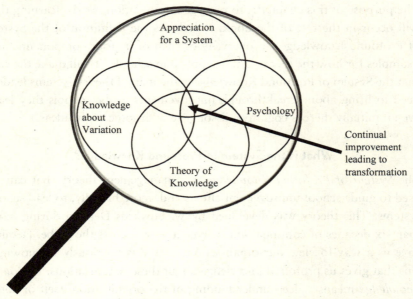

The use of the magnifying glass in Figure 1.1 was intentional; it signifies the idea of the System of Profound Knowledge as a lens through which to view our school systems as aided by each of the four components of profound knowledge. An introduction of each of the components follows.

Appreciation for a System

Dr. Deming recognized that organizations are indeed characterized by a set of interactions among the people who work there; the tools, methods, and materials they have at their disposal; and the processes through which these

SYSTEM OF PROFOUND KNOWLEDGE

people and resources join to accomplish its work. This is the essence of a system. *Appreciation for a System* quite literally means that we step back and see the organization we lead as a system. This results in management viewing the organization in terms of many internal and external interrelated connections and interactions, as opposed to discrete and independent departments or processes governed by various chains of command. When all the connections and interactions are working together to accomplish a shared aim, an organization can achieve tremendous results.[3]

In my experience, systems leaders fall short of this appreciation most commonly in two areas. First, we overemphasize the extent to which problems can be attributed to individual educators as opposed to the underlying system. Second, we often fail to appreciate the idea that improvement in one area of our school system can lead to a decline in performance in the system as a whole.

If you asked the typical school leader to show you their organizational structure, what would be produced would most likely look very much like Figure 1.2. It shows the 2018-19 organizational chart for one of the middle schools at United Schools Network.

Figure 1.2.
USN Middle School Organizational Chart (2018-19)

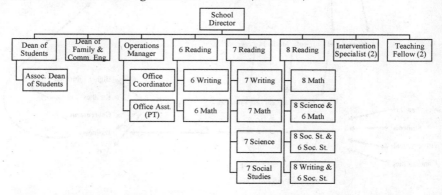

When this is the picture you have in your head when asked about the structure of your organization, it is only natural then that when developing improvement plans, you would almost exclusively focus on attempting to improve the people within the organization. This is what schools do when confronted with problems: they turn to professional development to improve the individual practice of teachers and administrators. However, despite spending billions on professional development activities in the United States, well-regarded studies by organizations such as the American Institutes for Research (AIR) and TNTP show no measurable results from this spending. This was the case even when the training was considered rigorously aligned to the tenets of best practice for educator professional development.[4]

I would contend that an underappreciation for systems and their complexity lies at the heart of this issue. After studying Deming's work in this area, I learned that one of the first things he taught the Japanese upon his arrival there in 1950 was that Japan must see itself as a system. A very different image begins to emerge when you view schools as a system, as do the possibilities for improvement. That same middle school whose organizational chart was displayed previously is illustrated in Figure 1.3 through a systems lens that I adapted from a diagram Deming displayed on a chalkboard in Japan.[5]

Figure 1.3.
USN Middle School: A Systems View

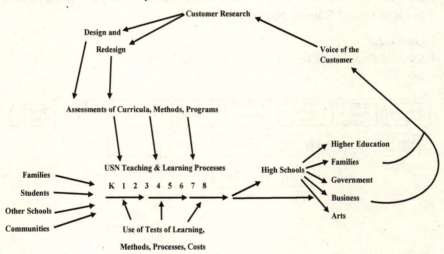

Source: Adapted from James F. Leonard, *The New Philosophy for K-12 Education: A Deming Framework for Transformation America's Schools* (Milwaukee, WI: ASQ Quality Press, 1996), 30.

SYSTEM OF PROFOUND KNOWLEDGE

Viewing the USN middle school as a system as displayed in Figure 1.3 opens numerous possibilities for improvement beyond simply working to improve the individuals who work in the school. In fact, it would be far more productive to work to improve the system in which the people work rather than solely focusing on the individual educator. To do this, it is helpful to see, understand, and improve the larger system in which the school operates. Deming stressed the following:

> *I should estimate that in my experience most troubles and most possibilities for improvement add up to proportions something like this: 94% belong to the system (responsibility of management), 6% special.*[6]

His point in saying this is that a tiny fraction of an organization's overall performance problems, the 6% special, can be attributed to individual performance issues. Instead, most of the causes of failure lie in how we organize the work we ask people to carry out. Deming taught us that improving quality in complex systems is not principally about individual competence, but rather about designing better systems.

When viewing the middle school through the lens of the organizational chart in Figure 1.2, that is hard to comprehend because all that you see is the individual workers. When viewing the system in which the middle school sits, as displayed in Figure 1.3, the view is far more revealing. The system is not only made up of the administrators and teachers within the school building, but also includes students and their families and the communities in which they live. It includes higher education as both a customer as well as a supplier of educators. It includes government and the resources it supplies to both the school and the community in which it is situated. The government also sets policies for the school, such as state learning standards and testing regimes. All of these are components of the system, and if, beginning with the school, you follow the arrows around the diagram, you start to appreciate the complexity. By following the arrows around the diagram, beginning with the school and moving to the right, then up, then left, and finally back down to the school, you see that the systems view also forms a feedback loop from which to learn. Viewed in this way, not only are there significantly more individual components to consider in the systems view, but there is also the interaction of these components that is important. Systems thinking expert

Dr. Russell Ackoff put it this way:

> A system is never the sum of its parts; it's the product of their interaction. The performance of a system doesn't depend on how the parts perform taken separately, it depends on how they perform together—how they interact, not on how they act, taken separately. Therefore, when you improve the performance of a part of a system taken separately, you can destroy the system.[7]

When the individual educators, organizational components, and the interactions between both the individuals and those components are considered, the idea that the system accounts for the vast majority of the variation in the outcomes that we see in schools becomes much clearer.[8] To be sure, there is a very small number of educators that do not belong in front of a classroom or leading a school building or district. However, most of the potential to eliminate poor performance in schools lies with improving the systems and processes through which work is done, not in changing the individual educators. Even in situations where it appears that an individual has done something wrong, the root of the problem often can be traced back to how that employee was trained, which is itself a type of systems problem. Once leaders recognize that systems create most of the problems, we can stop blaming individual educators and instead ask, "What in the system needs improvement?"[9]

Knowledge about Variation

Knowledge about Variation is a way of statistical thinking that allows us to distinguish between *common cause variation* and *special cause variation*, understand its causes, and predict behavior, all of which is key to management's ability to remove barriers and problems within a system.[10] This thinking is useful because there is variation in everything we observe and measure in schools. Knowledge about Variation provides a tool kit which allows us to understand this variation. Systems leaders are inundated with data, but what's much more difficult is knowing how to interpret and make sound decisions with it. Do this year's state test scores indicate that our district is improving? Was last month's drop in per pupil revenue a sign of things to come? Did attendance rates improve this week because of the intervention

SYSTEM OF PROFOUND KNOWLEDGE

we put in place or was it do to something else? The ability to answer questions like these is fundamental to our ability to make improvements.

USN's schools started the 2020-21 school year using a remote learning model. An 8th grade math teacher was concerned about daily engagement rates because of his experience with remote learning from the previous spring when schools were initially shut down due to the pandemic. He defined a student as engaged when they completed the math practice set that accompanied each lesson video. Table 1.2 displays the engagement rates for his students for the first 24 days of the school year.

Table 1.2.

8th Grade Math Engagement Data

Day 1	Day 2	Day 3	Day 4	Day 5	Day 6
62%	67%	75%	84%	77%	71%
Day 7	Day 8	Day 9	Day 10	Day 11	Day 12
58%	74%	64%	54%	61%	49%
Day 13	Day 14	Day 15	Day 16	Day 17	Day 18
75%	72%	72%	69%	60%	81%
Day 19	Day 20	Day 21	Day 22	Day 23	Day 24
72%	65%	55%	51%	68%	68%

If you were working with the 8th grade math teacher, what conclusions would you draw based on these data? Are engagement rates improving or declining? How do we improve engagement rates? Knowledge about Variation is needed to answer these questions and to take appropriate action.

W. Edwards Deming's understanding of variation was heavily influenced by Dr. Walter A. Shewhart, a physicist at Bell Labs who developed a theory for variation as well as a tool called a control chart in the 1920s. Control charts are sometimes referred to as Shewhart charts or process behavior charts. I've adopted the latter terminology because it better describes the purpose of the chart without the baggage of "control." As a result, I will use process behavior chart terminology going forward unless I am specifically talking about Shewhart's work.[11]

Shewhart's theory emphasizes the importance of plotting data over time, what I've come to call plotting the dots. Plotting data on a chart and connecting consecutive points with a line makes analysis far more intuitive than data stored in a table like Table 1.2. *Process behavior charts* examine data from a process (or system)[12] to determine if the process is predictable or unpredictable. Shewhart's Theory of Variation employs the process behavior chart to separate these two situations, the predictable and the unpredictable, based on the patterns of variation in our data over time. One pattern of variation includes common causes (aka *controlled variation* or *noise*). *Common cause variation* includes causes that are inherent in a process over time and affect every outcome of the process and everyone working in the process. A second pattern of variation includes special causes (aka *uncontrolled variation* or *signal*). *Special cause variation* is a name for sources of variation that are not part of the process all the time, or do not affect everyone, but arise because of specific circumstances. Figure 1.4 displays the math engagement data in a process behavior chart.

Figure 1.4.
X Chart: 8th Grade Math Engagement Data

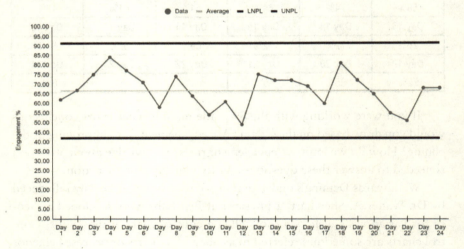

A process with predictable variation has only common causes affecting outcomes and is called a *stable process*. In this situation, the variation is the result of many different cause-and-effect relationships where no single cause is dominant over the others. Every process is subject to many cause-and-effect relationships, but in a stable process the net effect of all of these relationships is a sort of equilibrium.[13] This should not be taken to imply that there is no variation present or even that the variation is small within the process, but rather that it is predictable within statistically established limits.

SYSTEM OF PROFOUND KNOWLEDGE 11

The limits in the 8th grade math system are represented by the heavy black lines in Figure 1.4, the *Upper Natural Process Limit* (UNPL) and the *Lower Natural Process Limit* (LNPL). The limits and how they are determined will be discussed in greater detail in Chapter 7. The key take-way for now is that a system that is producing predictable results is performing as consistently as it is capable of doing. It is a waste of time to explain common cause variation in a stable system because there is no simple, single root cause for noise. Instead, if the results are unsatisfactory, the appropriate focus is working on fundamental changes to the system itself.

In contrast, a process whose outcomes are impacted by both common cause variation and special cause variation is called an *unstable process*. The instability does not in and of itself imply large variation, but rather that the changes from data point to data point are of such a magnitude as to be unpredictable. In an unstable process where special causes of variation are present, it is a waste of time to improve or change the system until it is stable and predictable. In this type of system, you must investigate and try to identify what causes the data points to be so different, and then to remove the special causes affecting the system in order to return it to a stable, predictable state.

The process behavior chart is the tool that allows us to determine what type of variation is present in our system and whether the system is stable or unstable. The inability to recognize the difference between common causes and special causes of variation is the source of tremendous confusion and wasted effort in the education sector. Deming categorized this misinterpretation as Mistake 1 and Mistake 2. *Mistake 1* occurs when we react to an outcome as if it came from a special cause, when it came from common causes of variation. Here we study and try to remove a non-dominant cause of the problem when the only way to improve is to fundamentally change the system. *Mistake 2* is the opposite. It occurs when you treat an outcome as if it came from common causes of variation, when it came from a special cause. Here we miss the opportunity to fix a specific, identifiable problem within our system.

In returning to the eighth-grade math engagement rates in Figure 1.4, we can learn a few important things. First, the data indicate a stable system because the plotted points for the first 24 days remain between the Upper and Lower Natural Process Limits. This means that we can reasonably expect that the engagement levels for this eighth-grade math class will produce similar results in the future. Second, in the first 24 days of remote learning, we don't see any signals or special causes of variation in the data. One indicator of a signal would be a single point outside of either of the Natural Process Limits. This means that there haven't been any significant events, either in a positive or a negative direction, to investigate in this eighth-grade math remote learning system. Third, it means that improvement can be achieved only through a fundamental change to the 8th grade math system.

Systems leaders equipped with Knowledge about Variation are able to determine if the variation of important outcomes of a process or system are due to common causes or special causes of variation. This knowledge can help you avoid Mistake 1 and Mistake 2. It can also assist you in charting a proper improvement roadmap while saving energy, time, and money.

Theory of Knowledge

How do we improve the math engagement rates displayed in Table 1.2? In other words, what would your theory be for improving these rates?

Don't get too caught up in the idea of theory. By *theory* I mean any set of assumptions that you use to predict what's going to happen in the future. Here, I simply mean the plan or strategy you'd suggest to improve those rates. The plan or strategy you choose is based on the prediction that it will improve the 8th grade math engagement rates, and your underlying rationale for your choice of plan or strategy is your theory. *Theory of Knowledge* then is the study of how what we think we know and claim to know actually is the way we claim it is.

Rational prediction requires theory. Theory is the basis of all investigation, and the basis for any action we take to attempt to improve systems within our organizations has to include testing our theories. W. Edwards Deming developed a tool called the Plan-Do-Study-Act cycle, or PDSA cycle, for this purpose. A PDSA is a learning cycle that mirrors the scientific method. A prediction (hypothesis) is detailed, data is collected to test the prediction, and the data is analyzed to determine to what extent the prediction was accurate. The accuracy of the prediction is an observable measure of the knowledge we have about the system under study. Given that all attempts to improve educational systems are social and human resource intensive activities, the critical question for PDSA cycles is not "What works?" but rather "What works, for whom, and under what set of conditions?" During the cycle, observed outcomes are compared to predictions and the differences between the two become the learning that drives decisions about next steps with the theory. The knowledge generated through each PDSA cycle ultimately becomes the evidence that some process, tool, or modified staff role or relationship works effectively under a variety of conditions and that quality outcomes will reliably ensue *in our system*.

The foundation of the Plan-Do-Study-Act cycle is the deductive and inductive learning that occurs as you move back and forth between the theory phase of the cycle and the application phase. The iterative nature of the PDSA cycle is illustrated in Figure 1.5.

Figure 1.5.
Learning and PDSA

Plan (theory) → Do-Study (application) → Act-Plan (theory) → Do-Study (application), etc.

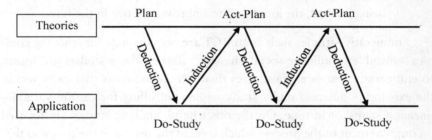

During the cycle, moving from planning to doing is deductive learning and moving from doing to studying is inductive learning. *Deductive learning* involves moving from a theory to the test of the theory. From Plan to Do is a deductive approach where a theory is tested with the aid of a prediction. In the Do phase, observations are made and differences from the prediction are noted. *Inductive learning* involves using results from the test to revise the theory. From Do to Study is an inductive approach where gaps or anomalies to the prediction are studied and the theory is updated accordingly. The final step in the PDSA cycle is to act on the learning from the phase which includes planning the subsequent cycle.[14]

Astute systems leaders reading this section on the Theory of Knowledge, especially those with a Ph.D., may very well be wondering by this point, "Where is the randomized trial?" The *randomized controlled trial* (RCT) sits atop the research method hierarchy in many fields, including education, and plays an important epistemological role as a mechanism to get at the "truth" about what works in schools. However, while the RCT is likely well-known as a research method amongst systems leaders, what is less appreciated are the limits of the RCT. Deming said that the purpose of any statistical study is to provide a rational basis for taking action, but that the important distinction between the type of study needed for a particular type of improvement centers on where the action will be taken. He classified studies into two categories according to the location of the action taken:

- An *enumerative study* is a statistical study in which action will be taken on the material within the frame being studied. The aim is estimation about some aspect of the group of items.

- An *analytic study* is a statistical study in which action will be taken on the process or cause system that produced the frame being studied, the aim being to improve practice in the future.[15]

Enumerative studies such as an RCT are not adequate for studying complex, unstable, nonlinear social change.[16] Rather, these studies are meant to enumerate, that is explain or evaluate, the conditions that exist within the existing population under study while controlling for certain variables during a snapshot in time. On the other hand, analytic studies are focused on improvement of the process which created the results of the past and that will continue creating future results. The domain of continual improvement is almost entirely focused on the ability to predict future performance using analytic studies within the local context, while including the variables for which the RCT controls.

Deming's conception of the Theory of Knowledge was significantly shaped by Shewhart's Theory of Variation. The process behavior chart displayed in Figure 1.4 is an attempt to define the actual present within the process limits. Shewhart used three-sigma, a concept that will be discussed in detail in Chapter 6, to define the limits; a choice he based on both statistical theory as well as his experience at Bell Labs.[17] The baseline 8th grade math engagement data provides an approximate range of the possible rates from that system in the future with the acknowledgement that you cannot determine with absolute certainty if the engagement rates will continue in a similar fashion or if special causes will occur. The engagement data is an example of an analytic study. Action would have to be taken on the 8th grade math causal system to improve performance in the future.

SYSTEM OF PROFOUND KNOWLEDGE

Like the engagement data, almost all data we are interested in to improve schools occurs across time, and in many cases this chronology is the point. It's the pattern that emerges from viewing the data in time order that gives us the most insight into what is happening with the data we are analyzing. This is what Deming indicated when he said that knowledge has temporal spread, meaning that our best understanding for how the processes and systems in our organizations are performing can only be interpreted after we view the variation of this data over time.

In addition to the PDSA, with its cycles of prediction and learning, the concept of operational definitions is another key component of the Theory of Knowledge. *Operational definitions* put communicable meaning into a concept and include a method of measurement or test as well as a set of criteria for judgment. Concepts that are important to schools, such as attendance, engagement, graduation, and learning, have no communicable value until they are expressed in operational terms. The learning that comes through PDSA cycles is meaningless in the absence of a shared definition for the concept under study because there is no true value for any measurement in and of itself.

Returning again to the 8th grade math engagement example, the importance of operational definitions became readily apparent as schools were shut down during the pandemic in the spring of 2020. Because of the speed with which schools had to transition to remote learning, we quickly learned that although the four schools within United Schools Network were reporting engagement levels, there wasn't a shared operational definition. There is no true value for this concept until there is a set of criteria to determine when a student has been engaged as well as a method for measuring engagement.

USN's two middle schools are located just five miles from each other, but they initially had two very different conceptions of engagement. In one middle school, students had to complete the lesson practice in its entirety to be counted as engaged. In the other middle school, students were counted as engaged if the lesson practice was at least partially completed. By the time the following school year began, both schools had elected to use the more rigorous definition of engagement where students had to complete the practice set that accompanied a lesson in its entirety. With the definition in place, we then were able to turn our attention to building a measurement system that allowed us to assess the capability, stability, and variation within our remote learning system. This example about the transition to remote learning exemplifies the power of operational definitions. They make it possible to share meanings for the concepts that we measure to avoid misunderstandings and conflicts, and ultimately so that we can both communicate during change efforts and have a clear yardstick to tell if these efforts did in fact lead to improvement.

Without theory, there is no way to use the information that streams into our educational systems. The Theory of Knowledge can assist us as systems leaders to accumulate local reports of effectiveness of improvement ideas juxtaposed against sometimes contradictory findings in the literature. This brings us to an important question. What happens when the learning from PDSA cycles suggests one course of action while evidence from more formal methods suggest another?

Here an analogy may help. If I am a ship's captain, then general navigation theory will serve me well while crossing the open ocean. However, as I approach the Eastern seaboard of the United States, say near the Port of Baltimore, at the point I enter the port I turn navigation over to the local harbormaster. This is done because the harbormaster has practical knowledge about how to take the ship in and out of this particular port. In the context of the 8th grade math system, the harbormaster is the teacher, the students, and others who are working on the ground in the USN school where the engagement data is being generated. General navigation theory is analogous to the teacher understanding the research-literature on engaging middle school students. This is the knowledge generated by controlled scientific studies. While important, the knowledge generated by the teacher running PDSA experiments with her or his students to increase remote learning engagement rates is an arguably more important and seldom appreciated component of the organizational improvement process. General navigation theory brings you to the entrance of the port where the local knowledge of the harbormaster becomes of supreme importance. Theory of Knowledge give us the tools to generate the local knowledge necessary to navigate the port, that is, the actual classrooms and schools where we find ourselves daily.

Psychology

The four components of the System of Profound Knowledge interact with each other and cannot be separated. For example, as outlined in the previous section, the Theory of Knowledge relies on one's ability to separate statistical variation into common and special causes to learn about and

SYSTEM OF PROFOUND KNOWLEDGE

improve a system. Each part of Profound Knowledge is interdependent and equal in importance. Nonetheless, in my study, if there is one of the four components that seems to flow through each of the others, it is psychology. *Psychology* involves understanding the actions and reactions of people in everyday circumstances.

An improvement leader must understand the psychology of individuals, the psychology of groups, the psychology of society, and the psychology of change. Knowledge of the human side of change helps us to understand not just the individuals within our education systems, but also how those individuals interact with each other, as well as how individuals interact with the system itself. The field also helps inform how people will react during improvement efforts, including their commitment to any changes being made to the system.

In any activity where we are the system and process owners, we know where we stand, what we are trying to accomplish, and why we are trying to accomplish it. This pride of ownership of the outcomes of any activity naturally leads to finding value in the activity itself. The psychological component of W. Edwards Deming's System of Profound Knowledge maintains that internal states within each of us explain and produce our behavior. When the focus is shifted to extrinsic incentives (e.g., merit pay, grades, etc.), the potential for system distortion and individual motivation to focus predominately on rewards becomes much more likely. In both our work and school systems, much game playing and manipulation takes place in getting into top positions. I believe it is in part this game playing and manipulation that led Deming to say that in large measure, school and work systems have eliminated natural joy in learning, personal motivation, and self-esteem, as well as decreased people's willingness to cooperate with each other. What then are the psychological concepts we must attend to as systems leaders to create systems where joy in learning, personal motivation, self-esteem, and cooperation are the norm?

Before exploring the concepts, let's ground ourselves in a basic orientation of systems leadership. If you asked the typical American manager, be it the superintendent of a school system or the CEO of a large corporation, "What is your job?," how would they respond? How would you respond?

My hunch is that most would say something to the effect of, "to motivate the employees in my organization to work hard and to do their best." This approach lacks an understanding of the basic principles of motivation.

We would be better served if we saw our role not as chief motivator, but rather as the person responsible for removing the obstacles to attaining joy in work within our system. It's a subtle but important distinction when you start thinking about removing obstacles versus spending time and energy constructing incentive systems that are misaligned to the important psychological concepts to which Deming pointed when developing the System of Profound Knowledge.

Returning to these concepts, first, we must avoid the cognitive bias social psychologists have dubbed the *Fundamental Attribution Error*. It describes the tendency to underestimate the impact of situational factors on other people's behavior and to overestimate the impact of individual factors. In describing our own performance, we do the reverse. For example, in the 8th grade math system discussed throughout this chapter, we may attribute low engagement rates to the teacher's lack of dedication and skill in creating strong remote lessons. If, however, we were the math teacher and got the very same results, we may attribute the low rates to a lack of technological resources rather than to our own skill as a teacher. It is easier to blame individual educators than to carefully consider how the system impacts performance.

Second, variation in personal preferences, motivations, and goals is the norm. This is likely obvious to educators who have spent any time in classrooms, as it is with parents with multiple children. Even within our own households, family members often differ in how they learn, in their needs, and in their beliefs and values. Given that these differences extend to those who share DNA and home environments, clearly this will be the case in educational systems with a diversity of people on any number of dimensions.

Third, behavior is driven by motivation. However, the behavior that we observe is only the tip of the iceberg where what remains unseen and unclear are the underlying motivations for the behavior. Taking the time to understand this underlying motivation rather than relying only on the observed behavior is a critical component of leading systems and improvement efforts within those systems.

Fourth, there are intrinsic and extrinsic sources of motivation. *Intrinsic motivation* is the natural form of positive motivation which comes from within the individual.[18] When motivation is intrinsic, satisfaction comes from the activity itself. *Extrinsic motivation* refers to external processes applied to individuals or organizations, such as rewards and punishments, used to influence people to improve performance (e.g., merit pay, grades, etc.).[19] When

SYSTEM OF PROFOUND KNOWLEDGE

motivation is extrinsic, the satisfaction people get from a learning or work activity comes from outside the activity itself. While people are differentially motivated by intrinsic and extrinsic factors, total submission to extrinsic motivators can be destructive. System leaders that have clearly articulated the core purpose of the organization can more readily tap into the intrinsic motivation of the people who work there when improvement efforts are aligned to the purpose that attracted people to the organization in the first place.

However, attracting a workforce aligned to your organization's core purpose is necessary, but insufficient during improvement efforts. Even if the core organizational purpose is well-understood, that doesn't mean that there will be automatic buy-in to proposed change ideas. For this purpose, at USN we've adopted a framework to evaluate the utility and buy-in of change ideas being tested through the PDSA cycle. The five dimensions include relative advantage; simplicity; trialability; measurability and observability;, and compatibility. These five dimensions are briefly defined in Table 1.3. They are very similar to the framework proposed by Everett Rogers to facilitate the adoption of innovations.[20]

Table 1.3.

PDSA Change Idea Scorecard

Dimension	Definition
Relative Advantage	The degree to which an innovation is perceived as better than the idea it supersedes.
Simplicity	The degree to which an innovation is perceived as simple to understand and use.
Trialability	The degree to which an innovation can be tested on a small scale.
Measurability & Observability	The degree to which the use of an innovation and the results it produces are visible and measurable to those who should consider it.
Compatibility	The degree to which an innovation is perceived as being consistent with the existing values, experiences, beliefs, and needs of potential adopters.

At the start of the psychology section, I mentioned the importance of the interactions between each of the four components of the System of Profound Knowledge. I gave an example of the connection between Knowledge about Variation and Theory of Knowledge. The PDSA Change Idea Scorecard offers another example of these interactions, this time between Theory of Knowledge and Psychology. Some knowledge of each of the four components is essential, including understanding the human side of change. A potentially effective change idea is useless without buy-in and understanding from those that will ultimately be responsible for its implementation. Understanding the psychological concepts discussed in this section—the Fundamental Attribution Error, differences among people, underlying motivations for observed behaviors, and extrinsic and intrinsic motivators—complement Appreciation for a System, Knowledge about Variation, and Theory of Knowledge as we learn to design better systems.

Endnotes

1. "Quotes," The W. Edwards Deming Institute, accessed October 5, 2021, deming.org/quotes/10148/.

2. Daniel J. Boorstin and Gerald Parshall, "History's Hidden Turning Points," *U.S. News and World Report,* April 22, 1991, 52-66.

3. "Appreciation for a System," The W. Edwards Deming Institute, accessed August 25, 2022, https://deming.org/appreciation-for-a-system/.

4. "The Mirage: Confronting the Hard Truth about Our Quest for Teacher Development," TNTP, accessed October 24, 2017, https://tntp.org/publications/view/the-mirage-confronting-the-truth-about-our-quest-for-teacher-development.

5. W. Edwards Deming, *The New Economics for Industry, Government, Education, 3rd ed.* (Cambridge, MA: The MIT Press, 2018), 39.

6. W. Edwards Deming, *Out of the Crisis* (Cambridge, MA: MIT, Center for Advanced Engineering Study, 1986), 315.

7. The Deming Cooperative, "2003 Ackoff Seminar Part 1 of 4," YouTube, July 1, 2019, https://www.youtube.com/watch?v=a0ooqJ-pOH4&t=366s&ab_channel=TheDemingCooperative.

8. Joseph Juran estimated this to be 85% system and 15% individual while Deming attributed up to 98% of the performance variance to the system, depending on the situation.

9. Peter R. Scholtes, Brian L. Joiner, and Barbara J. Streibel, *The Team Handbook*, 3rd ed. (Edison, NJ: Oriel STAT A MATRIX, 2010).

10. "Knowledge of Variation," The W. Edwards Deming Institute, accessed August 25, 2022, https://deming.org/knowledge-of-variation/.

11. For a more in-depth explanation for the rationale of using process behavior chart as opposed to control chart see: Donald J. Wheeler, *Understanding Variation: The Key to Managing Chaos,* 2nd ed. (Knoxville, TN: SPC Press, 2000), 139-143.

SYSTEM OF PROFOUND KNOWLEDGE

12. I use process and system to mean the same thing throughout the book. The 8th grade math class's remote learning system or process is what is under study. This system or process produced the engagement rates displayed in Table 1.2 and Figure 1.4.

13. Donald J. Wheeler, *Making Sense of Data: SPC for the Service Sector* (Knoxville, TN: SPC Press, 2003), 97.

14. Gerald J. Langley, Ronald D. Moen, Kevin M. Nolan, Thomas W. Nolan, Clifford L. Norman, and Lloyd P. Provost, *The Improvement Guide: A Practical Approach to Enhancing Organizational Performance,* 2nd ed. (San Francisco: Jossey-Bass, 2009), 82.

15. The W. Edwards Deming Institute, "Mike Tveite on Enumerative and Analytic Studies." YouTube, May 29, 2013, https://youtu.be/LqXKZv_uM8Q.

16. Donald M. Berwick, "The Science of Improvement," *Journal of the American Medical Association* 299, no. 10 (March 12, 2008): 1182-1184.

17. Rocco J. Perla, Lloyd P. Provost, and Gareth J. Parry, "Seven Propositions of the Science of Improvement: Exploring Foundations," *Q Manage Health Care* 22, no. 3 (July-September 2013): 170-186.

18. David Langford, *Quality Learning Training Manual,* Version 12.0 (Langford International, 2008), Reference Material – 9.

19. Ibid., Reference Material – 8.

20. Everett M. Rogers, *Diffusion of Innovations,* 5th Ed. (New York: Free Press, 2003).

CHAPTER TWO

Transformation from Mythology to the New Philosophy

People are asking for better schools with no clear idea how to improve education, nor even how to define improvement in education. [1]

—*W. EDWARDS DEMING*

A NATION AT RISK was published by the National Commission on Excellence in Education in April 1983. The report cited statistics such as: "The SAT demonstrates a virtually unbroken decline from 1963 to 1980. Average verbal scores fell over 50 points and average mathematics scores dropped nearly 40 points." The report did not mince words and, in addition to the alarming statistics, it included a number of memorable lines including the following:

> We report to the American people that while we can take justifiable pride in what our schools and colleges have historically accomplished and contributed to the United States and the well-being of its people, the educational foundations of our society are presently being eroded by a rising tide of mediocrity that threatens our very future as a Nation and a people.[2]

The purpose of the report was "to help define the problems afflicting American education and to provide solutions..."[3] In other words, it was meant to awaken the American public to the problems afflicting its schools. Awaken it did; the report has been referenced in countless books and articles in the subsequent four decades and served as the foundation for many of the education reforms that have been undertaken since the report was published, including Goals 2000, No Child Left Behind, and Race to the Top.

Less than a decade after *A Nation at Risk* was published, a far lesser-known follow-up report was commissioned by the Department of Energy. Prior to my research for this book, I in fact had never heard of the *Sandia Report* named for the engineers from the Sandia National Laboratories who authored it. They had set out to create economic forecasts and were not centrally concerned with education test scores. However, they were quite surprised by what they found when they completed their own analysis of the education data from *A Nation at Risk*. On nearly every measure of achievement, the Sandia analysts found steady or slightly improving trends.[4]

While it was true that SAT scores had declined from the early 1960s until the early 1980s as *A Nation at Risk* asserted, this data lacked important context. It is this context that led Sandia's authors to the conclusion that the decline in average scores did not mean that more recent high school students weren't as capable as their peers in the 1960s.

How could this be?

When the Sandia researchers broke the test scores out by subgroups of students (e.g., race, socioeconomic status, class rank, etc.), they found steady or improving scores for all groups. This seemingly confounding finding can be attributed to a statistical phenomenon called Simpson's Paradox, which occurs when trends that appear in an aggregated data set (as in *A Nation at Risk*) reverse when the data is separated into subgroups (as in the *Sandia Report*). In other words, the declining SAT results underscore a more diverse mix of students taking the test over time rather than decreasing student performance. Similarly, the Sandia researchers found steady or slightly improving trends on nearly every measure they investigated, including dropout statistics, standardized tests, postsecondary studies, educational funding, and international assessment comparisons.

There are two seemingly counterintuitive ideas here. On the one hand, I don't believe that there is evidence that schools have been on a steady decline for the last 50-60 years. This was the thesis of *A Nation at Risk*; one that many others have picked up on since then. On the other hand, I believe that to achieve equitable outcomes for all students, schools must undergo a transformation on an order of magnitude seldom seen in the history of organizations. On their face, these two ideas may seem to be mutually exclusive, but the opposite is true. Test scores are a narrow definition of success, and while they could potentially provide useful information to educators and policy makers, they are more of an inspection and sorting mechanism than an improvement tool.

The Sandia authors drew a similar conclusion in 1992 despite the steady or improving trends they noted in their analysis. An excerpt from their report stated

> First, it is not clear to us that all the measures analyzed by us and others are appropriate barometers of performance for the education system (recall that our selection criterion was that a measure be popular, not necessarily appropriate). Thus, the trend data on some of these measures, positive or negative, may be irrelevant. Second, even if a particular measure is appropriate, steady or slightly improving performance may not be adequate to meet future societal requirements in an increasingly competitive world. Finally, in some appropriate measures, the performance of the U.S. education system is clearly deficient.[5]

For most people, what they saw in the educational data from the last half century or so depends in large part on what they thought about our country's schools beforehand. The authors of *A Nation at Risk* started with the premise that our schools were on the decline, and that's what they found. That's what makes the *Sandia Report* so unique. The authors saw themselves as outsiders expecting to verify the findings of the commission. Instead, they came to very different conclusions. And yet, it is the central premise of *A Nation at Risk* that has come to dominate the narrative around our schools.

I chose to introduce Chapter 2 with the juxtaposition of these two reports to illustrate a key point about the education reform battles. There are so many agendas in these battles that it is hard to get to at the real truth about how our schools are performing. *A Nation at Risk* drew the conclusion that our schools were in decline, but this conclusion was based on oversimplified and cherry-picked data. A better, more nuanced analysis came along in the *Sandia Report*, but it has garnered significantly less attention and has had much less influence on the educational policy front. Test scores and other similar measures of performance change over time, sometimes improving and sometimes declining. The *Sandia Report* provided a number of useful insights that could potentially facilitate sound data-based decision-making. I'm certainly not arguing that this type of decision-making should be abandoned if it is as free as possible of preconceived notions and political agendas. But, and this is a big but, to achieve this, the decision-making must sit on top of a solid philosophical foundation.

Aim of this Chapter

The purpose of this chapter is to make the case for transformation from the prevailing style of management to the Deming philosophy. It is on this sound philosophical foundation that our education system should stand, rather than constantly shifting in the wind based on management mythology, the latest testing data points, and political pet projects. Perhaps the most radical idea put forth by Deming is the idea that any outcome we see within our system is the result of more than the skills and efforts of the individuals who work within the organization. Most of the performance differences observed between individuals are generated by the complex and dynamic system in which workers are only one part. Understanding this idea and moving away from a number of common management myths may be the most important part of the new philosophy.

What is transformation?

Transformation implies a change in state from one thing to another. W. Edwards Deming pushed us to transform from the prevailing style of management, a modern invention that seeds "competition between people, teams, departments, pupils, schools, universities," to a new philosophy of management. The transformation will allow everyone to work together as a system, with the goal of allowing everybody to win. He was advocating for cooperation and transformation to this new style of management.[6]

The route to transformation is what Deming called *Profound Knowledge*. Even though it has been three decades since he described his theory for transformation, the prevailing system of management is still the dominant management philosophy in school systems. This prevailing system is rooted in a management mythology, a false foundation. Table 2.1 outlines a few examples of faulty practices from the prevailing style of management and better practices from the new philosophy. The right side of the table outlines the relationship between each of the better practices to the four components of Profound Knowledge. It will be helpful to pause here and review Table 2.1. For each of the pairs of "Present Practices" and "Better Practices," put

TRANSFORMATION FROM MYTHOLOGY TO THE NEW PHILOSOPHY 27

a check mark in the box that best describes your organization. Then, study the relationship between the pairs of practices and Profound Knowledge. The System of Profound Knowledge is the light that illuminates the path to transformation and the new philosophy for educational systems leadership.

Table 2.1.

Transforming Faulty Practices Using Profound Knowledge

Present Practice	Better Practice	Relationship with Profound Knowledge			
		System	Variation	Knowledge	Psychology
Lack of constancy of purpose. Short-term thinking. Emphasis on immediate results. Think in the present tense; not the future.	Adopt and publish a constancy of purpose. Do long-term planning. Ask the question: "Where do we wish to be five years from now? Then ask, "By what method?	System has an aim. Stay true to the aim. The aim is a value judgment. The system includes the future.	Understand the distinction between enumerative and analytic problems (see p. 14).	A focus on common purpose enables better theory building. No number of successes in short-term problems will ensure long-term success.	Constant change confuses people who work in the system; working to a common purpose facilitates clarity, relationship-building, and trust.
Ranking students, teachers, teams, schools; reward at the top and punish at the bottom.	Abolish ranking. Manage the whole organization as a system. Study and understand how every component contributes to optimization of the system.	The system is responsible for most of the observed variation. Ranking does not help anyone improve nor help the system improve.	Ranking people within the common cause system is misleading. There will always be variation.	Ranking is a snapshot and does not take into account temporal spread (i.e., performance over an extended time period).	Debilitating and perceived to be arbitrary. Pygmalion effect[i] begins and destroys cooperation. People are different from one another.
Management by results. Take immediate action on any fault, complaint, delay, test data. Act on the last data point.	Understand and improve the process that produced the negative results within the system.	Most results belong to the system.	Understand the distinction between common and special causes to understand the kind of action to take (see p. 14).	Consistently making Mistake 1 or Mistake 2 (see p. 11).	People take credit or get blamed; fundamental attribution error (see p. 18).

Adapted from: Moen, Ronald D. & Norman, Clifford L. "Always Applicable." *Quality Progress,* June 2016, 52.

[i] In one landmark 1968 study, teachers were told by researchers that certain students in their classes had performed well on a test that predicts intellectual growth. In truth, these students had been randomly selected by the researchers to be described as high performing for the purposes of the experiment. These students were distinguished only by their teachers' expectations for their performance. Eight months later, those randomly selected scholars described to the teachers as high performing had significantly outperformed their peers on IQ tests. And the teachers themselves consistently described the "bloomer" students as better behaved, more academically curious, more likely to succeed, and more friendly than other students in the class.

Education Reform in the Age of Management Mythology

W. Edwards Deming often began his famous four-day seminars by saying that management is living in an age of mythology. This idea applies just as well today as it did in the 1980s and early 1990s when Deming was delivering these seminars to tens of thousands of people each year. It also applies just as well to educators as it did to the industry and government leaders that predominantly made up his seminar audiences. By "age of mythology," he meant that leaders of industry, government, and education alike operate according to assumptions and myths that harm their organizations. Transformation is the process of understanding these assumptions and myths and then working to move away from them. The rest of this chapter will describe the assumptions and mythology of the prevailing system of management on which Deming railed. Chapter 3 will describe a set of principles for transformation to the new philosophy.

Management Myth Origins

The evolution of management practices can be tracked across four broad themes over the last few centuries. First, there was management by doing the work yourself. Think here of farmers in their fields or craftsmen in their workshops. Second, there was management by directing. Think here of the craftsman taking on and teaching an apprentice. Third, there was management by results. Think here of numerical quotas and the quip, "I don't care how you do it, just get it done." Third-generation management practices were the dominant paradigm of the 20th century and continue in many organizations to this day. Fourth, there was management by method. W. Edwards Deming urged leaders to move from third-generation to fourth-generation management. He was calling on leaders to work with people on methods rather than judging them on results.[7]

While myths can help us understand the world, Deming saw many traditional management myths as erroneous and lacking sound theoretical foundations. Many school system leadership ideas have come from industry and government and are built on these same false premises and beliefs. A good example of a false belief is the idea that "if you can't measure it, you can't manage it." As I studied Deming's written work and watched recordings of his seminars over the last several years, I've gotten quite good at picking out quotes that have been misattributed to him or ideas of his that have been misunderstood. The aforementioned idea may be the most mis-quoted and misunderstood of all. What he actually said was, "It is wrong to suppose that if you can't measure it, you can't manage it—a costly myth."[8] Deming was a statistician, so of course he believed in the value of using data to help improve the management of organizations. However, he also believed that looking at data wasn't enough, that many things that cannot be measured must still be managed, and that there are many things that leaders must make decisions about that cannot be measured.

Another myth is rooted in the basic idea that we should rate and rank people in our society, be it in schools or at work, based on their individual performance. This assumes that problems are always the result of people working within the system, as opposed to the underlying system itself. This focus on individual performance is so fundamental to our society that I suspect many of us have never even stopped to question it. After a few years studying the Deming philosophy, I've become much more comfortable with this idea, but I type these words with trepidation about the pushback that may come as a result. Individuals have agency for sure, but that idea does not reduce the role of systems on performance.

The rest of this chapter will be spent describing other common management myths Deming worked to dispel. As you read the myths, it is important to keep in mind that you may very well experience some cognitive dissonance. For example, Deming went so far as to label the merit system among the forces of destruction, the costs to society for which he said were "unknown and unknowable."[9] There is a counterintuitive thread to much of the Deming philosophy, which of course makes sense given that he advocated for a change from the prevailing system of management to something better. It is also important to understand that there may be some kernels of truth within the myths that are explored; the key is to understand why the overarching idea is in fact a myth. It is with an eye toward nuance that I'll attempt to unpack the various myths in the following sections.

Myth of Best Practices

Over the last two decades, I've gone on dozens of school visits across the United States. My travels have taken me to traditional public, public charter, and private schools in the southern, midwestern, western, and northeastern parts of the country. On the one hand, these visits were extremely beneficial because I was able to observe classroom and school practices in many different places. I was able to speak with teachers, building administrators, and district leaders about innumerable challenges and how these leaders addressed the challenges with innovative solutions. While I was always careful to study the context of the places I visited, I repeatedly underestimated the challenges inherent in trying these innovative solutions in the schools where I worked.

Over time, I've grown more skeptical of best practices because of the importance of the context within which they evolve while, of course, assuming there is in fact evidence that they do work. On the former point, I've come to the realization that there is too often a significant underappreciation for the contextual elements in which "best practices" operate. For example, it is often assumed that a practice or program that works in one high-poverty school or district can be dropped into another such place that shares similar poverty rates without accounting for the myriad other factors that vary considerably between the two places. On the effectiveness of various best practices, I've found the evidence base in the educational literature is often exceedingly thin for many such practices and programs.

Because of this, we'd be wise to heed Deming's warning, "to copy is to invite disaster" to avoid the myth of best practices.[10] Studying a school and its practices without understanding the underlying theory for these practices as well as the context in which they work can in fact lead to disaster.

Myth of the Hero Educator

Similar to any area of life, there are outlier educators with exceptional and rare talents. One of the best-known movies depicting an outlier, a hero teacher if you will, is *Stand and Deliver*. The film famously depicts Jaime Escalante leading his 18 inner-city math students from basic math to calculus in just two years' time. In reality, it took Escalante eight years to build the math program depicted in the movie. During this time, he completely revamped the math department at Garfield High School, starting out by convincing the school's principal to raise math requirements. He also designed a pipeline of courses to prepare students for AP calculus, hand-selected top teachers to instruct those courses, and even convinced feeder junior high schools to offer algebra to 8th graders.

None of Escalante's students moved from basic math one year to AP calculus the following year.[11] Instead, progress was achieved over time through

TRANSFORMATION FROM MYTHOLOGY TO THE NEW PHILOSOPHY 31

system transformation at Garfield with the cooperation of many educators and students. Still, most educators won't rival Escalante's tenacity and results; his performance is so far outside the norm that a movie was made about him. However, Knowledge about Variation tells us that the vast majority of educators perform within the enabling or constraining forces of an organization's systems.[12] Our society has the tendency to create mythologies around heroes that are often embellished, leaving out important details (such as those in *Stand and Deliver*). On the other side of the performance spectrum, there are educators who are unfit for their present jobs. The heroes and those unfit for their present jobs represent a tiny fraction of the educator workforce. All of this points to the fact that focusing on the system is where the vast majority of the improvement potential lies. The hero educator myth makes for good drama in Hollywood, but a poor strategy for educational transformation and improvement.

Myth of Performance Appraisals (and Rating & Ranking Employees)

Organizational leaders must provide direction and feedback to team members, but this is far from synonymous with administering performance appraisals. Performance appraisals are more about control than they are about providing direction. They are more about evaluation and judgment than they are about giving feedback for improvement purposes. There are four parts to the typical performance appraisal. First, standards are set. Second, there is a time limit set by which to meet the standards. Third, observations and judgments are made. Finally, the evaluation is given to the individuals by those in the hierarchy. The problem is that performance appraisals fail to consider the role of the system on individual performance and fail to appreciate the variation in performance attributable to common causes.

The idea of the performance appraisal, or teacher evaluation system as it's called in our sector, is like a lot of management practices in educational systems. It has been my experience that discussions about these evaluation systems are always about how to improve them. In learning about the Deming philosophy, I've learned that a better line of analysis about any number of typical management practices in school systems is thinking through their purpose. Questions like, "Is management practice X useful in the first place?" or "On what premise do we know the usefulness of management practice X?"

In the case of the performance appraisal, another key question is, "What are the factors that differentiate highly-rated versus lower-rated people?" According to Peter Scholtes, there are five such factors:

A. Native ability and/or early education
B. Individual effort
C. Training and orientation on the job
D. Variability of processes and systems of work
E. The system of evaluation itself

If you look closely, only one item on this list is within the control of the individual employee. That is, individual effort. The other four factors have nothing to do with individual performance, and yet performance appraisal systems purport to be able to solve the following equation for the value of B: $A + B + C + D + E = 100$. If this equation is not solvable then you cannot evaluate the individual employee; in attempting to do so you must disregard the contributions of the system on the rating. Much of the credit and blame within the individual evaluation is actually attributable to others, an issue that will come up in the next section on merit pay as well.[13]

A by-product of performance appraisal as a management practice is that these systems actually make it more difficult to improve the organization as a whole. For one, they can result in mediocrity. Safe goals are set to protect the negative impact that falling short of goals could have on your rating; this is especially the case if the evaluations are tied to compensation. Even worse, systems are manipulated for individual gain rather than optimized for whole system improvement. Rating and ranking an employee instills fear and disincentivizes cooperation. Instead of performing this time-consuming sorting ritual, leaders' time would be better spent working to understand how the system interacts with employees to produce organizational performance.

Myth of Merit Pay (and Rating & Ranking Employees)

Merit pay has been proposed as a reform idea in education going back to at least the Reagan administration. Since the 1980s, the idea has been taken up by governors and presidents, most recently during the Obama administration through the Race to the Top legislation. The theory behind these proposals is that merit pay is a motivator; basically, that the chance to make more money will drive improvements in our schools. It is worth noting here that the discussion that follows is solely focused on merit pay in education and not on whether teacher base salary levels are adequate; that is a separate discussion topic altogether.

There are several problems with the merit pay theory. There is the problem of defining a meaningful measure of performance by which to judge individual educators. There have been advancements in statistical measures of academic growth and computing power since the Reagan administration, but Deming's assessment of the idea is as valid today as when he remarked on merit pay in *Out of the Crisis*. Upon learning of the merit pay idea proposed by President Reagan, Deming had this to say:

> The problem lies in the difficulty to define a meaningful measure of performance. The only verifiable measure is a short-term count of some kind... Where were the President's economic advisors? He was only doing his best.[14]

During his four-day seminars, when participants would ask him how much data they would need on an employee before an accurate evaluation could occur, he would say 15-16 years' worth. His primary point in answering this way was that it is nearly impossible to accurately disentangle the contributions of the employee, the contributions of the system, and the contributions of the interactions between the employee and the system on a short-term time frame.

Even now, with many states having teacher-level value-added data in some grade levels and subject areas, there are significant problems with the disentanglement problem. These Value-Added Models (VAMs) are statistical models that attempt to distinguish a teacher's causal impact on her students' learning from other factors. For example, in a 2016 working paper by University of California Berkeley economics professor Jesse Rothstein, he found the following:

> Teachers' VAM scores are evidently inflated or depressed in part due to the students who they teach, who differ in unobserved ways that are stable over time. This bias accounts for as much as one-third of the variation in teachers' value-added scores, enough to create a great deal of misclassification in VAM-based evaluations of teacher effectiveness.[15]

There are other problems with merit pay beyond the measurement problem. The theory suggests that the additional money will incentivize improved teaching and, in turn, improved student outcomes. For this to be true, it would mean that teachers were previously withholding their best efforts. I've not encountered a single educator in my nearly 20-year career for whom this would be true. I'm not saying that we as educators don't have room for improvement; there is always room improvement, no matter the level of experience. Instead, I'm saying that the lure of more money will not likely lead to improvement because it is completely disconnected from developing better educational methods.

More likely is that the environment created by a merit pay system would disincentive behaviors that are important to improving any complex system, such as cooperation and teamwork. The competition of merit pay in general, and especially where the merit pay calculation is viewed as opaque and unfair, could easily lead to undesired behaviors such as the unwillingness to share ideas or take on certain assignments. Returning to Rothstein's research, he in fact finds that

> Insofar as such biases are important, they create obvious problems for VAM-based teacher evaluations. A teacher whose VAM score is biased upward due to her student assignments might thereby qualify for bonuses that she has not earned, while one who specializes in tougher students risks being undeservedly dismissed for poor performance. This creates obvious incentives for teachers to avoid the latter assignments in favor of the former, potentially making it harder to staff certain courses and reducing the overall efficacy of the school.[16]

This is exactly the type of unintended consequence that is likely to flow from the merit pay idea. This problem is not unique to schools; similar issues occur in any work system that employs these practices. As Brian Joiner astutely notes in his work on understanding variation

> When people are pressured to meet a target value there are three ways they can proceed: (1) they can work to improve the system; (2) they can distort the system; or (3) they can distort the data.[17]

Performance appraisal and merit pay lead to suboptimization of the system. Unfortunately, without profound knowledge, these practices are continually recycled by education, policy, and political leaders. The main idea here is that joy in work, intrinsic motivation, and cooperation are key to a healthy organizational culture within schools. Practices like merit pay that rely on extrinsic motivation and competition are more likely to lead to distortions of the system or the data within the system than they are to lead to an improvement of the system. Here we would be wise to use Deming's theory to optimize the system rather than attempting to incentivize individual educators within those systems.

Myth of Accountability (Management by Objective)

In the K-12 education sector, one of the most visible uses of data is in state education department accountability systems. All 50 states now issue school district report cards typically based on various performance metrics such as proficiency rates on standardized tests, absenteeism rates, and college and career readiness indicators. In my home state of Ohio, individual schools also receive report cards, and the accountability system extends down from school districts and schools to individual educators.

Dr. Deming referred to accountability systems and other similar practices as *Management by Objective* (MBO) or management by the numbers. This is the practice of focusing on outcomes. Grading and rating school systems and individual schools is akin to the inspection of parts in a factory. One problem with MBO is that goals for accountability and goals for improvement are two very different things. Far too often, these two types of goals get conflated when we discuss educational improvement efforts. Inspection and accountability measures come after the fact, and do not improve the processes that produced the defective results. Accountability goals without a method do not improve the system of education much like the inspection of parts in the factory does nothing to improve the quality of the manufactured product.

The conflation of accountability and improvement goals can have unintended consequences. In the last section, I introduced three ways people can react when pressured to meet a target value, like those in an accountability system. The optimal response is to improve the system. However, the other two responses—distorting the system and distorting the data—are negative reactions. Think here of the schools that you've worked in across your career, assessing which of the three responses were most common in your experience. For example, if you were around for the implementation of the No Child Left Behind (NCLB) legislation, what did you experience? If you are like many educators, you probably experienced a version of the second bucket—distortion of the system. This occurs when people work to achieve expected results at the expense of other results. I saw this first-hand as a 5th grade teacher in the Atlanta Public Schools from 2001-2004. There was an increased focus on reading and math test results; we were told to spend approximately 180 minutes of the day on these two subject areas. Recess was cut from the elementary-level schedule altogether. Little time was left for science, history, art, music, and physical education. My hunch is that most educators would agree that this system distortion was not a net positive for kids.

I would also be remiss if I didn't mention the third bucket—distorting the data. This occurs when you get creative with the numbers. Think here of the state testing and other similar cheating scandals that have occurred in the last two decades. While it's true that the vast majority of educators and educational institutions do not engage in this type of behavior, it's also true that this is not a rare occurrence. The most egregious example may have occurred in the Atlanta Public Schools where the superintendent was accused of running a corrupt organization that used test scores to financially reward and punish teachers. Cheating on student standardized tests were reported in most states and the District of Columbia during the Bush and Obama administrations. The common thread of the cheating scandals is that they came during a time when standardized test scores had become the primary metric to evaluate educators, as well as K-12 schools and school districts. I'm not excusing the behavior of those that participated in the cheating, but it is important to learn what it is about the accountability system design that led to so many scandals.

The bottom line in the Deming philosophy is to stop holding people accountable in lieu of improving processes. Numerical goals do not produce quality, especially when those goals are outside the capability of the system as it is currently designed. Instead, they result in distortions of the system or distortions of the data or both.

Myth of Extrinsic Motivators

The basic premise of this myth is that employee performance is determined by putting the right extrinsic motivators in place. Under this supposition, the key is to find the right balance between reward and punishment. While it is true that people are differentially motivated by extrinsic and intrinsic factors, it is a false premise that leaders can improve performance using carrots and sticks. For one, extrinsic motivators do not work or improve performance in most contexts within complex systems like schools. These motivators typically only work in the short-term and even then, they only typically work for simple, repetitive tasks. There are also the unintended consequences that stem from practices like teacher evaluations and merit pay that rely on extrinsic motivation and are more likely to lead to distortions of the system or the data within the system than they are to lead to an improvement of the system. This is because they optimize competition instead of cooperation. All of this brings us to the primary issue with extrinsic motivators targeted at individuals. Individual performance only accounts for a tiny fraction of organizational performance. Deming estimated that 94% of the troubles and possibilities for improvement belong to the system and are the responsibility of management, so incentivizing individuals who have little control over the system as a whole is at best pointless. At worst, these incentive systems decrease organizational performance.

The New Philosophy

The common thread among all the management myths discussed in Chapter 2 is that they sub-optimize the system as a whole. This a key issue with the prevailing command-and-control approach to management. All of the myths—best practices; the hero educator; performance appraisals; merit pay; rating and ranking employees; accountability systems; Management by Objective; and extrinsic motivators—fragment the whole into parts and fail to appreciate the organization as a system. The Deming philosophy does the opposite. The four components of the System of Profound Knowledge work in concert to provide us with profound insights about how our organizations operate so that we as system leaders can in turn work to optimize the whole of our systems. Systems leaders must understand and avoid the management myths described in Chapter 2. However, there is a step beyond simply avoiding these management pitfalls. The next step is to be able to think and make decisions using the lens provided by the System of Profound Knowledge. Here a core set of principles will be helpful. In Chapter 3, I'll outline fourteen principles that will enable you to move from theory to practice with the Deming philosophy. These principles will provide system leaders with a strong philosophical foundation from which to make sound decisions.

Endnotes

1. W. Edwards Deming, *The New Economics for Industry, Government, Education,* 3rd ed. (Cambridge, MA: The MIT Press, 2018), 6.

2. U.S. National Commission on Excellence in Education, *A Nation at Risk: the Imperative for Educational Reform: a Report to the Nation and the Secretary of Education,* United States Department of Education, Washington, D.C.: Superintendent of Documents, U.S. Government Printing Office distributor, 1983.

3. This quote comes from the introductory letter included in *A Nation at Risk* written by David Pierpont Gardner, the chairman of the commission, to Secretary of Education T.H. Bell.

4. Various media articles I read referred to the report as the "Sandia Report." The research article I read for this report has the following citation: C.C. Carson, R.M. Huelskamp, and T.D. Woodall, "Perspectives on Education in America: An Annotated Briefing," *The Journal of Educational Research* 86, no. 5 (May-June 1993): 259-265, 267-291, 293-297, 299-307, 309-310.

5. Ibid., 259.

6. W. Edwards Deming, *The New Economics for Industry, Government, Education,* 3rd ed. (Cambridge, MA: The MIT Press, 2018), xix.

7. *The Deming Library,* Volume 30, "The Case Against Management by Objective," licensed to The W. Edwards Deming Institute, produced by Clare Crawford-Mason, narrated by Lloyd Dobbins, featuring Brian Joiner (1989; Wooten Productions, Inc., 1987; CC-M Productions, 1995), DemingNEXT.

8. W. Edwards Deming, *The New Economics for Industry, Government, Education,* 3rd ed. (Cambridge, MA: The MIT Press, 2018), 26.

9. Ibid., 84.

10. Ibid., 26.

11. Heather Kirn Lanier, "What Jaime Escalante Taught Us That Hollywood Left Out," *EducationWeek,* April 20, 2010, https://www.edweek.org/leadership/opinion-what-jaime-escalante-taught-us-that-hollywood-left-out/2010/04.

12. Edward Martin Baker, *The Symphony of Profound Knowledge: W. Edwards Deming's Score for Leading, Performing, and Living in Concert* (Bloomington, IN: iUniverse, 2017), 20.

13. *The Deming Library,* Volume 28, "The Case Against Performance Appraisal," licensed to The W. Edwards Deming Institute, produced by Clare Crawford-Mason, narrated by Lloyd Dobbins, featuring Peter Scholtes (1989; Wooten Productions, Inc., 1987; CC-M Productions, 1995), DemingNEXT.

14. W. Edwards Deming, *Out of the Crisis* (Cambridge, MA: MIT, Center for Advanced Engineering Study, 1986), 103-104.

15. Jesse Rothstein, "Measuring the Impacts of Teachers: Comment," *American Economic Review* 107, no. 6 (June 2017): 1656-84.

16. Ibid.

17. This is attributed to Brian Joiner, but I first read it in: Donald J. Wheeler, *Understanding Variation: The Key to Managing Chaos,* 2nd ed. (Knoxville, TN: SPC Press, 2000), 20.

CHAPTER THREE

Principles for Transformation

The transformation will release the power of human resource contained in intrinsic motivation. [1]

—*W. EDWARDS DEMING*

IN 1988, TYPICAL TEACHERS in the United States had an average of 15 years of experience under their belt. By 2017, he or she was a beginner in his or her first year of teaching. A significant part of this "greening" of the teaching force can be chalked up to the dramatic growth in the number of teachers during this period. That is, the elementary and secondary teaching force in the United States has significantly increased in size over the last three decades. It is also true that the teaching force has become less stable. Intuitively this makes sense; there are now more new teachers, and these beginners are less likely to stay in teaching than teachers with longer resumés. Taken together, the growth in the teaching force combined with greater turnover point to a decrease in the stability in the teaching profession. Increasingly in recent years, large numbers of people are entering teaching and large numbers of people are leaving the field.[2]

Education in the United States is a complex system. I'm not attempting to draw any causal relationships between the instability of the teaching force and the federal education policies (e.g., Goals 2000, NCLB, etc.) mentioned in the previous chapter. Nor am I attempting any evaluative judgments about the transformation of the teaching force that has occurred over the last thirty years. There isn't conclusive evidence to suggest that the teaching force is "better" or "worse" in one way or another now than it was prior the shake-up of the sector after the release of *A Nation at Risk*. These are the types of topics about our country's education system that rage on in the media and within the political sector that work to grab headlines but are good for little else. What should be of interest to educational leaders is the very large opportunity to transform the system. K-12 teachers represent one of the largest occupations in the United States; the philosophical foundations for educators and education institutions should be one of our highest priorities.

Aim of this Chapter

The purpose of this chapter is to list and describe the 14 principles for the transformation of school system leadership. They provide everyone in the education system a basis by which to answer the question, "How is our management doing?" The transformation is the job of management and can only be accomplished by system leaders, not by technology, curriculum, programs, or other similar measures. A school system cannot buy its way to quality.

What is the origin of the 14 principles?

The 14 principles, or as they are better known, the *14 Points for Management*, were developed by W. Edwards Deming as the basis for transformation of American industry. He described the points in detail in *Out of the Crisis* where he said, "Adoption and action on the 14 Points are a signal that the management intend to stay in business and aim to protect investors and jobs." He employed the 14 Points as the basis for the lessons he taught to top management leaders in Japan beginning in 1950 and in the decades that followed. Over the course of 60 years of continual improvement work, Deming worked with Japanese industry leaders and top companies in the United States. He was also a professor of statistics at New York University for decades. He not only taught the 14 Points to the leaders with which he worked, they also guided his own teaching practices as a professor. Thus, as Deming said, "the 14 Points apply anywhere, to small organizations as well as to large ones, to the service industry as well as to manufacturing."

Continual improvement leaders such as David Langford and James Leonard have translated the 14 Points into education system-friendly language. In addition to Deming's original version, as well as Henry Neave's analysis of the 14 Points[3], I also studied Langford's "Modified Deming Points for Continual Improvement of Education"[4] as well as Leonard's "14 Obligations of the School Board and Administration"[5] as I wrote the 14 Principles for Transformation. These four sources form the basis for the principles in *Win-Win*, with the aim being to preserve the original intent and spirit of Deming's 14 Points.

Experience Alone Teaches Nothing

Having sufficient numbers of veteran teachers in a school is important for both students and beginning teachers. They have a positive impact on new teachers' instructional quality, their likelihood to stay in the profession, and their ability to improve students' academic achievement.[6] As a systems leader, I'd take a school staffed with veteran educators as opposed to new teachers every day of the week and twice on Sunday. At the same time, having schools staffed with veteran educators does not guarantee quality schools. As I learned from Dr. Deming, experience in and of itself without the aid of theory doesn't teach us anything regarding how to improve quality.

In the absence of a theory of management for improvement of educational quality, we get education reform ideas grounded in the management myths outlined in Chapter 2. The major federal education initiatives since the 1980s have all fallen prey to one or more of these myths. Goals 2000 (1994), No Child Left Behind (2002), Race to the Top (2009), and the Every Student Succeeds Act (2015) all included some version of Management by Objective (MBO). Race to the Top was a grant competition among states. Beyond MBO, it also encouraged the design of teacher and principal evaluation systems that judged educators on student and school standardized test score performance. All of the federal initiatives were well-intentioned reforms attempting to shine the light on inequities and inadequacies in our educational system. In practice, they caused problems such as the narrowing of curriculum post-NCLB discussed in the last chapter.

In the absence of a set of guiding principles and a theory of management, we get tampering disguised as education reform. By *tampering*, I mean action taken to compensate for variation within the limits of a stable system; it increases rather than decreases variation. Think of tampering as changes in law, practice, or policy that makes it feel as if you are being yanked this way and that within your educational system for seemingly illogical reasons. Prior to understanding the Deming philosophy, I had this feeling without being able to give it a voice. With the System of Profound Knowledge, in particular the Knowledge about Variation, I can now put into words the disconnect between outcomes and plans to improve those outcomes (by outcomes I mainly mean standardized test results).

Most of the attempts at education reform that I've experienced have been overly focused on numerical goals and accountability. The problem is that these goals are hopes without a method to achieve them, and so they remain mere hopes. In other words, reform efforts like Goals 2000, No Child Left Behind, and the Every Student Succeeds Act have not brought about the improvement the reforms' designers have intended. Goals 2000 was replaced by No Child Left Behind, which in turn was complemented by Race to the Top and then replaced by the Every Student Succeeds Act. Pronouncements about lessons learned were made, but in reality, much of the emphasis on numerical goals can be found in each subsequent version of the federal legislation. This can be chalked up to the fact that there was not sound management theory underlying the various attempts at reform.

Unknown & Unknowable Figures

The management myths outlined in Chapter 2 do not work. In Chapter 3, I've again stressed the problems with the reliance on numerical goals and accountability systems in the education sector as mechanisms for improvement. This focus is due to the attention paid to numerical goals in schools; they may very well be the most common of the myths. Issues of system capability, variability, stability, and method are key considerations of healthy goal-setting, all of which are normally absent in the design of the vast preponderance of accountability goals in schools and school systems. But I also wanted to bring up one other important point prior to the introduction of the 14 principles. This is the issue of unknown and unknowable figures. Dr. Deming credited to his friend and contemporary Dr. Lloyd Nelson the idea that, "The most important figures needed for management of any organization are unknown and unknowable."[7]

The researchers at Sandia alluded to this idea in their report when they said, ". . . it is not clear to us that all the measures analyzed by us and others are appropriate barometers of performance for the education system (recall that our selection criterion was that a measure be popular, not necessarily appropriate)." There are important questions left unanswered within the state accountability systems, the unknown and unknowable figures that Deming

PRINCIPLES FOR TRANSFORMATION

referenced, such as: What effect does a hyper-focus on test scores have on a school's reading program? What effect does the testing regimen have on students' joy in learning and teachers' joy in teaching? Are our schools providing an educational foundation that will have a positive impact on students' long-term life outcomes?

An important point to understand is that unknown and unknowable figures nonetheless can and must be managed, and are in fact, the responsibility of systems leaders. In the absence of coherent guiding principles, I'm worried about the decisions we're making in response to the pressures applied by numerical goals, accountability systems, and the other management myths. Short-term gains in test scores are not a reliable indicator of performance of management. Those types of gains can be achieved by methods that are not in the best long-term interest of students or education systems.

Systems leaders cannot simply commit to quality; we must know what to do. Ohio's school and school district rating system recently switched from A-F school ratings to a five-star system. It's a delusion to think either rating system has anything to do with school quality or that switching from one rating system to another has anything to do with it. Similarly, we cannot improve quality by putting the screws to principals and teachers to do better work. Quality is the job of systems leaders; it cannot be delegated. The 14 principles in the next section will provide systems leaders with a basis for judgment of their own decisions and for transformation of the organizations to which they belong.

14 Principles for Educational Systems Transformation

Deming's 14 Points didn't exist in the 1950s when he started working with Japanese business leaders on how to transform their organizations. They were developed gradually over a roughly 20-year period from the 1970s to the early 1990s and didn't reach the number 14 until Deming started to present his four-day seminars in the United States. The list was expanded as the focus of his work shifted from Japan to the United States. There were certain principles such as "Drive out fear" and "Remove the barriers that rob the hourly worker of his right to pride of workmanship" that did not have to be told to Japanese management, but they did need to be addressed in the U.S.

Prior to describing the 14 Principles, there are a few items that are worth clarifying. First, Deming sometimes referred to the 14 Points as "Principles" or "Obligations" of management; I will refer to my list as the 14 Principles going forward. Second, Deming's 14 Points are not in and of themselves the philosophy, but they are important components of it. They are not a recipe or a checklist to be implemented, but rather principles that are meant to open up your mind to a whole new way of thinking regarding how we organize and run our educational institutions. Finally, and most importantly, Deming's 14 Points are interlinked principles within a larger management philosophy. As such, you can't simply put the points into action without first developing a deep understanding for why Deming wrote them in the way that he did. The transition to transformation must account for your organization's particular context, so the 14 Points should not be adopted without this deep understanding and appreciation for that context. Continual improvement guided by Deming's 14 Points is not a project or program to be implemented, but rather a never-ending commitment to quality. Committing to that mindset, a description of each of the "14 Principles for Educational Systems Transformation" follows.[8]

Principle 1: Create constancy of purpose toward continual improvement of high-quality learning systems. These systems should be designed in such a way that they enable joy in work for staff and joy in learning for students, with the aim that everyone can access opportunity-rich lives in our society now and into the future.

W. Edwards Deming spoke of two problems faced by organizations that hope to stay in business. First, there are problems of today. With all schools, but especially schools of choice like the network of public charter schools for which I work, student enrollment is of constant concern. Problems of today include ensuring quality of the learning experience while balancing the demands of local, state, and federal educational policies; attracting, training, and retaining employees; making sound budgeting decisions amid constantly changing financial conditions; recruiting and retaining students; fundraising from corporate, foundation, and individual donors; acquiring, upgrading, and maintaining school buildings; and so forth. It is self-evident to see how education leaders stay closely tied to the myriad problems of today.

One could become quite proficient in dealing with the problems of today even amidst this complex and quickly changing environment, but still go off track because of a lack of attention to the second type of problem. That is, the problems of the future for which the idea of constancy of purpose is especially

PRINCIPLES FOR TRANSFORMATION

important. Intertwined with constancy of purpose is the attention paid to the continual improvement of the school or district's competitive position within the educational ecosystem (e.g., parents seeking out a particular school because of its learning program). Here it is important to consider the following question: Is the school board and the superintendent dedicated to the short-term or to the long-term future of the institution? Both short-term and long-term commitment to the constancy of purpose are important. We do not want to sacrifice one for the other. In the business world, the short-term is quick profits at the expense of the existence of the company 10, 20, or 30 years from now. In schools, a short-term mindset is one that is overly focused on state testing results rather than the existence of the school 10, 20, or 30 years from now. Most importantly, the long-term approach would put more emphasis on the success of its students 10, 20, or 30 years after graduating from the school system rather than solely on shorter term measures such as test scores.

The commitment to constancy of purpose, aligned both for the short-term and long-term comes with the acceptance of three obligations. First, schools need to innovate by allocating resources for long-term planning. Future planning calls for a number of considerations, some of which include new educational services that better prepare students for the future; new materials such as curricular resources and educational technology and the associated costs; new pedagogical approaches grounded in neuroscientific discoveries; new skills required of teachers and administrators; training and retraining of staff; training of managers; costs of running a school or district; costs associated with staff and student recruitment; effectiveness of educational services; and satisfaction of the customer (and society in the case of public schools). Faith in a future is a prerequisite for innovation. It cannot thrive unless top management has stated an unshakable commitment to quality, without which middle management (i.e., principals, teacher leaders), teachers, and students will be skeptical of putting forth their best efforts.

Second, resources must be put into research and education. Research may focus on areas such as curricular options or staying abreast of developments related to the science of learning. Education means self-improvement and acquiring new knowledge. Deming made a point of differentiating between training and education. Training is learning methods that should later be observed in the person's behavior, whereas education is more focused on continuing education and gaining new knowledge (see also Principles 6 and 13).

Third, systems leaders must continually improve the design of educational services with prime importance placed on the key product produced in schools, which is, of course, quality learning. This obligation never ceases. It is not only possible, but quite easy, for a school system to go downhill or even out of operation altogether by designing and offering the wrong type of learning systems, even though everyone in the organization performs with admirable devotion and efficiency.

Customers (i.e., families, higher education, government, industry, etc.), suppliers (i.e., families, other school districts), and employees need to know and understand the organization's constancy of purpose. In other words, they need to understand that it is your intention to stay in business by providing valued educational services that will help them all live better, and which will still have a market in the future. Committing to the three obligations described in the preceding paragraphs—innovation, research and education, and continual improvement of educational services—will help to achieve long-term success.

Principle 2: Adopt the new philosophy. System leaders must awaken to the fact that education reform movements lack a sound philosophical foundation, must learn their new responsibilities, and take on leadership for improvement.

The Deming philosophy stated as a new philosophy for education could be framed by studying and applying the System of Profound Knowledge in order to (1) view teaching and learning as dynamic processes that occur within a system and (2) understand the nature of variation of teaching and learning processes so that appropriate action can be taken to accomplish improvement on a continual basis.[9] The 14 Principles serve as a practical guide by which systems leaders can lead. Some of the principles tell us what to do, such as "creating constancy of purpose," while others instruct us on ways to remove barriers to create an environment which is conducive to the new philosophy, such as "abolish management by objective." The backbone of the philosophy is transformation from the paradigm of the "I win, you lose" or "I lose, you win" culture to a Win-Win paradigm based on a culture of cooperation. The Win-Win philosophy includes new thinking about leadership of people, where a primary concern is developing joy in work and learning among students and staff as a prerequisite to achieving the core purpose of the organization.

PRINCIPLES FOR TRANSFORMATION

49

This transition will not happen overnight, or as Deming put it, there is no "instant pudding."[10] Instead, a more realistic goal is constant, consistent movement toward the new philosophy where there is total involvement in continually improving quality of all systems, processes, and activities within the school system.

Principle 3: Cease dependence on standardized testing to achieve quality, and work to abolish grading and the harmful effects of rating people. Eliminate the need for inspection on a mass basis (i.e., standardized testing) by building quality into the product in the first place. The product in education systems is high-quality learning.

There are two different concepts to deal with in Principle 3, standardized testing and grading, and the proscription is different for each following Deming's teachings. Close reading of the 14 Principles is paramount because Dr. Deming chose his words very carefully. If your initial reaction to these requirements is to scoff or laugh, then this demonstrates how far away your standards are from those which he demanded.

Is Deming saying that we should abolish inspection using standardized tests or assessment in general? No, of course not. After all, without assessment we would not be able to answer the critical question, "How are we doing?" However, our sector is overly reliant on mass inspection (i.e., state testing) as the way of life to try to ensure that customers of the education system get some type of quality. Principle 3 calls for eliminating *dependence* on standardized and other tests as the sole measure of quality, not for their elimination altogether. There is a tremendous difference between mass testing as an attempt to provide the customer with something they won't complain about and the use of assessments to provide guidance toward improvement of a learning process. Mass inspection through testing is costly and generally unproductive since it aims to sort out good from bad but does not contribute to progress. Beyond the cost and unproductive nature of mass inspection through testing, it also introduces the idea of a supposedly acceptable level of defectives. The goal for state testing in grades 3-8 in Ohio is for 80% of students to meet the proficiency standard, which means that one in five students not meeting the standard is acceptable. This is a direct contradiction to the philosophy of continual improvement. The Deming philosophy is to build quality into the process in the first place. Quality does not come from inspection, but from going upstream to the improvement of teaching and learning processes. Classroom assessments are a much better tool for identifying these upstream processes. Deming said that the system of make-and-inspect if applied to toast would be expressed, "You burn, I'll scrape,"[11] which is obviously an unacceptable approach when dealing with anything involving the education of children.

Turning to grading, Deming did not suggest that we merely cease dependence on grades, but that we abolish them. It is worth noting that this has nothing to do with making things easier for students nor does it have anything to do with low-scoring students' self-esteem. Instead, it is based on the more fundamental premise that we want students to experience success and failure on school work as information rather than as reward and punishment. Grades are inherently about experiencing things as reward and punishment. When author Alfie Kohn completed a comprehensive review of the research literature on grades that compared students who got grades to those who didn't, he found three robust differences. First, kids who are graded tend to become less interested in whatever topic they were studying. This includes the specific topic as well as the subject-area in general, such as math or writing, compared to students that get the identical assignment but with no grades involved. Second, kids who are graded, when they have a choice to pick, pick the easiest possible task. If the point is to get a high grade, it is rational to pick the easiest book or assignment. Grades inherently lead students to avoid intellectual risk-taking. Third, kids who are graded are more likely to think in a superficial or shallow fashion, and more likely to ask questions like, "Do we have to know this?" as opposed to more thoughtful questions about the content itself.[12]

It is this fundamental displacement of priority from the learning to the grade that is at the heart of both Deming's and Kohn's philosophy in this area. The specific losses from grading practices are unknown and unknowable, but very likely catastrophic.

Principle 4: Maximize high-quality learning and minimize total cost of education by improving the relationship with educational institutions from which students come and to which they matriculate. A single source of students coming into a system, such as elementary school students moving into a middle school, is an opportunity to build long-term relationships of loyalty and trust.

United Schools Network began as a single middle school serving eastside neighborhoods in Columbus, Ohio, where I served as the founding school

PRINCIPLES FOR TRANSFORMATION

director (principal). We elected to open a middle school because this was the point in a student's educational career where they could fall so far behind that they ended up dropping out a few years later. This meant that before we were a network of schools, we were one school serving grades 6-8. There were 15 or so elementary schools from the city school system that served as de facto feeder patterns into our middle school. Many of these elementary schools were performing in the bottom 5% of schools in the state, which meant that the average student that enrolled with us did so 2-3 years below grade level. There was no way for me to run the USN middle school and all that entailed, and form relationships with the 15 principals leading the elementary schools from which our students came. As a result, when we had the opportunity to grow from one school into a network of four schools, we elected to grow down to include elementary schools. The point in doing so was to move toward the single supplier relationship that Dr. Deming outlined with his Point 4. The school directors of our middle and elementary schools can work together on a whole host of quality characteristics, such as vertically planning curriculum across the K-8 pipeline. While the students that enroll in USN middle schools still come from a number of elementary schools, we are increasingly moving toward the single supplier model. In addition to maximizing high-quality learning, this also works to minimize the total cost of education. One of the paradoxes of continual improvement is that as quality goes up, price goes down. In the case of USN, this occurs as we have to do less remediation with students as they increasingly come from USN elementary schools and will not be as far behind when they arrive at the middle schools.

Because Deming mainly worked in industry, his Point 4 read, "End the practice of awarding business on the basis of price tag. Instead, minimize total cost. Move toward a single supplier for any one item, on a long-term relationship of loyalty and trust."[13] I translated Deming's framing to one that applies directly to students as they move through the K-12 pipeline. However, there is also a second component to this principle that is more directly analogous to his point and definitely applicable to the business of running school systems. That is the idea of ceasing dependence on price alone when selecting curriculum, technology, supplies, etc. and any number of goods and services that school systems regularly buy. The main idea here is to understand the difference between the lowest bidder and the lowest qualified bidder. Price has no meaning without a measure of the quality of the goods and services being purchased, including after-sale service.[14]

Developing partnerships with suppliers within both the K-12 pipeline and in making purchases for the school system helps to engage those suppliers in the effort to continually improve processes throughout the system. On the purchasing front, decisions driven by concern for this year's budget alone may impede long-term improvements and constancy of purpose.

Principle 5: Improve constantly and forever the system of planning, teaching, learning, and service to improve every process and activity in the organization and to improve quality and productivity. It is management's obligation to work continually on the system (school design, curriculum, incoming supplies and materials, technology, supervision, training, retraining, etc.).

Principle 1 and 5 are very similar in that they both talk about improvement of the system and its processes over the long term. The distinction is that Principle 1 (constancy of purpose) facilitates Principle 5 (continual improvement of systems and processes). A key idea to keep front of mind is that quality must be built in at the planning and design stage of the work. For example, when a school system selects a curriculum, this selection will have downstream effects on teacher lessons and student learning. How many individual teachers selected their district's curriculum? That's a number that is usually close to, if not, zero. There are many other components to education systems that are analogous, which is why it's management's obligation to continually improve the system.

Management must be able to deal with the day-to-day issues of the organization while also moving toward continual improvement. While putting out fires is important, it does not result in improvement. Similarly, detection and removal of a special cause does not improve a process. At best, fighting fires and detecting special causes returns a process back to its previous state. This means that systems leaders must strive to make unstable processes stable and to make stable but incapable processes capable, and to make capable processes ever more capable.[15]

While problems are opportunities for improvement, a commitment to never-ending improvement can be daunting. Fortunately, there are a number of methods and tools that can be deployed by improvement teams, such as the process behavior chart introduced in Chapter 1. It allows us to differentiate between common and special causes in our data, as well to help us determine

PRINCIPLES FOR TRANSFORMATION

the capability, variation, and stability of the process under study. This and other methods and tools such as the Plan-Do-Study-Act Cycle will be discussed throughout the book.

Principle 6: Institute thorough job-related training for students, teachers, staff, and management, so that everyone can make better contributions to the system. New skills are required to keep up with changes in cognitive science, curricula, methods, learning experience design, technology, teaching techniques, services, etc.

There is an important distinction between Principle 6 (institute training) and Principle 13 (institute a vigorous program of education). Principle 6 refers to the foundations of training for management and for new employees whereas Principle 13 refers to continual education and self-improvement on the job. Training is for skills. Education is for the development of knowledge. Training involves learning how to do a particular job within the system using a particular set of methods and tools. Its purpose is to allow a worker to know exactly what their job is.

A major aim of training is reduced variation in methods. Educators at all levels are likely familiar with the problems that occur when classroom management practices and teaching methods vary widely from classroom to classroom within the same school. In many schools, some teachers have highly structured and disciplined classrooms while other teachers allow almost anything to go. What are the effects of these mixed messages on the overall culture of the school?

On the instructional side, what happens when three third grade teachers each have their preferred methods and sequencing for teaching math? Some combination of these third graders wind up in the same fourth grade classroom the following year, and this creates significant issues for the teacher. Remember the systems view illustrated by Figure 1.3; the fourth-grade teacher is the customer of the three third grade classrooms. However, those individual third grade classrooms were optimized instead of the system as a whole, and this very well may be an issue that can be tied back to training.

Training involves learning methods that should later be observed in the person's behavior. As a result, a trainer needs good understanding of operational definitions (see Chapter 1, Theory of Knowledge) because they must understand that particular job in a clear-cut way. For example, a trainer working with new teachers on their ability to deliver an effective lesson must have a clear operational definition for effective lesson. Without this understanding on the trainer's part, the new teachers will not be able to do their job in the way the school system has intended.

When planning any training, systems leaders also must keep the following formula in mind:

Training effectiveness = f[(Quality of subject matter) x (Probability of use)][16]

This equation is seemingly obvious, just as is the idea of instituting a thorough job training program in the first place. It simply states that the effectiveness of any training will be the function of the quality of the subject matter times the probability of its use. My sense is that most systems leaders recognize that there might be issues on both fronts—quality of training and probability of use—within their organizations. Less appreciated is the idea that in order for training to be used, there often have to be changes to organizational systems that enable the training to be put to use.

One way systems leaders can provide a high probability of use for training is by placing new employees on process improvement teams. At United Schools Network, the improvement process (see Appendix A) used by these teams is built around three questions:

1. What are we trying to accomplish?
2. How will we know a change is an improvement?
3. What change can we make that will result in improvement?[17]

Within each of these questions there are process steps, guiding questions, and tools for visualizing the team's thinking. For example, Step 1 in the improvement process is "See the System." Here team members define the system for improvement, state the system aim, identify opportunities for improvement within the target system, prioritize those opportunities, and charter the project. It should be apparent how participation on such a team would help train the new employee in a process that allows them to understand the system within which they are working in a much deeper way than if they sat through a presentation on the organizational structure of the school system. Students also can participate in these teams. In doing so, they come to learn a scientific approach to improving problems through training in im-

PRINCIPLES FOR TRANSFORMATION

provement methods and tools. Involving students in improvement work will be discussed further in Chapters 6 and 10.

The benefits of training fall into the category of "unknown and unknowable" measures that systems leaders must manage. However, training is often one of the first things to be eliminated when finances become tight. This is exactly the wrong way to think about its benefits. Proper training of new employees and students costs very little in proportion to the total costs involved with those that are new to your system over the months and years they are associated with the organization. The benefit of new employees and students understanding their role within the system gives you a fighting chance of achieving your mission. And this benefit does not even include the unknowable benefits to the school system when the employee or student gains satisfaction from doing a good job, and thus becomes more committed to continual improvement in the future.

Principle 7: Adopt and institute leadership aimed at helping people to do a better job. Management's responsibility must shift from focusing solely on outcomes to focusing on the quality of learning experiences and services produced by the educational system.

The prevailing style of leadership in most American organizations has embedded within it barriers to long-term constancy of purpose (Principle 1) in the form of the management myths (e.g., MBO) discussed in Chapter 2. In addition, there is often the creation of hero leaders through short-term crisis management instead of a commitment to continual improvement (Principle 5). The required transformation includes the transition of managers and supervisors to become leaders. Focus on outcome (i.e., management by numbers, numerical goals, MBO, performance appraisal, merit pay) must be abolished with leadership installed in its place. Leadership following the Deming philosophy is responsible for creating an environment where educators and students have genuine interest in their work and are supported to do it well. These are mutually reinforcing activities, meaning that if people are interested in their work and learning then they will want to do it well and will accept help to improve their performance. If the conditions set them up to do well, then their interest will increase, and a *virtuous cycle* is created. However, the opposite can and often is created where a *vicious cycle* occurs. The system is set up in such a way that it leads to the likelihood of people doing a bad job, interest in the work or learning plummets, which in turn causes them to do an even poorer job, which in turn lessens interest even further. The constant churn of new teachers is a good example of this vicious cycle.

The virtuous cycle is more likely to occur when transformation is guided by the System of Profound Knowledge. As systems leaders learn and apply this system, they in turn exhibit certain behaviors that lead people and organizations toward continual improvement of planning, teaching, learning, and service processes (Principle 5) on an ongoing basis. As it relates to managing people using the Deming philosophy, leadership behaviors are guided by appreciation for a system, logical theories of variation and knowledge, and understanding psychological concepts such as intrinsic motivation.

The adoption of Principle 7 can sound a bit soft and maybe even a bit scary. Typical questions from staff (and questions I asked when first learning the 14 Points) include, "How do you motivate educators and students in the absence of numerical goals? How do you hold people accountable for their work or learning without performance appraisal?" These questions are more than reasonable, until you realize what Deming meant by adopt and institute leadership. To make this clear, he circulated a document at several of his four-day seminars toward the end of his life called "Some Attributes of a Leader" that paints a clear picture.[18] I've reproduced this list below with some adjustments to wording with the intention of keeping the spirit of the list in place while translating it for an education audience.

Some Attributes of a Leader

1. Understands how the work of his or her department, school, or classroom fits into the overall aim of the system. The assumption is that the school board and senior administrators have done their job to clearly define and communicate the system aim, so classroom and building leaders can figure out how they and their students fit in.

2. Works with preceding stages and with following stages within the systems view of the organization (Figure 1.3). Focuses on the customer, both internal and external.

3. The leader tries to remove the barriers to joy in work and learning for everybody. He or she tries to optimize the education, skills, and abilities of everyone and help everyone to improve.

PRINCIPLES FOR TRANSFORMATION

4. Is coach and counsel, not a judge.

5. Uses figures to help them to understand the people and themselves. They understand variation. They use statistical calculation to learn who, if anybody, is outside the system and in need of special help. Effective leaders understand that the question is not, "Are employees/students different?" but rather "Are they significantly different?" Statistical methods and Knowledge about Variation help leaders answer that second question and take appropriate action to improve teaching and learning processes accordingly. Figure 3.1 illustrates this leadership attribute.

Figure 3.1.
Leadership of People Using the Theory of Systems and Variation

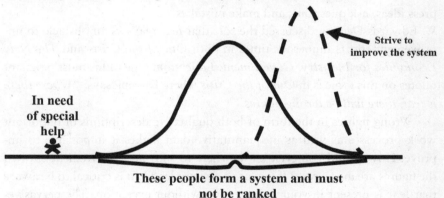

Source: Adapted from Henry R. Neave, *The Deming Dimension* (Knoxville, Tennessee: SPC Press, 1990), 335.

6. Works to improve the teaching and learning processes within which employees and students work. Effective leaders continually improve these processes instead of sorting, tracking, grading, and ranking students, and rating and ranking employees.

7. Creates trust. Leaders are aware that the creation of trust requires them to take risks.

8. Does not expect perfection; forgives a mistake.

9. Listens and learns without passing judgment on those who they listen to.

A key concept implied by the attributes and illustrated in Figure 3.1 is Deming's focus on variation as opposed to the traditional focus on averages. Average values can be useful, but Figure 3.1 makes it clear that improving a system includes both decreased variation around some optimal value as well as a better process average. A reduction in variation often also results in the improvement of the average level of performance.

As reported by Henry Neave in *The Deming Dimension*, when Deming was asked about what qualifications we should look for in candidates for promotion he answered, "What better than the ability to be a leader?" Of leaders he said, "Why lead? People happier, quality up, productivity up, everybody wins."[19]

Principle 8: Drive out fear, so that everyone may work effectively for the school system. No one can perform their best unless they feel secure to express ideas, ask questions, and make mistakes.

W. Edwards Deming discussed the role that fear plays as an obstacle to improvement efforts numerous times in both *Out of the Crisis* and *The New Economics for Industry, Government, Education*. One of his most poignant quotes on this topic is in *Out of the Crisis* where Deming says, *"Where there is fear, there will be wrong figures."*[20]

Wrong figures in the form of both qualitative descriptions of important work processes as well as in quantitative data makes it impossible to improve. How would you even know where to start an improvement effort if the figures are inaccurate? If you are a systems leader, it is critical to be aware that fear is present in your organization without exception. The pervasiveness certainly will vary in terms of the severity of the fear and its impact on employees and students, but it is present. Its presence is guaranteed under the prevailing style of management because it's a by-product of Management by Objective, performance appraisal, and any type of rating and ranking system. Within organizations that employ these methods, the goal becomes for the individual to optimize their own performance instead of optimizing the organization as a whole. Likewise, management must cease blaming employees for problems of the system which account for the vast majority of problems in all organizations. Faults of the system are the responsibility of management because they have the authority to change the design of the system. Educators and students cannot work effectively if they dare not ask about the purpose of their work or have the ability to offer suggestions for

PRINCIPLES FOR TRANSFORMATION

improvement of the system that are in turn considered by management. Not every suggestion leads to a change to the system, but there has to be a process to make the suggestions, as well as follow-up communication to indicate what, if any, system changes will be made as a result. There also should be sound rationale for the decision.

Principle 9: Break down barriers between departments and grade levels and develop strategies for increasing cooperation among groups and individuals. Administrators, business & financial managers, operations staff, support staff, students, teachers and others must work as a team to foresee problems in the production and use of high-quality learning experiences.

As a starting point, it is important to be very clear on what is being produced by school systems, something that is clarified when viewing it through the model we've visited multiple times in the form of Figure 1.3. Stop and think about this idea. What exactly is being produced by a school system? The answer is much simpler in industry where it is easy to see the product coming off the line in the form of a car, a laptop, or a refrigerator. Your first instinct may have been to answer "students" in response to the question about what is being produced. However, if you really stop and think about it, this is not quite right. Rather, the aim in school systems is to produce high-quality learning (i.e., knowledge and skills) and not the students themselves. This is an idea that will be revisited Chapter 4.

The key is to think about how we've organized our school systems to accomplish this aim. Most institutions, including school systems, are organized functionally to be efficient, but they need to operate cross-functionally. The problems that occur because of barriers relate to the quote we saw from Dr. Ackoff in Chapter 1. In essence, he stated that when you improve the performance of a part of a system taken separately, you can destroy the system. Deming gave us his Point 9, which shifts the focus from barriers and competition between departments to cooperation and his Win-Win philosophy. Barriers lead to suboptimization because individual departments or grade levels focus more on achieving their goals than on improving the whole system. The bigger and more entrenched the barriers, the worse the effects of this suboptimization on other departments or grade levels in the school system.

In the systems view of schools illustrated by Figure 1.3, you'll notice that there are no horizontal lines (i.e., walls), but those artificial barriers have been erected by management in almost all systems. In Chapter 5, we'll explore an example of such barriers where a student recruitment department suboptimized the system as a whole by placing more importance on meeting their goals without considering how recruiting very young students to kindergarten would impact the whole system. Just as top management erected the barriers, and in this case, set the recruitment goals, it is their responsibility to break them down. Unfortunately, unlike physical barriers such as a wall made of brick or stone, barriers between departments and grade levels operate in the reverse. Physical barriers take time to build but can be destroyed quickly. Barriers in school systems can be erected quickly but must be taken down with deliberate thought and patience. This is because you are replacing one system that serves a purpose with another system that serves a very different purpose.

Barriers between departments and grade levels not only impede improvement efforts, but also can act as an impediment to innovation. When barriers are up, the emphasis is on "my departmental goals" or "my grade level's goals" instead of on "my school's goals." In this type of environment, the communication and the sharing of ideas necessary for innovation are lacking. A crucial difference between the prevailing style of management and the Deming philosophy is how people at all levels of the organization view their jobs. In the prevailing style, workers tend to look out for themselves. In the Deming style, the focus is on system optimization. The key here is to realize that the system itself has a major influence on how the people working within it operate. In what way does the system of management, including the system of reward, guide the administrators, business and financial managers, operations staff, support staff, students, and teachers in the school system?

A critical role to consider in the school system is that of the business and financial managers, especially given the cost-conscious nature of public education systems. For the Deming philosophy to bring about improvement, these leaders must realize that their role is certainly to carefully steward public moneys, but this should not be achieved by beating down costs. Instead, the emphasis should be to optimize the system, remembering from Principle 4 that the main idea is to understand the difference between the lowest bidder and the lowest qualified bidder. Imagine a scenario where the school system picked a curriculum at least in part because of the cost, and then teachers end up printing other materials on their classroom printers because the curriculum that was purchased isn't serving their needs. Price has no meaning without a measure of the quality being purchased, including after-sale service and use. This can only be realized if all people, including the finance people, see the organization as a system.

Principle 10: Eliminate slogans, exhortations, and targets for educators and students that ask for perfect performance and new levels of productivity. Such exhortations only create adversarial relationships, as the bulk of the causes of low quality and low productivity belong to the system and thus lie beyond the power of teachers and students.

What is wrong with slogans, exhortations, and targets for educators and students? The main problem is that they are directed at the wrong people. They are based on the premise that teachers and students could, by simply putting in more effort, work to improve quality, productivity, and all else that is desirable. However, the slogans, exhortations, and targets do not account for the fact that most trouble within schools come from the system. Recall here the quote from Chapter 1 which stated, "most troubles and most possibilities for improvement add up to proportions something like this: 94% belong to the system (responsibility of management), 6% special." A primary tool for management should be the process behavior chart introduced in Chapter 1, and which will be discussed in depth in Chapters 6 and 7. It's able to indicate which problems come from the system (responsibility of management) and which problems come from other causes.

This problem becomes particularly pernicious when exhortations of some type are deployed in a stable system with defective items. Setting goals for people to work towards seems like a good idea. However, not only is goal-setting useless in this situation, it's often an act of desperation that has the opposite of the intended impact. Think back to the 8th grade math engagement data presented in Chapter 1. Imagine if the principal created posters with the exhortation, "100% ENGAGED . . . WE CAN ACHIEVE IT IF YOU BELIEVE IT!!!" with the remote learning engagement data listed below the proclamation. The data in the poster and shown in Figure 3.2 shows a stable system of output with 67% average daily engagement. School leadership obviously wants to see higher engagement rates and fewer days with low rates. The problem is the exhortation is asking the teacher to do what they are unable to do. As designed, this system is not capable of achieving 100% engagement, so the effect of the goal is fear and mistrust towards leadership.

Figure 3.2.
X Chart: 8th Grade Math Engagement Data with Goal Line

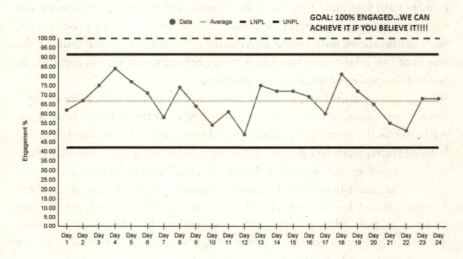

Better content for the posters would be to explain to everyone in the school what the leadership is doing month-by-month to improve the remote learning engagement system. This may include strategies such as making sure that every student has access to a device and reliable internet connectivity at home and that every teacher has been trained in remote learning methods. Leadership to improve quality and productivity is completely different from exhortations to achieve a goal. Teachers would then understand that the leadership is taking some responsibility for the lack of engagement and trying to remove obstacles.

All of this talk of goal setting is not to suggest that individuals should not set goals. You may have a goal to complete your master's degree in the next two years. I had a goal to finish writing this book by October 1, 2022. Goals are helpful and necessary tools for individuals. However, numerical goals set for other people without an accompanying set of methods by which to accomplish the goals have an effect opposite to what is intended.

Principle 11: Eliminate arbitrary numerical targets in the form of work standards that prescribe quotas for teachers and numerical goals for people in management. Substitute leadership to achieve continual improvement of quality and productivity.

PRINCIPLES FOR TRANSFORMATION

Let's start with work standards that prescribe quotas for teachers. When you think of quotas, you probably think of workers in a production facility, and this was in fact Deming's focus when explaining his Point 11. I decided to keep this part of my Principle 11 because it does show up in different ways in the classroom setting. For example, when I was the school director (principal) of a USN middle school, the school had a quota of sorts for homework. Teachers had to assign homework nightly, grade two to three assignments a week, and return the graded assignments to students within 24 hours. However, I've learned that this is the wrong approach. Deming powerfully said that a quota is "a fortress against improvement of quality and productivity . . . totally incompatible with never-ending improvement."[21]

There was a noble premise behind the quota, which was that students needed frequent feedback on their work. The problem was that while the work standard was well-intentioned, the actual effect was that teachers spent less time on giving feedback and more time grading a high volume of work. The focus was on meeting the quota (grading two to three assignments per week) rather than on giving quality feedback to students. The numerical target for graded assignments superseded the quality of feedback as is often the case when quotas are used in practice.

What was the teacher's job? Grading two to three homework assignments per week or giving students quality feedback? It cannot be both.

A better approach would have been to assure that there was a well-articulated aim for giving homework that included a process for ensuring that students received timely and high-quality feedback. The job of management is to replace work standards with knowledgeable and intelligent leadership, including having some understanding of the job (teaching in this case). Replacing work standards with leadership leads to higher quality and productivity, resulting in people who are happier on the job. In the homework example, time spent grading homework was probably the number one complaint I received from teachers. A better approach to the two to three assignments per week quota would have been to work with teachers to design a system that delivered high-quality feedback to students on a timely basis.

The second part of this principle is eliminating numerical goals for people in management, which has been discussed extensively throughout the early chapters of the book. Even so, it's worth discussing a few key points.

An organization and the various departments and teams within the organization should have an aim, a statement that clearly defines the purpose of the team without being so specific in detail that it stifles initiative. A clear aim statement is something different from numerical goals. Internal goals set in the management of an organization are a burlesque if they do not include a method. Examples include goals such as "increase student attendance rates by 10%" or "increase math state test scores by 5%." Inevitably, natural variation in the direction of good is viewed as a success, while fluctuation in the other direction sends everyone running around looking for explanations akin to writing fiction (more on this later). I've been guilty of setting goals such as declaring that "we're going to improve test scores by 10% next year" without providing a clear plan for doing so. In these instances, a fair question would have been: "If we can do it next school year with no plan, why didn't we do it this past year?" And "If we can do it with no plan, why not increase the scores by 20%?" One important caveat when it comes to numerical targets are those in the category of *facts of life*. These are plain statements of fact with respect to survival. For example, unless student enrollment improves by 10% next year, the school will have to shut down. This is something altogether different from the arbitrary test score targets.

The main point of Principle 11 is that leaders must understand system capability; in a stable system you get what the system will deliver. If you have an unstable system, there is no way to predict capability. Of course, organizations and individuals need goals, but they do not need arbitrary numerical goals. Unfortunately, the vast majority of the goals that I have experienced in the education sector over the last two decades have been arbitrary and often without a method attached. This is inevitable in a sector that lacks an understanding of both the theory of systems and the theory of variation. The result of this lack of understanding is the tendency to blame individuals working within educational systems as opposed to working to improve the system itself. The Deming philosophy offers systems leaders a better way to lead if we so choose. **Principle 12: Remove barriers that rob educators and students of their right to joy in work and learning. This means, *inter alia*, working to abolish the system of grading student performance, the annual or merit rating of staff, and the Management by Objective of schools and school systems. The responsibility of all educational leaders must change from sheer numbers to quality.** The unifying theme of Principle 12 is the concern with pride of workmanship, what I call "Joy in Work" and "Joy in Learning" throughout the book. Bar-

PRINCIPLES FOR TRANSFORMATION

riers against the realization of Joy in Work and Joy in Learning may be one of the most important obstacles to improvement of the quality of our educational systems in the United States. These barriers must be removed at three levels of our educational system. One level is students, where the barrier is the system of grading student performance and the ratings and rankings that are a by-product of the grading system. A second level is teachers, principals, and other educators, where the barrier is the annual rating of performance or merit rating, especially teacher and principal performance appraisals that include student test data as a part of the rating system. The third level is the grading, rating, and ranking of schools and school districts within public school accountability systems. There is a common problem with the grading and rating systems at all three levels. That is, they involve the judgment and ranking of people, while failing to recognize that most of the variation in performance comes from the system within which the people live, learn, and work rather than from the people themselves.

Deming has indicted the system of reward as being one of the main constraints holding us back from a Win-Win culture. Grades at all three levels of the education system—the grading of students, the grading of educators, and the grading of educational institutions—are reward systems. In Chapter 2, I spent considerable time discussing the Myth of Performance Appraisal as well as the Myth of Merit Pay, which both have to do with rating and ranking educators. In Principle 3, I outlined some of the most important problems with grading students. In addition to those previously mentioned problems, I'll add the Pygmalion Effect to the list.

In one landmark study documenting this powerful effect, teachers were told by researchers that certain students in their classes had performed well on a test that predicts intellectual growth. In truth, these students had been randomly selected by the researchers to be described as high performing for the purposes of the experiment. These students were in fact only distinguished by their teachers' expectations for their performance. Eight months later, those randomly selected scholars described to the teachers as high performing had significantly outperformed their peers on IQ tests. And the teachers themselves consistently described the "bloomer" students as better behaved, more academically curious, more likely to succeed, and more friendly than other students in the class.[22] The Pygmalion Effect, coupled with the issues of grading from Principle 3, should leave us with serious concerns for student grading systems.

State accountability systems have extended the grading, rating, and ranking from individual students and educators to schools and school systems. As previously mentioned, schools and school systems in Ohio receive report cards with an overall grade, as well as grades in various performance categories. What are school report card grades measuring exactly? Are those grades a fair representation of the activities occurring within the school? Or can a significant portion of those grades be attributed to the larger context in which a school sits? Systems thinking assigns most differences in school performance to the system and not to individual schools.

One way to consider the theory behind the systems thinking perspective is to try to solve the equation below for the Performance Index component of Ohio's school report card. The Performance Index (PI) is a measure of the test results of every student and is reported as a numerical value with a top score of 120.

If $A + B + C + D + E + F = 71$ (PI score), what is the numerical value of F?

Obviously, the equation cannot be solved without knowing the values of A through E, or at least their sum. However, the report card system in Ohio suggests that we can assign a value to F (the school) with no knowledge of the values or effects of the other variables. The accountability system accomplishes this impossible task as follows:

Table 3.1.

An Impossible Equation

$A + B + C + D + E + \ldots$	$+ F$	$= 71$
State standards, test design, laws & policies school funding, facility access, community resources, neighborhood safety, household income, household wealth, home environment, access to healthcare, access to healthy food, housing stability, teaching methods, technology, and many (if not countless) other variables...	+ School	= Performance Index

PRINCIPLES FOR TRANSFORMATION

As systems leaders, instead of developing ever more complex systems for grading, rating, and ranking students, educators, and schools, we instead should shift our thinking to figuring out how to remove barriers to Joy in Work and Learning. This will help put us on the path to transforming those systems.

Principle 13: Institute a vigorous program of education and encourage self-improvement for everyone. A school system needs not just good people, but people that are improving with education. Advances in teaching and learning processes will have their roots in knowledge.

As discussed in Principle 6, training for a skill is finite because it ends when performance has reached a stable state. Principle 13 is focused on education, which is for growth and is never-ending. Where training is focused on skills, education is focused on knowledge and theory. The distinction is an important one; training and education are complementary components of an effective school system. Training for the current job as it is currently structured is necessary. It has been my experience that new teachers often arrive at United Schools Network without the classroom management and lesson planning and delivery skills they need to be successful in the classroom. In the absence of a vigorous training program for these skills, new teachers may very well flounder. This is unacceptable from the standpoint that USN is a young organization with a high proportion both of early career teachers and students with significant needs. This means that these teachers need to acquire basic skills to run a classroom in an efficient manner. Because of this, we have a robust summer training program for first- and second-year teachers that begins three weeks prior to the start of the school year and continues through weekly and full-day training sessions throughout the year.

However, broader education is also needed, which is an investment in the future. Things change fast in the modern world; in schools, change is brought about through advancements in many areas, such as increased knowledge of cognitive science. Systems leaders should not be enticed by every fad that comes along, but when there is a change that represents a potential advantage, such as increased understanding for how students learn, the school system must be in a position to benefit from it. On this front, Deming advocated for organizations to support and encourage the education of employees at all levels, with very wide latitude for the types of courses they were allowed to pursue (Deming said he wouldn't draw the line anywhere when it came to allowable educational pursuits!).[23]

The main point is that systems leaders should encourage education among the work-force with wide latitude for allowable pursuits. Educators that actively seek such opportunities offer a model of continual learning to students as well as benefits to the school system that fall into the category of unknown and unknowable.

Principle 14: Clearly define top management's commitment to continual improvement of quality and its obligation to implement the 14 Principles. Plan and take action to put everyone in the organization to work to accomplish the transformation; the transformation is everyone's job. Start with education for all in positions of leadership.

Management in authority will struggle over every one of the 14 Principles discussed in Chapter 3, as well as the management myths discussed in Chapter 2. To effectively address the obligations inherent in Principle 14, school systems should start by providing education for all in positions of leadership. The initial education should include an introduction to the System of Profound Knowledge, with emphasis placed on helping leaders to understand the systems view of organizations as well as the Theory of Variation. In *Out of the Crisis*, Dr. Deming offered several steps to get started on transformation. Organizational context will play a critical role in your own process, but I've paraphrased and translated the steps for an education-sector audience that can serve as a starting point:

The school board and superintendent must study the 14 Principles, understand their implications, agree on a strategic direction, and make a deliberate decision to adopt and implement the new philosophy.

Transformation implies a change of state. The school board and superintendent must feel a burning dissatisfaction with past procedures and a strong desire to transform their management approach. They must have the courage to break with tradition, even to the point of exile among peers.

The school board and superintendent must explain by seminars, community meetings, and other means to a critical mass of school system staff, students, and parents why change is necessary and that the change will involve everybody. People across the organization must understand the System of Profound Knowledge, the 14 Principles, and the management myths to ensure that enough people know the *what* and the *how* of transformation.

Every job and every activity within the school system is a part of a process that can be improved. A flow diagram for an activity such as teaching and learning processes will divide the work into stages, which as a whole form a process. The goal is to optimize the process as a whole, not to optimize individual stages.

Figure 3.3.
A Flow Diagram of Teaching & Learning Processes

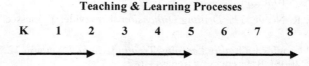

Students and teachers work together at each stage to produce high-quality learning. As students move from early elementary to late elementary to middle school and beyond, each stage is also working with the preceding stage toward optimization. Ultimately, all stages are working together toward quality about which the ultimate customer will boast!

Utilize the Plan-Do-Study-Act cycle as a procedure to learn how to improve the organization's processes (more in Chapter 8).

Everyone in the school system can take part in a team, the aim of which is to improve the input and output of any stage of the process. A team may very well be composed of people from different functional areas and can also include student participants. Transformation is everyone's job, which means everyone has a part in dealing with one or more of the issues facing the school system (e.g., drive out fear, working to improve a specific process).

Deliberately construct the school system for quality with certain percentages of staff understanding continual improvement and statistical methods at a basic, intermediate, and advanced level.

The 14 Principles for Educational Systems Transformation serve as a logical extension of the System of Profound Knowledge applied to schools. They proscribe the management dos and don'ts for a healthy environment for work and learning during the process of transformation. They are not a checklist to be completed in sequence, but rather an interdependent and mutually supporting set of guiding principles for systems leaders working to transition to the Deming philosophy. In the chapters that follow, we'll dive deeply into each of the components of that philosophy.

Endnotes

1. W. Edwards Deming, *The New Economics for Industry, Government, Education,* 3rd ed. (Cambridge, MA: The MIT Press, 2018), 85.

2. Richard Ingersoll, Elizabeth Merrill, Daniel Stuckey, Gregory Collins, and Brandon Harrison, 'The Demographic Transformation of the Teaching Force in the United States," *Education Sciences* 11, no. 234 (May 14, 2021): 1-30, https://doi.org/103990/educsci11050234.

3. Henry R. Neave, *The Deming Dimension* (Knoxville, Tennessee: SPC Press, 1990).

4. David Langford, *Quality Learning Training Manual,* Version 12.0 (Langford International, 2008), Reference Awareness – 6-7.

5. James F. Leonard, *The New Philosophy for K-12 Education: A Deming Framework for Transforming America's Schools* (Milwaukee, Wisconsin: ASQ Quality Press, 1996).

6. Richard Ingersoll, Elizabeth Merrill, Daniel Stuckey, Gregory Collins, and Brandon Harrison, 'The Demographic Transformation of the Teaching Force in the United States," *Education Sciences* 11, 234 (May 14, 2021): 12, https://doi.org/103990/educsci11050234.

7. W. Edwards Deming, *Out of the Crisis* (Cambridge, MA: MIT, Center for Advanced Engineering Study, 1986), 20.

8. Henry R. Neave, *The Deming Dimension* (Knoxville, Tennessee: SPC Press, 1990).

9. James F. Leonard, *The New Philosophy for K-12 Education: A Deming Framework for Transforming America's Schools* (Milwaukee, Wisconsin: ASQ Quality Press, 1996).

10. W. Edwards Deming, *Out of the Crisis* (Cambridge, MA: MIT, Center for Advanced Engineering Study, 1986), 126.

11. Joseph Sensenbrenner, "Quality Comes to City Hall," *Harvard Business Review,* March-April 1991, https://hbr.org/1991/03/quality-comes-to-city-hall.

12. "Schools and Grading," September 8, 2021, in *Munk Debates*, Season 2, Episode 42, produced by Stuart Coxe, hosted by Rudyard Griffiths, podcast, 51:07, munkdebates.com/podcast/schools-and-grading.

13. W. Edwards Deming, *Out of the Crisis* (Cambridge, MA: MIT, Center for Advanced Engineering Study, 1986), 23.

14. Walter A. Shewhart, *Economic Control of Quality of Manufactured Product* (Van Nostrand, 1931; reprinted edition, American Society for Quality Control, 1980; reprinted by Ceepress, The George Washington University, 1986).

15. Henry R. Neave, *The Deming Dimension* (Knoxville, Tennessee: SPC Press, 1990), 42.

16. James F. Leonard, *The New Philosophy for K-12 Education: A Deming Framework for Transforming America's Schools* (Milwaukee, Wisconsin: ASQ Quality Press, 1996), 201.

17. Gerald J. Langley, Ronald D. Moen, Kevin M. Nolan, Thomas W. Nolan, Clifford L. Norman, and Lloyd P. Provost, *The Improvement Guide: A Practical*

PRINCIPLES FOR TRANSFORMATION

Approach to Enhancing Organizational Performance, 2nd Ed. (San Francisco: Jossey-Bass, 2009).

18. The version of the list I used is from: Henry R. Neave, *The Deming Dimension* (Knoxville, Tennessee: SPC Press, 1990), 335. There is a similar list on pages 117-118 of *Out of the Crisis.*

19. Henry R. Neave, *The Deming Dimension* (Knoxville, Tennessee: SPC Press, 1990), 339.

20. W. Edwards Deming, *Out of the Crisis* (Cambridge, MA: MIT, Center for Advanced Engineering Study, 1986), 266.

21. Ibid., 71.

22. As described in: Steven Farr, *Teaching as Leadership: The Highly Effective Teacher's Guide to Closing the Achievement Gap* (San Francisco, CA: Jossey-Bass, 2010), 26-27.

23. Henry R. Neave, *The Deming Dimension* (Knoxville, Tennessee: SPC Press, 1990), 397.

CHAPTER FOUR

System Basics

The aim of the system must be stated by the management thereof. Without an aim, there is no system. The components of a system are necessary but not sufficient of themselves to accomplish the aim. They must be managed. [1]

—W. EDWARDS DEMING

IN JUNE 2013, MY colleague Kathryn Anstaett and I were sitting in my office at Columbus Collegiate Academy (CCA) evaluating teaching candidates. At the time, I was entering my fifth year leading CCA, which by this time was a fully built-out middle school serving grades 6-8 on Columbus' eastside. Kathryn and I had previously worked together for several years at CCA before she was tapped to found and lead our new middle school on the other side of town, Columbus Collegiate Academy-West (CCAW). She had just wrapped up her first year as the school director of CCAW, and it was growing from serving just 6th grade to 6th and 7th grade for the 2013-14 year.

Given a limited pool of prospective teaching candidates, Kathryn and I would come together when both of us wanted to hire the same person. Over the course of the hiring season, we decided that the fairest approach was to alternate turns in these situations. On this particular day, we both wanted to hire the same reading teacher, but it was my turn in the rotation. However, it was readily apparent as we reviewed rosters that the better decision in terms of optimizing the whole system was for Kathryn to hire this teacher at her school. This was because I had a very capable group of reading and writing teachers at CCA despite the one opening. Thinking through this whole systems lens, I agreed that Kathryn should hire the applicant. At the time, I hadn't yet heard of Deming's philosophy, nor had I been exposed to the idea of Appreciation for a System. My decision-making was simple. We were working to build a strong network of schools and working together with my colleague across town was the most obvious way to bring this to fruition.

It certainly helped that by the time I made the decision described above, I was well-established as a leader at United Schools Network. I had a close working relationship with the staff, as well as with the network's founder and superintendent. Truth be told though, even within this context, whole system thinking was not easy. As a relatively young organization there was still the question of survival, and as such, there was tremendous pressure on me as the school leader to achieve high test scores and to establish the reputation of CCA as a strong educational option on the eastside of the city. Thankfully, I had the backing of both my superintendent and the school's board to make these types of decisions; whole system thinking was at least the implied *modus operandi* as we were growing the network. This thinking has been strengthened by naming the System of Profound Knowledge as our management philosophy as well as by making the 14 Principles explicit.

My point in opening this chapter with this anecdote is to illustrate a straightforward example of whole system thinking. However, it is easy to imagine contexts where fear would prevent such decision-making. If I had been held accountable for my school's results in the absence of considering the impact of my hiring decision on the entire network, I would have been hard-pressed to hand over my pick to Kathryn. Under these circumstances, I would have been more likely to guard my corner of the system at the expense of the whole system. This is why the adoption of the new philosophy, and the 14 Principles has to start at the top with the system leader and the board. Without this commitment, there is no way to utilize the power of the System of Profound Knowledge.

Aim of this Chapter

The purpose of this chapter is to define what a system is and describe the basic structure and components of a system. Understanding systems may be our best hope for making meaningful change across the many dimensions of our lives at home, at school, and at work. The system lens will help you see events as a part of trends and those trends as a part of an underlying structure. This understanding will provide you with improved ways of managing in this world of complex education systems.

SYSTEM BASICS

What is a system?

In a general sense, a *system* is "a set of elements or parts that is coherently organized and interconnected in a pattern or structure that produces a characteristic set of behaviors, often classified as its 'function' or 'purpose'."[2] Most typically, when I refer to a system in *Win-Win*, I am referring to an organization (e.g., United Schools Network). Thus, a useful definition of a system is "an organization characterized by a set of interactions among the people who work there, the tools and materials they have at their disposal, and the processes through which these people and resources join together to accomplish its work."[3]

Systems Must Have an Aim

The *aim* of a system is a qualitative statement with methods attached that details a system's long-term constancy of purpose. Dr. Deming taught us the following about the aim of a system:

> A system must have an aim. Without an aim, there is no system. The aim of the system must be clear to everyone in the system. The aim must include plans for the future. The aim is a value judgment. The secret is cooperation between components toward the aim of the organization. We cannot afford the destructive effect of competition.[4]

It will be helpful here to start with some characteristics of an *aim statement* in terms of what it is and what it isn't. The bulleted lists in both categories that follow come from a careful study of Deming's writing about the aim of a system.

What it is:

- Long-term constancy of purpose
- Value judgement/clarifies values
- Relates to a better life for everyone
- Purpose with a method attached
- Includes the future
- Aspirational
- Precedes the organizational system
- Guides behavior
- Everyone must understand it

- Tied to and guides the system
- Transcends individual preferences; group calling
- Cooperative in nature
- Focused on the whole organization
- Set by leadership
- Coordinates efforts

What it isn't:
- Not a specific activity or method
- Not a numerical goal
- Not tied to a specific outcome
- Not Management by Results or Objective
- Not a way to control or punish
- Not a product of external pressure

It will be useful to revisit the systems view of organizations first introduced in Chapter 1 and mentioned several times since. In Figure 4.1 below, four components of the system have been labeled and appear in the black boxes. Those four components include (1) Suppliers, (2) Processes, Responsibilities, & Activities, (3) Customers, and (4) System Measurements and Feedback.

Figure 4.1.
USN Systems View with Four Labels

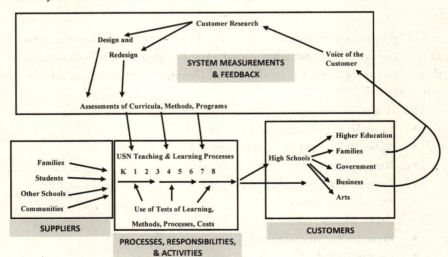

SYSTEM BASICS

Suppliers are the inputs to the system. In the case of schools, this includes the families, other school districts, and communities from which students come. The processes, responsibilities, and activities are the throughputs in the system. In schools, these largely are made up of the teaching and learning processes that take place in classrooms. The customers receive the outputs from the system. Families are customers of the school system, but so are high schools (remember USN is a K-8 system) and other parts of society, such as the business and arts sectors. The fourth and final component is the system measurements and feedback that inform the design and redesign of the school system.

More attention will be paid to these components in Chapter 5, especially regarding the role of students, teachers, building administrators, system leaders, and board members. For now, this introduction to the four components will suffice; the purpose of the reintroduction of the systems view is focused on the following question: What is the aim that provides purpose and direction to the system? By now, the importance of a clearly defined aim to guide the system and all its components should be clear. An organization must have an aim to ensure that everyone across all four components of the system is moving in the same direction.

At United Schools Network, we recently added a system aim as a complement to our vision and mission statements. Taken together, USN's vision, mission, and aim statements help align the work of everyone in the network. USN's vision, mission, and aim are listed in Table 4.1 below.

Table 4.1.

USN's Vision, Mission, & Aim Statements

	Statement
Vision	For every child, an open door.
Mission	Transforming lives and our communities through the power of education.
Aim	USN aims to create and continually improve high-quality learning systems that enable joy in work for staff and joy in learning for students, so that everyone can access opportunity-rich lives in our society now and into the future.

Each statement articulates an important aspect of the core purpose of United Schools Network. The vision statement is a picture of USN's desired future. "For every child, an open door" implies both a welcoming environment and an education that opens future doors. The mission statement is the why behind what we do, USN's reason for existing. It states for what, in the end, we want USN to be remembered. For us this is "Transforming lives and our communities through the power of education." The aim statement, which provides direction and long-term constancy of purpose to the USN system, has been added as a part of the network's most recent strategic planning in order to guide and coordinate organizational improvement efforts. The aim statement is: "USN aims to create and continually improve high-quality learning systems that enable joy in work for staff and joy in learning for students, so that everyone can access opportunity-rich lives in our society now and into the future."

This aim should be utilized by subcomponents within the system, such as grade levels and departments to guide their work. For example, there is a dean of students at each USN school. One of the elementary schools is currently working on improving various aspects of school culture. The first step for the improvement team working on this project was to write an aim to guide this work. USN also has an alumni services department that assists our 8th grade students and families as they make the transition to high school. This work continues as alumni move through high school and even as they explore college and career options after graduation. They too are working to improve their services and wrote an aim for the department. The aims for both the Dean's Office as well as the Alumni Services Department were written to align with the overarching system aim. This alignment between system and subsystem aims is illustrated below in Figure 4.2.

Figure 4.2.
USN System & Subsystem Aim Alignment

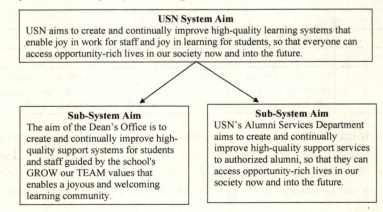

SYSTEM BASICS

USN is a system, an interdependent group of people, processes, and resources working together toward a common purpose. Alignment between the whole system and all of the subsystems is a critical component of thinking in systems, the topic for the next section of this chapter.

Thinking in Systems

As a starting point, it will be helpful to revisit the definition of a system from the start of this chapter and add to it the definition of systems thinking. A *system* is a set of elements interconnected in such a way that it produces its own pattern of behavior over time. They are coherently organized in a way that achieves something. The system may be impacted by outside forces, but its response to these forces is characteristic of the system itself, and that response is seldom simple. As you may notice from the definition, systems must have *elements*, *interconnections*, and a *function* (nonhuman systems) or *purpose/ aim* (human systems).[5] *Systems thinking* then is a way of thinking that focuses on recognizing the interconnections between the parts of a system and synthesizing them into a unified view of the whole.

A defining property of a system is that none of the individual elements have all the properties of the whole. Think about the example of the automobile as a system. No part of an automobile can take you from one place to another, only the whole automobile can do that. Dr. Ackoff, the eminent systems thinker quoted earlier, explained that a system is more than the sum of its parts using this classic example of the automobile as a system.

> When the whole automobile (system) is disassembled it loses its essential properties and so do all of its parts. The automobile is the product of the interaction of the parts, not the sum of the parts taken separately. This has an incredibly important implication for management that the Western world has not yet learned. Divide and conquer is the basic principle of Western management. Manage each department separately and in turn the whole will be run as well as possible. But this is absolutely false.
>
> In any system, when one improves the performance of the parts taken separately the performance of the whole does not necessarily improve and frequently gets worse. When the system is being run as well as possible, none of its parts may be. This simple example demonstrates it. The NY Times reported that there are 457 automobiles available in the U.S. If you

had engineers find the best part from each car, the best motor from say a Rolls Royce, the best transmission from a Mercedes, etc. and have engineers remove the best parts from each car and instruct them to assemble them. Do we get the best automobile? Of course not, we don't even get an automobile. Because the parts don't fit together.[6]

Ackoff's automobile as a system example illustrates the four defining characteristics of systems. First, systems have a function or purpose/aim. The function of the automobile is to provide transport from one place to another. This function is a property of the automobile as a whole and cannot be achieved by any of the parts alone—be it the wheels, the transmission, or the engine. The function of the automobile is what defines it as a discrete entity. Second, all parts of the system must be present for it to carry out its function optimally. If pieces can be taken away from something without impacting its function, then you have a collection of things and not a system. The wheels, transmission, and engine (and many other parts) cannot be taken away from the automobile without it losing its ability to transport. Third, the order in which the parts are assembled impacts the performance of a system. Not only that, but those parts must fit together; the arrangement of the parts matters a great deal. That is why assembling the best parts in the anecdote above results in a pile of junk rather than a luxury automobile. They do not work together as a system. And finally, systems attempt to maintain stability through feedback. *Feedback* is the return of information within the system about the status of a process. Its most important feature is that it provides information about system performance relative to some desired state. If you brake too hard as you approach a stop light, you receive feedback in the form of screeching tires and the automobile abruptly stopping. From there, you can use the feedback to make the braking smoother at the next light.

As I've characterized them throughout *Win-Win*, a school is a system. The elements are the students, teachers, administrators, curriculum, technology, buildings, etc. Its interconnections are the many written and unwritten rules, policies, procedures, lessons, teacher-student, teacher-principal, and school-family relationships that hold the elements together. The purpose/aim of a school will vary based on who you ask. Some may think it is to educate students and prepare them for college, military service, or work. Others may focus on scoring high on state tests. Still others may see schools as providers

SYSTEM BASICS

of childcare while parents go to work. Many believe that schools should do all the above.

The elements of the school system are typically the easiest to notice because many, but not necessarily all of them, are visible. I listed a few of those elements above, but there would be almost no end to the list (e.g., paper, pencils, chairs, desks, etc.). The interconnections are often harder to see than the elements; some are physical flows, like students progressing from one classroom to the next. Other interconnections include how students are assigned to schools; exams and grades; promotion requirements; budgets and resource allocation; and perhaps most importantly, the interaction of students and teachers during lessons.

While the interconnections are harder to see than the elements, the purpose or aim of the system is even more difficult to see. If you've ever found yourself doubting the purpose of an organization, be it a school or otherwise, that's likely because there is a mismatch between the organization's stated purpose (goals or other rhetoric) and its actual behavior. Fixing this mismatch is extremely difficult for three reasons. First, a critical function of almost every system is to perpetuate its own existence. Second, the system's purpose is not always what any one individual within the system intended. Third, and most importantly, even though we frequently refer to "school systems," it is not always evident that systems thinking is going on in our schools nor that this type of mindset is common among those that make education policy.

There may be no better example of non-systems thinking in education than when the issue of poverty is discussed. In one camp, you have people who insist that in order to fix underperforming schools, you must fix poverty. In the other camp, you have the people who insist that to fix poverty, you have to fix underperforming schools.

So, which camp has it right? From the systems thinking perspective, the answer is neither. This type of simplistic, linear, cause-and-effect way of viewing the world doesn't work in complex social systems. Instead of seeing only that A causes B, the systems thinker will ask how B may also influence A and how A might reinforce or even reverse itself. When someone tells you that poverty causes underperforming schools, you'll ask yourself how underperforming schools may cause poverty. The main point is that once you have the systems lens, you'll start thinking about the world and the systems in which you are embedded as dynamic and interconnected. Instead of looking

82   *Win-Win*

for someone to blame as in the case of underperforming schools, you'll start asking, "What's the system?"

System Structure

United Schools Network, where I work, is a system made up of four public charter schools and a nonprofit hub that serves as the central office for the schools. It is also a subsystem of the system of education in Columbus, in Ohio, and in the United States. This illustrates the point that a system contains subsystems and is itself a subsystem of a system in which it is contained. The point is not to go off the rails with divisions smaller and smaller or inclusion into larger and larger systems. Instead, the point is that it is nearly impossible to see the whole system all at once because it is spread over many places and operates over time. Too often we over-emphasize the people and processes that are within our view presently without an appreciation that actions and consequences for those current problems may have occurred in other times and places.[7]

When we draw the boundaries of a system to tackle a problem, it is critically important to operationally define that system prior to beginning the improvement work. Equally important is recognizing that no matter where those boundaries are drawn, there is always a larger system beyond them that is impacting the one that is within those boundaries. A useful way for thinking about this hierarchy of embedded systems is to look at it as three levels including the *core system*, the *subsystem*, and the *supra system*, each of which is described in Table 4.2.

Table 4.2.

Hierarchy of Embedded Systems

System Level	Supra System	Core System	Subsystem
Description	Contains subsystems	System in focus contains subsystems and is contained in a supra system	Contained in the core system

Think here about the arbitrary boundaries you have drawn or seen others draw in various educational improvement efforts for which you have been a part. In the No Child Left Behind era, the most typical example of this was drawing the boundary around reading and math to the exclusion of science, social studies, and enrichment classes. Even if you weren't explicitly

SYSTEM BASICS

83

thinking in these terms, you can likely in hindsight see how systems thinking would have been beneficial.

Another common issue is the lack of acknowledgement of the supra system because it is "out there" and not within our immediate sight. An example from my own work at USN and its four schools may help illustrate this point. Before diving into the anecdote, a quick refresher on our organizational context will be helpful. Table 4.3 gives a timeline and orientation to USN's growth into an educational system as it was first described in the Introduction.

Table 4.3.

United Schools Network's Organizational History

Organization	Grades	Founded	Neighborhood
Columbus Collegiate Academy	6-8	2008	Near East Side
Columbus Collegiate Academy-West	6-8	2012	Franklinton
Home Office (district office)	---	2013	Franklinton
United Preparatory Academy	K-5	2014	Franklinton
United Preparatory Academy-East	K-5	2017	King-Lincoln

USN started as a single middle school in 2008 and has since grown to include two middle schools, two elementary schools, and a home office. The basic design of the network is that one elementary and one middle school serve the east side of Columbus and one elementary and one middle school serve the west side of Columbus. Of note is that the newest elementary school, United Preparatory Academy-East is still in its start-up years and didn't serve its full K-5 grade level capacity until the 2022-23 school year. It launched in 2017 with kindergarten and first grade and has been adding one grade level per year since then.

This means that United Preparatory Academy-East won't feed into the middle school on the east side, Columbus Collegiate Academy (CCA), until the fall of 2023. For the first 15 years of Columbus Collegiate Academy's operations, it would not have its own feeder elementary school. The elementary schools that feed into it are a part of Columbus City Schools (CCS), and those fifteen or so schools have been among the lowest-performing in Ohio over the last decade and a half. There is an additional complication because these "supplier" schools are from outside of the USN system in terms of organizational governance. In other words, those elementary schools are governed by Columbus City School's board of education, while CCA has its own board. Both the CCS elementary "feeder" schools and Columbus Collegiate Academy are a part of the supra system of education within the city of Columbus. Imagine the possibilities if the USN system of schools and the Columbus City Schools system worked together to benefit the students on the east side of Columbus in the same way that Japanese industry thought of itself as a system working toward a common aim when working with Dr. Deming. Unfortunately, attempts at this type of collaboration have never materialized because of the artificial boundaries erected between public charter and traditional public school systems in the city. This hierarchy of embedded systems is illustrated in Table 4.4.

Table 4.4.
USN as the Core System

System Level	Supra System	Core System	Subsystem
Description	Contains subsystems	System in focus contains subsystems and is contained in a supra system	Contained in the core system
System Name	System of education in Columbus, Ohio	United Schools Network	Columbus Collegiate Academy
Function/Purpose	Provide the educational & social supports from birth through higher education to residents of the city and surrounding areas	Educate students in grades K-8 that attend USN schools	Educate middle school students on the east side of Columbus
System Components (Elements or Subsystems)	Traditional public schools, public charter schools, private schools, child care providers, social services, education nonprofits, colleges & universities	Home Office, Columbus Collegiate Academy, Columbus Collegiate Academy-West, United Preparatory Academy, United Preparatory Academy-East	Facility, teachers, school leaders, students, support staff, technology, curriculum, etc.

As you begin to view the world through a systems lens, the idea of improving the core system of which you are a part becomes more challenging. However, seeing the world in this way also opens a number of possibilities for improvement for which you may have been previously unaware.

SYSTEM BASICS

At the very least, this helps in understanding the various system levels in which your organization is situated. If I created another table, but this time with the system of education in Columbus as the core system, I could then make the city and its neighborhoods as the supra system. In doing so, you'd quickly recognize why those fifteen Columbus City elementary schools that form the *de facto* feeder system to Columbus Collegiate Academy are struggling so mightily. The neighborhoods in which those schools are situated are faced with numerous challenges including high poverty rates, violence, and housing instability, among others.

When well-intentioned educational leaders, policy makers, legislators, and reformers take up these issues, they often fail to do so with a systems lens. Accountability systems, school report cards, and any number of other legislative proscriptions crafted with school improvement in mind underappreciate the systems view. We all would do well to heed the words of noted systems theorist Donella Meadows as we undertake these improvement efforts

> The world is a complex, interconnected, finite, ecological-social-psychological-economic system. We treat it as if it were divisible, separable, and infinite.[8]

Viewing Education as a System

W. Edwards Deming's teachings are most widely known in industry and government. However, his teachings and principles apply to educational institutions, which, of course, is the very point of *Win-Win*. He taught the Japanese, and later American companies that would listen, to adopt a systems thinking perspective. The key point to what Dr. Deming called Appreciation for a System in the manufacturing setting is that most of the differences observed in workers' performance are caused by sources of variation within the production system itself and not by the workers. The skills and efforts of workers do impact the outputs of the manufacturing process, but are far less significant than the effect of the system on those outputs. Once management began to look outside the walls of their factories to external suppliers and customers as integral parts of their manufacturing system, they discovered numerous opportunities for improving quality, productivity, and competitive position. When they looked inside the walls of their own organization, they also found vast opportunities for improvement.

Before I go any further with the analogy between manufacturing and schools, I want to explicitly make a pre-emptive strike to objections from educators about the comparison between production work and educating students. The comparison between business and education settings have been made many times over the last few decades, often in objectionable ways. However, the analogy that I am going to outline is useful, and if you stick with me, is the exact opposite of treating teachers and students like inanimate products or widgets within an education production system. In fact, the framework I'm about to present is the very one that most dramatically shifted my own thinking regarding how we need to rethink our attempts at school improvement. As I dive into this example, it will be useful to take another look at Figure 4.1 to think through the insights that can be extrapolated from applying this systems perspective to schools.

Figure 4.1 illustrates K-12 education as a system that produces knowledge and skills. Roles within the system will be clarified later in this section, but it is an important distinction that what is being produced is high-quality learning (i.e., skills and knowledge) and not the students themselves. Like the performance of production workers, most of the differences in achievement and test scores at the individual student level are caused by sources of variation embedded within the complex and dynamic system in which they are being educated. Peter Scholtes gave us a very useful way to think about this dynamic

> The old adage, "If the student hasn't learned, the teacher hasn't taught" is not true or useful. Instead a much more useful characterization is, "If the learner hasn't learned, the system is not yet adequate."[9]

By taking the systems view, numerous opportunities for improvement that were hidden from view nearly jump off the page. This could include a method for regularly collecting feedback from high school graduates five to ten years after graduation. Think of the power of asking graduates from your education system the following question: Did we make a difference in your life? Alumni answers to this question will let you know the true purpose of your organization, and if you are fulfilling the mission statement on the wall.

It would be obvious and non-controversial to most educators to highlight the important role that parents and families play in the education sys-

SYSTEM BASICS

tem. If you look at the right side of Figure 4.1, families are customers of the K-12 education system just as are higher education institutions, local businesses, and society at large. However, families also show up on the left side of the model as suppliers. In the role of customer, and as I'm certain educators have heard, families may regularly ask their child's teachers, "What have you done for us lately?" On the flip-side though, and this would very likely be much more controversial in most places, the K-12 education system also should be able to ask of its suppliers, "What have you done for us lately?" The point isn't to assign blame, but rather that no one within the system gets to assume a passive role. When we define a school system as the employees that work within the district, you lose this perspective. Taking a systems view helps everyone to recognize that they have a stake in making our education institutions as strong as possible.

The final insight from the systems view is the role of feedback within the system. A deep and technical dive into feedback loops goes beyond the scope of this text; I'd encourage readers to check out Donella H. Meadows' *Thinking in Systems: A Primer* for anyone interested in an accessible introduction to learning more about this critically important concept. However, it is worth touching on a few important points.

Feedback loops are continuous. As a result, there is no such thing as an "optimum curriculum" or an "optimum school design." Ongoing research into child development and the science of learning as well as feedback from customers about their needs (e.g., changes in skills that are important to industry) drive never-ending efforts to improve teaching and learning processes. At the classroom level, this means that teachers are continually improving their lessons based on what is learned each school year, or even within the year, based on informal and formal assessments of learning.

In addition to the feedback that comes from customers of the K-12 education system (e.g., families, higher education, industry, etc.), there should also be feedback mechanisms within the school system itself. In the case of United Schools Network, the westside middle school is a customer of the westside elementary school. Each year, the elementary school supplies fifth grade students to the middle school as those fifth graders matriculate to sixth grade. One important loop involves having the elementary school collect feedback from the middle school to ensure that the K-5 curriculum is aligned to and adequately prepares its students for middle school.

The example of collecting feedback from alumni five and ten years after high school graduation, as well as the example of the fifth graders matriculating to middle school, introduces an important consideration with the use of feedback loops. That is, what makes understanding the behavior of complex systems like schools so challenging is the existence of delays in the feedback. Feedback delays can be imperceptibly short, as when you are the lead car at a stop light, the light turns green, and the car behind you honks to prompt you to accelerate through the intersection. Other times, the feedback we need about our system is far from immediate, as in the case of students matriculating to middle school. Still longer yet is the feedback we need from alumni five to ten years after graduation from the K-12 system to understand if we have adequately prepared them for success in society.

Delays in feedback are not inherently good or bad, but we do need to understand that they exist and that they are important to regularly analyze. In our sector, we operate with a sense of urgency, especially when we know the students in our care are not performing well. We must be careful here though as we tend to underestimate the true feedback delays in the system and/or ignore them. Systems often behave in counterintuitive ways; attempts to fix problems often just make them worse, and we often don't understand why. The answers may be elusive but recognizing that delays exist is an important first step. Additionally, having clearly defined system roles and adopting whole system thinking are part of the formula for overcoming challenges such as feedback delays. Both will be addressed in the next chapter.

Endnotes

1. W. Edwards Deming, "A System of Profound Knowledge" (working paper, March 10, 1990), 3.

2. Donella H. Meadows, *Thinking in Systems: A Primer* (White River Junction Vermont: Chelsea Green Publishing, 2008), 188.

3. Anthony S. Bryk, Louis M, Gomez, Alicia Grunow, and Paul G. LeMahieu, *Learning to Improve: How America's Schools Can Get Better at Getting Better* (Cambridge, MA: Harvard Education Press, 2015), 198.

4. W. Edwards Deming, *The New Economics for Industry, Government, Education, 3rd ed.* (Cambridge, MA: The MIT Press, 2018), 29, 36.

5. Donella H. Meadows, *Thinking in Systems: A Primer* (White River Junction, Vermont: Chelsea Green Publishing, 2008), 11.

6. "Systems Thinking Speech by Dr. Russell Ackoff." YouTube, November 1, 2015, https://www.youtube.com/watch?v=EbLh7rZ3rhU&ab_channel=awalstreetjournal.

SYSTEM BASICS

7. Edward Martin Baker, *The Symphony of Profound Knowledge: W. Edwards Deming's Score for Leading, Performing, and Living in Concert* (Bloomington, IN: iUniverse, 2017), 118.

8. Donella H. Meadows, "Whole Earth Models & Systems," *CoEvolution Quarterly,* Summer 1982.

9. Peter Scholtes, *The Leader's Handbook: A Guided to Inspiring Your People and Managing the Daily Workflow* (New York: McGraw-Hill, 1998), 36.

CHAPTER FIVE

Using Systems Thinking

If we wish to make breakthrough improvements in our schools and school systems (similar to the transformation in Japan after World War II that Deming supported), we must make time to work on the system of learning and to continually improve it with the help of our students. The System of Profound Knowledge provides the theoretical foundation for the transformation of conventional classrooms to those guided by quality learning principles. [1]

—DAVID LANGFORD

W. EDWARDS DEMING STRESSED the importance of leaders understanding the idea of a stable system. He asserted that "the performance of anyone that can learn a skill will come to a stable state upon which further lessons will not bring improvement of performance."[2] This was an interesting revelation for me because, for many years, I had heard policy makers and education reformers lament the fact that a teacher's improvement largely levels off in about year five of their career. More recent research on longitudinal teacher effectiveness has added nuance to this observation. The basic concept is that experience is positively correlated with student achievement gains across a teacher's career, although the gains in effectiveness are steepest in the initial years.[3]

When I read Deming's ideas around stable systems, it dawned on me that this was a perfect explanation for this phenomenon. In their first five years, novice teachers acquire many foundational skills. After this period of rapid improvement, there is a leveling off at the individual level because most of the potential for organizational improvement lies with the system and not with improving the individual. It is not that the individual teacher stops learning or gaining new skills, but rather that it gets more and more difficult to differentiate between the individual and the system after a certain level because most of the potential for improvement lies in the system itself. I'd speculate that this is just as true in other sectors such as medicine.[4]

The inability to understand the stable state of systems can have disastrous consequences in schools. Without this understanding, system leaders could draw the conclusion that experienced educators are not that important, since it appears that they either stop improving or improve less quickly in the later years of their careers. This is completely the wrong conclusion to draw. Experienced teachers are incredibly important exactly because of the stability they provide to a school, their ability to mentor inexperienced teachers, and their relationships with students and families. Most importantly, once teachers have a baseline level of knowledge and skills, it becomes much easier to work on the system where the real potential for organizational improvement lies.

Aim of this Chapter

The purpose of this chapter is to define systems thinking, as well as the roles of students, teachers, administrators, and school board members within organizations that are utilizing the System of Profound Knowledge to guide transformation. Perhaps the most radical idea put forth by W. Edwards Deming is the idea that any outcome we see within our system is the result of more than the skills and efforts of the individuals who work within the organization. Most of the performance differences observed between individuals are generated by the complex and dynamic system in which educators are only one part. Understanding this idea is critical for systems leaders because one of their primary responsibilities in this process is to work to remove the obstacles to whole system thinking within their districts.

What is systems thinking?

As first introduced in Chapter 4, this approach is a way of thinking that focuses on recognizing the interconnections between the parts of a system and synthesizing them into a unified view of the whole. Peter Scholtes referred to systems thinking as the "general reflex or habit of conceiving of reality in terms of interdependencies, interactions, and sequences. It is a way of thinking at the broadest macro-level (the galactic system) or the smallest micro-level (the genetic DNA system)."[5] As educational leaders, we work with systems somewhere between those two extremes, be it on whole system reform or on specific processes within our schools.

USING SYSTEMS THINKING

Individuals and Interactions

One of management's main responsibilities is to understand that the organization is not the sum of the abilities of the people that make up the organization, but rather the product of the interactions between those people and between the people and the organization. Ranking people in the hopes that it leads to organizational improvement is futile because of these interaction effects. Dr. Deming demonstrated these effects with the equation $x + (yx) = 8$ where x is the contribution of some individual and (yx) is the effect of the system on the individual's performance. Because there are two unknown variables and only one equation, there is no way to solve for x, but this is exactly what a ranking system attempts to do.

Another way to think about this is to consider the interactions of the individuals that work in organizations. If we use A, B, C, D, etc. to represent the separate abilities of the people in the school system, the full capability of these people working together can be expressed as follows:

Figure 5.1.
Individuals and Interactions

Individuals $A + B + C + D + ...$

Interactions
$$+(AB) + (AC) + (AD) + ...$$
$$+ (BC) + (BD) + ...$$
$$+ (CD) + ...$$
$$+(ABC) + (ABD) + (BCD) + ...$$
$$+(ABCD) + ...$$

Note 5.1. *Source:* W. Edwards Deming, *The New Economics for Industry, Government, Education,* 3rd ed. (Cambridge, MA: The MIT Press, 2018), 90.

The top equation represents the sum of the individual abilities of the people in the organization. The parentheses represent interactions between people, supporting or hurting each other in pairs, triads, grade level teams, departments, classrooms, etc. These interactions can result in negative, zero, or positive contributions to the organization as a whole system. Therefore, any organization is not the sum of the abilities of the individuals, but rather the product of their interactions.

A simple sports analogy may help bring this into focus. Think of a team filled with stars that significantly underperforms, and on the flipside, a team without much star power that goes on and wins a championship. In either case, this is a perfect illustration of the power of systems thinking and the importance of the interactions of the individuals on the team. In the first case, the product of the interactions was zero or negative despite the individual star power. In the second case, the interactions were overwhelmingly positive and a good example of optimization of a system.

Most of the potential for organizational improvement, be it in schools or in sports, lies within the system itself, rather than on focusing solely on improving the individuals working within the system. As we think about the role of students, teachers, administrators, and school board members within a school system, and their ability to drive improvement, there is a key point to consider. That is the idea of identifying those individuals who have the authority to work ON the system, as opposed to those individuals working IN the system without this authority. Systems thinker Daniel H. Kim helps illustrate the difference between working ON the system and working IN the system in the following example.

> If I were to ask you who has the greatest impact on the safety and comfort of your flight on a commercial airline, what would you say? You might answer that it is the pilots; after all, they're the ones who handle the takeoffs and landings and directly control how the plane operates under various circumstances. But then again, you might answer that it's the flight attendants, given that they have more contact with you during the flight. But if you really think about it, you may want to credit the designers of the aircraft, since they put the systems and structures of the airplane in place. (Now you know who to complain to about the carry-on luggage restrictions!) Whereas pilots and flight attendants work in the system, the aircraft designers work on the system—and therefore have the most influence on your experience of flying.[6]

An argument could be made that the complaints should rest with the executives who decided how much could be spent on the plane's design in the first place, rather than with the designers. However, the example gets at the main point, which focuses on who has the authority to work ON the system. After I read this example, I stopped complaining to flight attendants as I tried to cram my carry-on luggage into the overhead compartment. As is

USING SYSTEMS THINKING

often the case, front line workers such as flight attendants are only one part of a complex system, and they often have no control over the design of the system. This is a very important point to ponder as we start to define the cast of characters and their roles within our K-12 education systems. It is also an important consideration when forming interdisciplinary teams charged with improving some aspect of our education system.

System Roles: Students & Teachers

Let's start by looking at the role of the student within the school system. How should the student's role be defined? We've been comparing the educational system to a business system in the past couple chapters, but the analogy can start to break down when discussing the student's role within the system's view. This is where some may make the analogy that students are the raw materials coming into the system, while others may look to the other side of the model and see students as the products. Still others may see students as the customers of the school system that consume the teaching and learning processes. However, all three of these analogies—students as inputs (raw materials), students as outputs (product), and students as consumers (customers)—all miss the mark. William Glasser, the world-renowned psychiatrist, characterized the role of the student this way:

> If we accept the idea that the purpose of any organization, public or private, is to build a high-quality product or perform a high-quality service, then we must also accept the idea that the workers in that organization must do high-quality work . . . In our schools, the students are the workers, and today almost none are doing high-quality work in their regular academic classes.[7,8]

If we want high-quality work from production workers in a factory or similarly out of the flight crew on a commercial airplane, they must be provided with high-quality machines, training, tools of the trade, materials, methods, and other resources. Defining students as workers means that if we want to see high-quality learning and achievement, then we must likewise provide them with high-quality curricula, instruction, facilities, and other resources.

Development progresses from a dependent state to an independent state to an interdependent state. When children enter the education system in kindergarten they are in a dependent state. This should not be taken to mean that they are not capable of high-quality work, but rather that they are not ready to do classwork and homework on their own. As students develop over time, they increasingly become able to do work in school and at home independently. Certainly, by the time students leave the K-12 system, and ideally well before, they've achieved a state of interdependence where they are not only able to work on their own but also in cooperation with others. The key takeaway is that while a student's level of dependence will shift over time across their K-12 experience, at all points in the process they are the ones producing the learning. And learning is the product of an educational system.

If we take the systems view and define the primary role of the student as that of the worker, this has implications for the teacher role as well. First, and foremost, teachers are leaders. The nine attributes of a leader from Chapter 3 (see Principle 7 of the 14 Principles) apply to teacher leaders just as they do to systems leaders. Additionally, and in continuing the analogy of the student as worker, the role of the teacher is that of supervisor. This label doesn't imply that they are an authoritarian boss-type, but rather they are a facilitator working with students to support them in the production of high-quality work. However, while the student-teacher relationship should be collaborative in nature, we should resist the temptation to go as far as to say that teachers and students are co-workers. On this point, Jim Leonard captures this sentiment precisely:

> After all, if I have to undergo open heart surgery, the last thing I want to hear from the surgeons as I sink into anesthesia is the comment, "Let's brainstorm on how to best make this cut!" I do not want my surgeon to be a coworker, along with others on the operating room support staff. I want a surgeon who knows what to do and how to utilize the talents of others on the support staff.[9]

Teachers are the surgeons in this anecdote while students are the patients. Like surgeons, teachers have expertise that students do not have, just as surgeons have expertise that their patients do not have. However, in the medical example, what is being produced is health, and the patient is an important component in the production of their own health. The surgery could go off without a hitch, but if the patient doesn't do their physical therapy, eat a healthy diet, and follow post-operative instructions, then their health

USING SYSTEMS THINKING

will be compromised. Similarly, the teacher could teach the greatest lesson in the world, but if the student is not an active participant in the process, high-quality learning will not be produced.

This is why collaboration between the components of a system is so important. Students and teachers must be supported by an environment that makes this type of collaboration possible. Creating these conditions, and a healthy organizational environment in general, is the responsibility of top management. In a school system, this responsibility sits squarely on the shoulders of the school board and administration.

System Roles: School Board & Administration

My study of Deming's life and work has led me to think of him as a leader of leaders. He never led an organization of his own, but rather worked with industry leaders and chief executives in Japan and later in the United States. Deming long ran a successful consulting business, and later he led packed seminar halls attended by senior executives from all over the country. While he would be accompanied by experts from many different fields to support him as he led these seminars, they all came by invitation and were not employees. His professional stationary simply stated "W. Edwards Deming, PH.D. - Consultant in Statistical Studies" at the top (see Figure 5.2).

Figure 5.2.
Deming's Stationary

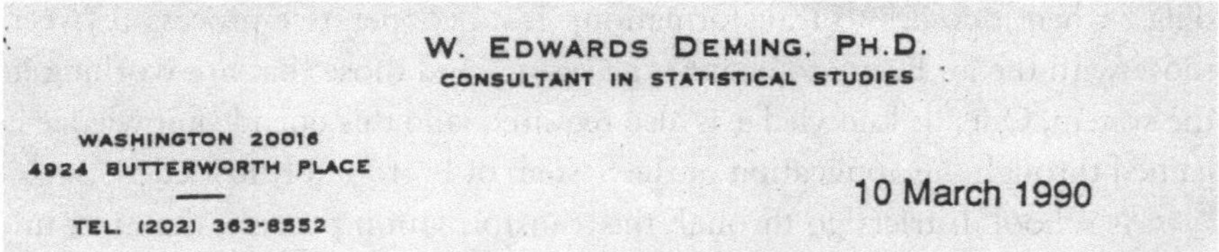

W. EDWARDS DEMING, PH.D.
CONSULTANT IN STATISTICAL STUDIES

WASHINGTON 20016
4924 BUTTERWORTH PLACE
—
TEL. (202) 363-8552

10 March 1990

Note 5.2. *Source:* The snapshot of Deming's professional stationary is taken from a 1990 outline of *A System of Profound Knowledge* that was emailed to me by David Lanford. David told me that this was known as The Butterworth Paper, a name that came from Deming's home address.

In his consulting work, he would insist that the chief executive officer or president of the company be heavily involved in the work prior to accepting an engagement. This was true even when he was working with very large companies such as Ford or Xerox, and yet, he was doing this work without his own team. This approach was effective because Deming knew that the key to organizational improvement did not lie in the size of the team of consultants, no matter how good their ideas. Rather, the key idea was that transformation takes place under a leader through the adoption of the systems perspective with a stated aim that guides the organization on a path to transformation.

In school systems, this leadership must start at the top with the school board and the superintendent adopting the new philosophy. A key understanding of the Deming management philosophy is that the individual components of the system, be it divisions in a business or departments in a school, should not be competitive but rather must reinforce each other through cooperation. The job of leadership then is to accomplish the transformation of the organization by helping everyone to understand that they must work in cooperation to optimize the system. The System of Profound Knowledge is the theory or lens through which one begins to understand why the transformation would bring gains to the organization.

Deming said that once leaders understand the System of Profound Knowledge, there is a compulsion to accomplish transformation as an obligation to themselves and the organization. This certainly rings true from my experience as I began to understand that there was a far better way by which to provide leadership to my own organization. Almost immediately, I started viewing United Schools Network in a different way and had this drive to spread Deming's ideas. This transformative change in state does not occur overnight, but instead is a process that unfolds within an organization over the course of perhaps five to ten years (Deming often said that there is "no instant pudding" when it comes to transformation). It's a cooperative process between those with the authority to change the system and those that are working in the system. Outside knowledge is also required, and this outside knowledge is gained through the application of the System of Profound Knowledge.

As school districts go through the transformation process, the most important role for the school board and senior administrators is to create an environment where teachers and students can fulfill their roles without fear. This new focus on the continual improvement of teaching and learning processes can only be sustained if the school board and senior administrators create the environmental conditions conducive to this new paradigm for schooling. Adoption of the System of Profound Knowledge as the core management philosophy as well as adoption of the 14 Principles for Educational Systems Transformation can serve as a guide. The 14 Principles introduced in Chapter 3 have been summarized and listed in Table 5.1 for your reference.

USING SYSTEMS THINKING

Table 5.1.

14 Principles for Educational Systems Transformation

14 Principles
1. Create constancy of purpose toward continual improvement of high-quality learning systems. These systems should be designed in such a way that they enable joy in work for staff and joy in learning for students, with the aim that everyone can access opportunity-rich lives in our society now and into the future.
2. Adopt the new philosophy. System leaders must awaken to the fact that education reform movements lack a sound philosophical foundation, must learn their new responsibilities, and take on leadership for improvement.
3. Cease dependence on standardized testing to achieve quality, and work to abolish grading and the harmful effects of rating people. Eliminate the need for inspection on a mass basis (i.e., standardized testing) by building quality into the product in the first place. The product in education systems is high-quality learning.
4. Maximize high-quality learning and minimize total cost of education by improving the relationship with educational institutions from which students come and to which they matriculate. A single source of students coming into a system, such as elementary school students moving into a middle school, is an opportunity to build long-term relationships of loyalty and trust.
5. Improve constantly and forever the system of planning, teaching, learning, and service to improve every process and activity in the organization and to improve quality and productivity. It is management's obligation to work continually on the system (school design, curriculum, incoming supplies and materials, technology, supervision, training, retraining, etc.).
6. Institute thorough job-related training for students, teachers, staff, and management, so that everyone can make better contributions to the system. New skills are required to keep up with changes in cognitive science, curricula, methods, learning experience design, technology, teaching techniques, services, etc.
7. Adopt and institute leadership aimed at helping people to do a better job. Management's responsibility must shift from focusing solely on outcomes to focusing on the quality of learning experiences and services produced by the educational system.
8. Drive out fear, so that everyone may work effectively for the school system. No one can perform their best unless they feel secure to express ideas, ask questions, and make mistakes.
9. Break down barriers between departments and grade levels and develop strategies for increasing cooperation among groups and individuals. Administrators, business & financial managers, operations staff, support staff, students, and teachers, etc. must work as a team to foresee problems in the production and use of high-quality learning experiences.
10. Eliminate slogans, exhortations, and targets for educators and students that ask for perfect performance and new levels of productivity. Such exhortations only create adversarial relationships, as the bulk of the causes of low quality and low productivity belong to the system and thus lie beyond the power of teachers and students.
11. Eliminate arbitrary numerical targets in the form of work standards that prescribe quotas for teachers and numerical goals for people in management. Substitute leadership to achieve continual improvement of quality and productivity.
12. Remove barriers that rob educators and students of their right to joy in work and learning. This means, inter alia, working to abolish the system of grading student performance, the annual or merit rating of staff, and the management by objective of schools and school systems. The responsibility of all educational leaders must change from sheer numbers to quality.
13. Institute a vigorous program of education and encourage self-improvement for everyone. A school system needs not just good people, but people that are improving with education. Advances in teaching and learning processes will have their roots in knowledge.
14. Clearly define top management's commitment to continual improvement of quality and its obligation to implement the 14 Principles. Plan and take action to put everyone in the organization to work to accomplish the transformation; the transformation is everyone's job. Start with education for all in positions of leadership.

Improvement Secret Weapons

There are two key revelations that I want to highlight here. First, underlying systems thinking and all continual improvement work in general is tapping into the insight of those working in the system. In the manufacturing setting, it is the production worker that is working in the system. In the airline example given earlier in this chapter, it is the pilots and flight crew that are working in the system. In our schools, it is the students who are working in the system. Remember that the product we are creating in schools is quality learning and the primary group among the cast of characters working to produce that quality learning is the students. They are the workers. However, as Deming pointed out, the worker can know everything about their work, except how to improve it. This means that tapping into student insight during the process is a necessary but insufficient component of improvement work. Teachers and school leaders are the supervisors overseeing students in their production of high-quality work. The school board and senior administrators are charged with creating the conditions for a healthy work environment. Like student insight, strong supervisors with subject-matter knowledge and a healthy culture are also necessary but insufficient components of the school improvement process.

This brings me to my second important point. A key concept of the systems view of organizations is that improvement efforts require someone from the outside that has Profound Knowledge to collaborate with the people working in the system (i.e., students) and the managers that have the authority to work on the system (i.e., teachers, school leaders). This means that students as well as someone from outside the system with Profound Knowledge (or someone internally that taps into outside knowledge gained through the Deming philosophy) are the substantially underutilized secret weapons of continual improvement efforts in schools. School and district-based improvement teams are typically missing both. Students working in the system can help identify the waste and inefficiency in the system. They must be paired with teachers and principals that have the knowledge and authority to change the system. Both must be guided by someone from outside the system with an understanding of the System of Profound Knowledge.

As an important part of this process, students must be regularly shown the data on which the improvement efforts are focused. By regularly, I mean daily or weekly routines by which teachers and students are examining the

USING SYSTEMS THINKING

most important data with guidance from the outsider. The data they are looking at should be displayed over time using a run chart or process behavior chart; students must see and understand this data, as well as be a part of the conversation to systematically improve it. This type of collaborative improvement work between those working in the system, those with the authority to make changes to the system, and the outsider with Profound Knowledge has tremendous potential as a powerful lever for school improvement. However, in my experience this almost never happens in our schools because of obstacles that regularly get in the way, and because very few in the education sector have an awareness of the System of Profound Knowledge.

Obstacles to Systems Thinking

The 14 Points for Educational Systems Transformation, along with clear roles for the cast of characters within an organization, help to create the underlying conditions for system optimization. There are also conditions and practices in organizations that can make systems thinking difficult for leaders, many of which you will no doubt recognize in your own school or school system: [10]

- Isolation from the customers of your organization. The most important customer of K-12 school systems are the students and their families, but also includes higher education, businesses, the military, etc.

- Central office department leaders and building principals have little awareness of, and no responsibility for, the entire system, only for their individual functional units or buildings (this silo effect can also happen within a single school building).

- Central office department leaders and building principals, and the people that work in those units, are often recognized based on how well they help those individual units succeed.

- Plans don't cut across individual classrooms, grade levels, or schools, nor is planning done cross-functionally.

- Success is measured by indicators important to internal leaders rather than by measures important to the customer (e.g., families, higher education, businesses, etc.).

- There is a focus on short-term thinking by which leaders look ahead only to the next month, grading period, or school year.

- Fostering and sustaining a culture of blame.

- Jockeying to be important and look good as an individual or as an individual unit within the organization.

- Strategic initiatives are not well-planned nor monitored and studied to see if they accomplish their intended effects. We simply put initiatives into action and do not see the system underlying the problems we seek to solve. Because of this, today's solutions become tomorrow's problems.

Two closely related themes to these obstacles emerge from the list above. The first theme centers on the idea that organizations often lack constancy of purpose. In other words, people do not have a shared understanding for why the organization exists. The second theme is a natural outgrowth of the first. When you lack a shared purpose, organizations are divided into functional silos that operate as independent fiefdoms, each with their own set of goals. The focus on the silo's goals, be it a department in the central office or a single school building or a grade level within a school building, has the potential to suboptimize the system as a whole, even if the individual unit's goals are met.

The main point of all of this is to recognize that overall performance suffers when individual parts of the system work to maximize their own performance instead of working together to optimize the performance of the whole system. This is illustrated in Table 5.2 through an example from a public charter elementary school I became aware of some years ago.

Like most charter schools, its students did not come from a defined geographic boundary but instead had to be recruited from the local community. At the same time, the academic program was being redesigned to meet the expectations of more rigorous state standards. The recruitment director was given very ambitious goals to meet, and in working to meet those goals had formed partnerships with many nearby preschools. The recruitment director worked extremely hard to meet the goals, but in doing so, recruited many four-year-old students to the school's kindergarten. As you will see in the table, this had several negative, unintended consequences. Most importantly, a much larger number of students who were not kindergarten-ready were being enrolled at the school to meet the recruitment goals.

USING SYSTEMS THINKING 103

Table 5.2.

Maximizing Subsystem Performance Lowers Overall Performance

(1) Subsystem Actions	(2) Effects on Recruitment Department	(3) Effects on Academic Department	(4) Effects on Support Services Department	(5) Effects on the Whole System
(2) Recruitment: Sources high number of young students	+ Exceeds student recruitment goals	- Significant redesign of kindergarten program	- Spend too much time administering readiness assessments	-1
(3) Academics: Redesigns curriculum & instruction aligned to higher standards	- Once year begins, recruitment spends much time explaining struggles of young students to parents	+ Higher quality and more rigorous lessons aligned to college & career readiness	+ High-quality lessons require less redesign for students in need of extra support	+2
(4) Support Services: Designs tools for assessing very young kindergartners	- Parents unaware that very young students need readiness assessment	- School leaders spend a lot of time explaining process to parents	+ Fair and transparent readiness assessment process	-1
(5) Results attributed to Subsystems	-1	-1	+1	-1

Table 5.2 shows that overall performance suffers when individual departments work to maximize their own performance and do not work together to optimize performance of the school as a whole system. The independent plans of each department subsystem appear in Column 1. However, the problem is that each department not only influences its own performance, but it also influences the whole system as it interacts with the other departments. These effects appear in the shaded cells on the diagonal whereby each department has developed and acted on plans to produce a + for

itself. As expected, the overall result of these actions is +3, but this is where things get interesting.

The recruitment department (Row 2, Column 1) sourced a very high number of four-year-old students from preschools, a high percentage of whom were not ready for the rigors of an all-day kindergarten program. This helped the recruitment department exceed the goals that had been set by district leadership; it gets a + for itself in Row 2, Column 2. The academic department (Row 3, Column 1) redesigned curriculum and instruction to align to the more rigorous state standards. It gets a + for itself (Row 3, Column 3) because the redesign improved overall curriculum and lesson quality. Student support services (Row 4, Column 1) designed tools for assessing very young kindergarten students. The team worked to ensure the policy was aligned to state requirements for early kindergarten entry. It gets a + for itself (Row 4, Column 4).

Each department also influences the performance of the other departments. These interaction effects can be seen in the non-shaded cells of Rows 2, 3, and 4 in Columns 2, 3, and 4. For example, recruitment (Row 2) negatively impacted the academic department (Row 2, Column 3) because they had to redesign segments of the kindergarten program a second time to accommodate very young learners. The recruitment department also negatively impacted student support services because they had to reallocate time to administering an overabundance of readiness assessments instead of working on other important beginning-of-year tasks. Both effects in turn negatively impacted the recruitment department, which had to spend more time explaining to parents why their child was struggling in the kindergarten program (Row 3, Column 2) once the school year started. Recruitment also had to spend time assisting with scheduling the readiness assessments (Row 4, Column 2) because this task was not a part of the originally designed orientation process.

These interactive effects clearly show that the individual units of an organization have an important impact on each other and cannot operate independently. The effects of one department on another can be positive, as was the case where high-quality lessons designed by the academic department required less redesign for students in need of extra support by student support services (Row 3, Column 4). However, this gain was offset by the extra time student support services had to spend administering readiness assessments to the four-year old students (Row 2, Column 4).

USING SYSTEMS THINKING

The totals in Row 5, Columns 2, 3, and 4 show the results for each department. Interestingly, in the absence of systems thinking, the recruitment director would likely receive positive feedback and a positive performance evaluation for meeting her or his departmental goals. However, the recruitment department produced a negative result on the system because of the impact that meeting their goals had on the other departments. The effects of each department on the system are shown in Column 5. Recruitment (Row 2, Column 5) and student support services (Row 4, Column 5) each caused a loss to the system even though they both met their own departmental goals (shaded cells). While the academic department produced an overall positive effect on the system (Row 3, Column 5), the interactions between departments produced a loss (Row 5, Column 5). The individual optimization (i.e., meeting departmental goals) of each department resulted in the suboptimization of the system as a whole.

The main point of this example is that the quality of the interactions between departments significantly impacts visible results. However, traditional performance evaluation methods assume that performance and its results are only produced and controlled where it appears, in this case within a department, but this is not the case. The interaction effects between departments are not considered even though they very much impact both the results of each subsystem as well as the system as a whole. The results produced by any individual within the department, or the department as a whole, cannot be separated from the interaction effects.

Whole System Thinking

W. Edwards Deming gave us a map of theory, the System of Profound Knowledge, by which to lead organizations as a whole system. In *Out of the Crisis,* he wrote:

> The job of management is not supervision but leadership. The required transformation of Western style of management requires that managers be leaders. Focus on outcome (management by numbers, MBO, work standard, meet specifications, zero defects, appraisal of performance) must be abolished, leadership put in place.[11]

The basis for seeing and leading our organizations as whole systems is the knowledge we acquire by using the System of Profound Knowledge. Like the departments in a school, the four individual components of the System of Profound Knowledge – Appreciation for a System, Knowledge about Variation, Theory of Knowledge, and Psychology – cannot be separated. On this point, Edward M. Baker said the following in *The Symphony of Profound Knowledge*:

> Although the four components are labeled separately, being a system, they can't be separated in thinking and practice, action, and application. The system, as a whole, is not the simple addition of the components. It is a system, which means that the four parts are inseparable and in a mutually reinforcing relationship, working together to provide knowledge and insight about whatever systems and performance are of interest. In application, the components function as a dynamic system of thought, interacting simultaneously, much like musicians playing in concert.[12]

This is the same way of thinking that applies to our organizations. Perhaps the central insight of systems theory is that systems for the most part cause their own behavior.[13] When something goes wrong in our organizations, the systems thinker doesn't look for someone to blame but rather will first look to the system for underlying causes of the problem. Whole system thinking is not just seeing the forest for the trees, as the saying goes, but understanding the interrelationships and interactive effects that give and maintain life within the system. The tricky thing to understand is that many relationships in systems are nonlinear, meaning that a cause does not produce a proportional effect. Whether we are thinking about an ecological system or an organizational system, as leaders we often fail to anticipate the nonlinearities and complexities of system behavior. Instead, we employ language that downplays the unintended consequences. Ecologist Garrett Hardin put it this way:

> When we think in terms of systems, we see that a fundamental misconception is embedded in the popular term "side effects". . . This phrase means roughly "effects which I hadn't foreseen or don't want to think about". . . Side effects no more deserve the adjective "side" than does the "principal"

USING SYSTEMS THINKING

effect. It is hard to think in terms of systems, and we eagerly warp our language to protect ourselves from the necessity of doing so.[14]

The school-based recruitment example illustrates the point that it is much easier to set goals by department than it is to step back and see how meeting those goals is impacting the whole system. Thinking in this way takes more awareness; it takes time to listen to the people that make up the organization and understand how decisions in one area impact those in another area. In addition to the mental challenge of systems thinking, there is also another obstacle for adopting this new management philosophy. Organizational leaders who have the authority to transform the system are typically in their roles because of success within the current system. It is reasonable for them to ask why they should change their management mindset. The question can be answered by turning this question on its head and asking: "Do you want to continue to face the day-to-day challenges that are costly in time and resources, or do you want to consider rethinking your approach to alleviate many of these challenges?"

The revolution of thinking that Deming preached is rooted in whole system thinking, grounded in the idea of cooperation for the benefit of all. He called this Win-Win. In Deming's words:

> We have grown up in a climate of competition between people, teams, departments, divisions, pupils, schools, universities. We have been taught by economists that competition will solve our problems. Actually, competition, we see now, is destructive. It would be better if everyone would work together as a system, with the aim for everybody to win. What we need is cooperation and transformation to a new style of management.[15]

In returning to the sub-optimized system example in Table 5.2, there is a better way to approach managing our organizations using the whole system lens. To optimize system performance, a good first step is for leaders to conceptualize the organization as a social system rather than analogizing the organization to a machine. Combining this conceptualization with giving individuals working within the organization the freedom to make purposeful decisions that impact their work facilitates effective adaptation of the organization. This is especially important during times of unpredictability and uncertainty; capable organizations are able to adapt and innovate and take advantage of opportunities.[16] The organization is whole when it operates as interdependent rather than separate parts, and when the individuals working within the organization are whole as well. The policies, procedures, evaluation methods, rewards, and punishments have a very real possibility of dividing and suboptimizing the individuals and, in turn, the organization. Optimization is only possible when everyone is cooperating to achieve the full capabilities of the organization by integrating the knowledge and skills of all its people. The leaders' responsibility is to ensure the conditions are in place for this to occur. Using the 14 Principles for Educational Systems Transformation is a good place to start. It is only when those principles are put into practice, when people have the information they need about how their actions impact the whole system, and when people are willing and able to work toward the purpose of the organization, that it is possible to fulfill the mission of the organization.

In the recruitment example, after realizing the unintended results, the school departments should collaborate to redesign their approach with a whole system lens. A summary of an improved process is shown in Table 5.3. As the table shows, this optimization process would only be possible if both the recruitment department (Row 2, Column 2) and student support services (Row 4, Column 4) departments were willing to incur what would typically be considered a loss. They would have to create plans that affect those departments negatively in the short term; this is what is demonstrated by the -1 notation in the shaded cells for each of them. The recruitment department could spend additional time visiting preschool programs to find more students that are of the typical age for kindergarten enrollment. The student support services department could design a pamphlet that clearly articulates the process for enrolling four-year-old students. Both tasks would be undertaken to enable the whole organization to perform better. The result would be optimization of the whole system, which is notated by the +6 (Row 5, Column 5). This contributes to the school being able to provide a better overall educational experience to its students and families, as well as contributes to the organization fulfilling its mission.

It is worth noting that this idea of whole system thinking and optimization would be new to the three departments that have been highlighted in the examples in Tables 5.2 and 5.3. This way of thinking would also be new to those leaders responsible for the financial aspects of the organization. The

USING SYSTEMS THINKING

Table 5.3.

Whole-System Cooperation Leads to Optimization

(1) Subsystem Actions	(2) Effects on Recruitment	(3) Effects on Academics	(4) Effects on Support Services	(5) Effects on Whole System
(2) Recruitment: Finds additional preschools from which to market the school	- Increases the amount of time visiting preschool programs	++ Time reallocated to coordinating lessons with support services	+ Better designed lessons make instruction more effective	+2
(3) Academics: Redesigns curriculum & instruction aligned to Common Core	+ Students more engaged in classes, higher retention rates	+ Higher quality and more rigorous lessons aligned to college & career readiness	+ High-quality lessons require less redesign for students in need of extra support	+3
(4) Support Services: Design pamphlet outlining 4-yr old assessment process	+ Parents aware that very young students need readiness assessment	+ School leaders spend time discussing readiness at orientation	- Incremental cost incurred for pamphlet design and printing	+1
(5) Overall Results	+1	+4	+1	+6
(6) Credit Given to Subsystems	+2	+2	+2	+6

cooperation between departments does not end with their work together; the same way of thinking must also make its way to financial discussions. Even though it would not be logical to try to identify the separate contributions of the departments, this is what happens routinely in most organizations. In the example, the recruitment department and student support services have added cost and taken a loss within their department while the academic department shows a gain on paper. However, it is critical to understand that because all three departments are interacting and inseparable parts of the overall system, they share the credit equally for the optimization of the system and the total results illustrated in Row 6. Any failure to equitably recognize the contributions of the subsystems (departments) is antithetical to Deming's guidance to have an Appreciation for a System. Conversely, a lack of Appreciation for a System, which is the usual condition of how we manage and are managed, would inevitably lead to demoralization, and create internal competition that would undermine the collaboration and cooperation needed to continue working in a way that leads to optimization.

As first discussed in Chapter 2, when people are pressured to meet a target value such as a departmental goal, there are three ways they can proceed: (1) they can work to improve the system; (2) they can distort the system; or (3) they can distort the data. It would be my humble opinion that if our efforts were divided among these three buckets, and then our efforts filled those buckets according to what actually happens in our school systems, buckets 2 and 3 would be considerably fuller than bucket 1. Whole system thinking is the antidote to these misplaced efforts, and the only thing I've discovered that ensures our efforts are better focused on bucket 1, improving the system.

Deming was very concerned with schools, which is why the final book of his long career was titled *The New Economics for Industry, Government, Education*. In the book he noted that people were asking for better schools, not only without a clear method for how to improve them, but also without a clear definition for improvement. Whole system thinking, through the four elements of Deming's System of Profound Knowledge, provides not only a good first step toward this end, but also toward the complete map of theory needed for system transformation.

Endnotes

1. This quote from David Langford came from my notes from an executive coaching session between he and I on October 26, 2020.

2. W. Edwards Deming, *The New Economics for Industry, Government, Education,* 3rd ed. (Cambridge, MA: The MIT Press, 2018), 87.

3. Tara Kini and Anne Podolsky, "Does Teaching Experience Increase Teacher Effectiveness? A Review of the Research" (Palo Alto: Learning Policy Institute, 2016), https://learningpolicyinstitute.org/product/does-teaching-experience-increase-teacher-effectiveness-review-research.

4. For an excellent discussion of the performance of individuals and systems in the medical field, see Chapter 1: On Washing Hands and Chapter 10: The Bell Curve in: Atul Gawande, *Better: A Surgeon's Notes on Performance* (New York: Picador, 2007).

USING SYSTEMS THINKING

5. Peter Scholtes, *The Leader's Handbook: A Guided to Inspiring Your People and Managing the Daily Workflow* (New York: McGraw-Hill, 1998), 58.

6. Daniel H. Kim, "Introduction to Systems Thinking." *Pegasus Communications' Innovation in Management Series,* 1999, *https://thesystemsthinker.com/introduction-to-systems-thinking/,* Retrieved 5 February 2021.

7. William Glasser, "The Quality School." *Phi Delta Kappan*, February 1990, 426.

8. For a more recent analysis of this issue, a TNTP report found that most students—and especially students of color, those from low-income families, those with mild to moderate disabilities, and English language learners—spent the vast majority of their school days missing out on four crucial resources: grade-appropriate assignments, strong instruction, deep engagement, and teachers with high expectations. The full analysis can be accessed in: "The Opportunity Myth: What Students Can Show Us About How School Is Letting Them Down—and How to Fix It" (TNTP, 2018), https://tntp.org/assets/documents/TNTP_The-Opportunity-Myth_Web.pdf.

9. James F. Leonard, *The New Philosophy for K-12 Education: A Deming Framework for Transforming America's Schools* (Milwaukee, WI: ASQ Quality Press, 1996), 47.

10. Peter Scholtes listed the obstacles to systems thinking in *The Leader's Handbook*, and I adapted them to an education setting. His original list can be found in: Peter Scholtes, *The Leader's Handbook: A Guided to Inspiring Your People and Managing the Daily Workflow* (New York: McGraw-Hill, 1998), 83-84.

11. W. Edwards Deming, *Out of the Crisis* (Cambridge, MA: MIT, Center for Advanced Engineering Study, 1986), 54.

12. Edward Martin Baker, *The Symphony of Profound Knowledge: W. Edwards Deming's Score for Leading, Performing, and Living in Concert* (Bloomington, IN: iUniverse, 2017), 40.

13. Donella H. Meadows, *Thinking in Systems: A Primer* (White River Junction, Vermont: Chelsea Green Publishing, 2008), 1-2.

14. I saw this reference to Garrett Hardin's work in *Thinking in Systems*: Garrett Hardin, "The Cybernetics of Competition: A Biologist's View of Society, *"Perspectives in Biology and Medicine 7,* no. 1 (1963): 58-84.

15. W. Edwards Deming, *The New Economics for Industry, Government, Education,* 3rd ed. (Cambridge, MA: The MIT Press, 2018), xix.

16. Edward Martin Baker, *The Symphony of Profound Knowledge: W. Edwards Deming's Score for Leading, Performing, and Living in Concert* (Bloomington, IN: iUniverse, 2017), 148. Baker also references the following source in his book: Russell L. Ackoff, *The Democratic Corporation* (New York: Oxford University Press, 1994), 32-33.

CHAPTER SIX

Understanding Variation

"Management must understand the theory of variation: If you don't understand variation and how it comes from the system itself, you can only react to every figure. The result is you often overcompensate, when it would have been better to just leave things alone." [1]

—*W. EDWARDS DEMING*

WITHOUT POSSESSING KNOWLEDGE ABOUT systems and variation, there's a propensity to misinterpret data, which can take the form of over-reaction or underreaction. This lack of knowledge is exacerbated by the fact that our biases make interpreting data extremely difficult. One such bias is that we tend to default to an assumption that there is a single, specific, and often readily observable reason for why results vary.[2] This is almost never the case and becomes particularly problematic when these misinterpretations become the basis for policies and blame in our school systems.

There will always be variation in how well individual students, teachers, schools, and school systems perform. In the face of this fact of life, we need to consider three questions as we work to understand variation:

- What is the variation telling us about our educational systems and about the people who work in them?

- When is it worthwhile to reduce variation versus accepting it?

- What are the best methods to use to reduce variation?

W. Edwards Deming's teachings help us address all three questions. He taught us that outcomes are either good or bad by the time we look at them. The enemy is variation and the sources of variation in and around the process that produced the outcome. From the systems perspective, variation is the enemy because it means there is loss of performance within an important process. The wider the variation around our target, the lower the quality of our process. The tighter the variation around our target, the higher the quality of our process. Without an understanding of variation and the ability to differentiate between common and special causes of this variation, leaders lack the ability to properly interpret data and, in turn, decide on a course of action that will lead to quality improvement. Deming's Knowledge about Variation is crucial for guiding leaders' decisions and actions throughout the transformation process.

Failure to understand and differentiate between the two types of variation leads to mistakes and staggering waste (more on the two types of variation and mistakes later).[3] As discussed earlier, in the K-12 education sector, one of the most visible uses of data is in state education department accountability systems. All 50 states now issue school district report cards typically based on various performance metrics such as proficiency rates on standardized tests, absenteeism rates, and college and career readiness indicators. Unfortunately, as we'll learn in this chapter and Chapter 7, absent an understanding of the Theory of Variation, any discussion of accountability is little more than a burlesque.[4]

Aim of this Chapter

The purpose of this chapter (and Chapter 7) is to outline three important concepts related to the Theory of Variation. First, I'm going to describe what Dr. Donald Wheeler calls "numerical naiveté" and explain its impact on the use of data in our schools. Second, we'll revisit the definitions of common cause variation, special cause variation, Mistake 1, and Mistake 2 first introduced in Chapter 1. Third, I'm going to posit a different set of methods for thinking about, visualizing, and acting on data using a set of "10 Key Lessons for Data Analysis" as a framework. These methods are not my own; rather they come from many of the improvement leaders mentioned throughout this book (e.g., Dr. Shewhart, Dr. Deming, Dr. Wheeler, etc.). These methods have revolutionized my own approach to just about everything I do as an education systems leader and will serve as the foundation to your own learning about the Theory of Variation.

What is the Theory of Variation?

While working at Bell Labs in the early 1920s, Dr. Walter A. Shewhart, who was first mentioned in Chapter 1, conducted studies of variation. Through this work he concluded that some processes display controlled variation while others display uncontrolled variation. W. Edwards Deming was introduced to Shewhart's ideas while working at Western Electric's Hawthorne Works during the summers of 1925 and 1926, and he later invited Dr. Shewhart to lecture at the USDA Graduate Schools where he oversaw courses in mathematics and statistics. Over time, Deming refined Shewhart's theory by adding the concept of a process to the theory; specifically, he started to refer to *controlled variation* as common cause variation and to *uncontrolled variation* as special cause variation. This was because common causes from within the process or system itself produced the outcomes.[5]

Variation within a process brings loss; the Theory of Variation gives us a framework by which to search for and appropriately respond to the source of this variation. The presence of common causes of variation indicates that the barriers to better performance are coming from within the process. The presence of special cause variation indicates that the barriers to better performance are coming from outside the process. With this understanding in hand, we can then take the appropriate improvement strategy for reducing undesirable variation. The response to random, common cause variation is to improve the process. On the other hand, special causes produce outputs that are not just different but significantly different. This type of variation indicates that the source of the problem is coming from outside of the process, so the appropriate improvement approach is to identify and deal with the special cause. No amount of work on the process will improve special cause variation.

Understanding variation in this way also allows you to avoid the two costly mistakes Deming identified, Mistake 1 and Mistake 2, that were also introduced in Chapter 1. They are worth revisiting here. *Mistake 1* occurs when we react to an outcome as if it came from a special cause, when it came from common causes of variation. Here we study and try to remove a non-dominant cause of the problem when the only way to improve is to fundamentally change the system. *Mistake 2* is the opposite. It occurs when you treat an outcome as if it came from common causes of variation, when it came from a special cause. Here we miss the opportunity to fix a specific, identifiable problem within our system.

Shewhart's theory coupled with Dr. Deming's contributions give us a powerful set of data analysis methods that came to be the Knowledge about Variation component of the System of Profound Knowledge. Without this knowledge, we as systems leaders are susceptible to the many problems in interpreting data that are discussed in the coming pages including "numerical naiveté," "noisy data," and "writing fiction."

Numerical Naiveté

My hunch is that you will quickly recognize how the affliction of "numerical naiveté" shows up within your own education institution. Leaders of most modern organizations—in education, in industry, in healthcare, and in government—encounter an overwhelming amount of information in their day-to-day work, and much of this information comes to us in the form of numbers. This data often flows in like a torrent from a mountain stream after the winter thaw. This implies that one of the challenges for leaders of today's organizations is the sheer volume of data they have at their fingertips. Technological advancements have allowed us to organize this data information in sophisticated spreadsheets and databases, and fancy visualization tools such as data dashboards often sit on top of those storage tools. But what do we do with this data as it inevitably moves up and down from week-to-week, month-to-month, and year-to-year?

It is very likely that most of us are doing what Deming cautioned against in the quote that opened this chapter, which is to react to every figure, often overcompensating when it would have been better to do nothing. Think about what happens as you look at data that comes to you regularly in a school setting. The monthly attendance report for the school in which you are the principal has come across the superintendent's desk. The attendance rate is down this month! Or maybe the annual state test scores have just been released. Reading scores decreased in 6th grade from last year to this year! The form of what comes next from the top is something along the lines of "Don't just stand there, do something!" The delivery of that message may vary a bit depending on your district's culture, but the core message is likely unchanged from this characterization. And so, you move into action. You may shoulder the blame yourself or look for a scapegoat. You may type up a lengthy email with detailed bullet points attempting to explain the results. You may go back to your team with steadfast resolve to get to the bottom of

UNDERSTANDING VARIATION

the decline in the attendance rate or in the test scores and to set new goals for the next month or next year. It is very likely that this process repeats itself month after month and year after year. This year it was a decline in 6th grade reading scores and perhaps next year those scores rebound but now the 6th grade math scores have declined. However, have you ever stopped to ask yourself: "Does the decline in my data represent something meaningful?" And just as importantly, you would ask yourself that same question even if the data was moving in the other direction. That is, "Does the increase in my data represent something meaningful?"

For a moment, let's take it as fact that the attendance rate and test score declines were *not* meaningful. I'll show you how you can tell for sure with actual data sets in this chapter and the next. But taking this point as true, imagine the waste of time and effort that is spent worrying about, explaining, and redesigning plans, all in the name of something that didn't represent a statistically significant change in performance. Scurrying around in reaction to the call to "Just do something!" is likely the modus operandi in most schools and organizations. Why is this the case if we now have these sophisticated data tools at our fingertips? What underlies all this wasted time and energy? The answer at least in part is *numerical naiveté*, a concept Dr. Donald Wheeler captured perfectly in his book *Understanding Variation*, aptly subtitled *The Key to Managing Chaos*. Wheeler puts it this way:

> This process of digesting data has been widely neglected at all levels of our educational system. Managers and workers, educators and students, accountants and businessmen, financial analysts and bankers, doctors and nurses, and especially lawyers and journalists all have one thing in common. They come out of their educational experience knowing how to add, subtract, multiply, and divide, yet they have no understanding of how to digest numbers to extract the knowledge that may be locked up inside the data. In fact, this shortcoming is also seen, to a lesser extent, among engineers and scientists.
>
> This deficiency has been called "numerical naiveté." Numerical naiveté is not a failure with arithmetic, but it is instead a failure to know how to use the basic tools of arithmetic to understand data. Numerical naiveté is not addressed by the traditional courses in the primary or secondary schools, nor is it addressed by advanced courses in mathematics. This is why even highly educated individuals can be numerically naive.[6]

The antidote to this terrible affliction is the component of the System of Profound Knowledge that Deming called Knowledge about Variation. The statistical techniques that underlie understanding variation were pioneered by Dr. Walter Shewhart in the 1920s and thoroughly vetted over the next century by Deming and many others across all sectors. Practicing these techniques with real data within the organization where I work has completely shifted how I use data in my career. I'll attempt to make the case that they are worthy of your study in these two chapters on variation.

Data in Context

Dr. Wheeler's first principle for understanding data is, "No data have meaning apart from their context." This principle serves as a summary of two rules that Dr. Shewhart gave for the presentation of data. In *Understanding Variation,* Wheeler paraphrased Shewhart's original rules, and it will be helpful here to review the original versions in this section. To bring these two rules to life, I'll first provide Wheeler's summary of the rules, and then I'll outline a real-life example of how we break the rules in practice in the education sector. Shewhart's Rule One for the presentation of data is as follows:

> Data should always be presented in such a way that preserves the evidence in the data for all of the predictions that might be made from these data.[7]

The implications of this rule are significant. As a starting point, the context from which the data was collected should not be divorced from the data itself. Even in presentation form, anyone looking at the data should be able to answer some basic questions such as:

- Who collected the data?
- How was the data collected?
- When was the data collected?
- Where was the data collected?
- What do these values represent?
- What is the operational definition of the concept being measured?

UNDERSTANDING VARIATION

- How were the values of any computed data derived from the raw inputs?
- Have there been any changes made over time that impact the data set (i.e., a change in the operational definition of the concept being measured, a change in the formula being used to compute the data, etc.)?

We typically organize data sets into a table of values (e.g., a spreadsheet). However, tables are necessary but insufficient in the analysis of this data. It is very difficult for people to see trends or patterns when data is only displayed in table or spreadsheet format. These displays become even more problematic when color-coding (i.e., red, yellow, green) or other similar graphics are added to the table for the purpose of comparing the data to each other or to a target. Furthermore, data in a table does not provide a meaningful time series nor any sense of whether the data was expected or a surprise. The simple fix on this front is to include a time series graph along with the table. This brings us to Shewhart's Rule Two for the presentation of data:

> Whenever an average, range, or histogram is used to summarize data, the summary should not mislead the user into taking any action that the user would not take if the data were presented in a time series.[8]

The main reason that Dr. Wheeler stresses this point is because almost all data occurs across time, and in many cases this time order *is* the point. In other words, it's the pattern that emerges from viewing the data in time order that gives us the most insight into what is happening with the data we are analyzing. This is a demonstration of what Deming indicated when he said that knowledge has temporal spread (more on this later in the chapter). Wheeler takes Shewhart's two rules and summarizes them in one succinct first principle for understanding data, the aforementioned: *"No data have meaning apart from their context."*[9]

It will be helpful here to turn to an example to bring this principle alive. Each year in the Buckeye state, the Ohio Department of Education releases a summary of state testing results in a five to six-page document. A snapshot from the 2017-18 results is shown in the Table 6.1.[10]

120   *Win-Win*

Table 6.1.
Ohio School & District Results 2017-18, Page 2

Ohio students continue to show improved achievement in academic content areas

Achievement increased in multiple areas – and with most subgroups of students. Overall proficiency rates increased by 1.6 points in English language arts, with a slight increase in math. Increases were especially notable in fourth, fifth, and seventh grades. Algebra I had an over 4 percentage point increase and biology almost an 8-percentage point increase in first-time test takers meeting proficiency. Third grade saw decreases this year but has maintained higher proficiency than two years ago. Sixth grade had small decreases compared to last year.

Grade	Subject	2015-2016	2016-2017	2017-2018	
3	ELA	54.9%	63.8%	61.2%	↓
	Math	65.8%	70.6%	67.0%	↓
4	ELA	57.5%	62.8%	66.4%	↑
	Math	69.2%	72.4%	72.5%	↑
5	ELA	60.2%	67.7%	70.2%	↑
	Math	62.4%	61.6%	62.9%	↑
	Science	67.5%	68.3%	68.5%	↑
6	ELA	54.0%	60.2%	59.9%	↓
	Math	56.7%	60.2%	59.4%	↓
7	ELA	53.6%	59.2%	63.9%	↑
	Math	55.3%	56.1%	59.4%	↑
8	ELA	47.5%	50.3%	54.5%	↑
	Math	52.7%	54.9%	54.3%	↓
	Science	64.9%	65.8%	67.6%	↑

The headline for the full document is stated in red in all caps on page 1 of the full report (not included here): "STUDENT ACHIEVEMENT INCREASES SEEN STATEWIDE IN 2018 OHIO SCHOOL REPORT CARDS." This is followed by the headline on page 2 that accompanies the data table in Table 6.1: "Ohio students continue to show improved achievement in academic content areas." The data table shows all the grades and subject areas where state tests are given each year in grades 3-8 in the first two columns. In the next three columns, proficiency rates for the 2015-16, 2016-17, and 2017-18 school years are listed. In the column on the far right, there is an arrow pointing up to show that test scores increased from 2016-17 to 2017-18 or there is an arrow pointing down to show that test scores decreased from 2016-17 to 2017-18. There is no doubt that the average proficiency rates with up arrows had a year-to-year increase. For example, the percentage of proficient students in 4th grade math went from 72.4% in 2016-17 to 72.5% in 2017-18. On the flip side, there is no doubt that the average proficiency rates with down arrows had a year-to-year decrease. For example, the percentage of proficient students in 3rd grade reading went from 63.8% in 2016-17 to 61.2% in 2017-18.

UNDERSTANDING VARIATION

The key question though is not whether there was an increase or decrease in the data, but rather if that change is meaningful. Does an increase in proficiency rates in the state testing data represent improvement? Does a decrease in proficiency rates in the state testing data represent a decrease in performance? To answer these questions, we need to do two things. First, we need a clear definition of improvement, which I first reviewed in the introduction. For outcomes to be considered an improvement, they must result from fundamental changes you've made to some component of your system that do the following: alter how work or activity is done or the make-up of a tool; produce visible, positive differences in results relative to historical norms; and have a lasting impact. When improvement is viewed through this lens, the description of "accountability as burlesque" comes much more into focus. Second, we need to understand the two types of variation and the two types of mistakes we can make in interpreting variation in our data mentioned at the beginning of this chapter. There is no way to claim improvement or the lack thereof without first understanding the type of variation present, as well as what the state testing results look like beyond simply comparing two years' worth of data points. We'll first turn to making sure we have a firm understanding of common and special cause variation as well as Mistake 1 and Mistake 2 before returning to Table 6.1 to learn why the narrative that accompanies the table is akin to writing fiction.

Understanding Variation

The primary purpose in understanding variation is that it allows us to increase quality. Let's begin this understanding by defining quality and quality improvement. When we say we are striving for *quality* outcomes, what we are really saying is that we are striving for minimal variation around some target or optimum value. *Quality improvement* work then is the idea of reducing variation around that target. It is also important here to revisit the two types of variation. We've established that there are common causes of variation which are sources of variation that are inherent in a process over time. They affect every outcome of the process and everyone working in the process. There is also special cause variation, the source of variation in a process that does not come from the system itself, but from something acting on the system, which makes it much more likely that we can identify and address it.

A key to quality improvement is being able to differentiate between common and special cause variation within a process that is important to us. Remember the idea that the human brain tends to default to an assumption that there is a single, specific, and often readily observable reason why results vary. This is almost never the case and results in the misinterpretation of data along two fronts—what Deming called Mistake 1 and Mistake 2. Mistake 1 occurs when we react to an outcome as if it came from a special cause, when it came from common causes of variation. Deming referred to this as tampering with the system. *Tampering* is action taken to compensate for variation within the control limits of a stable system; tampering increases rather than decreases variation. Mistake 2 is the opposite. It occurs when you treat an outcome as if it came from common causes of variation, when it came from a special cause. This is akin to not studying a data aberration when you should have done so.

From the systems perspective, variation is the enemy because it means there is loss of performance within an important process. The wider the variation around our target, the lower the quality of our process. The tighter the variation around our target, the higher the quality of our process. This is shown in Figure 6.1, which is focused on some assessment of student achievement. The aim of quality improvement work is to both increase the average of the assessment scores and to reduce the variation around that average. In the diagram, this improvement is illustrated by moving from the solid line distribution to the dashed line distribution. However, without an understanding of variation and the ability to differentiate between common and special causes of this variation, leaders lack the ability to properly interpret data and in turn decide on a course of action that will lead to this type of quality improvement.

Figure 6.1.
Results of Quality Improvement of Teaching and Learning Processes

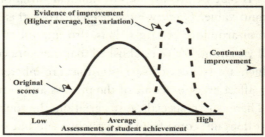

Note 6.1. *Source:* I first saw a version of this diagram in: James F. Leonard, *The New Philosophy for K-12 Education: A Deming Framework for Transforming America's Schools* (Milwaukee, WI: ASQ Quality Press, 1996), 60.

UNDERSTANDING VARIATION

A key step in the improvement process is to employ a statistical tool called a *process behavior chart*, first introduced in Chapter 1, that differentiates between common and special cause variation. Process behavior charts turn the normal distribution on its side, extend the upper and lower limits (plus and minus three-sigma) of controlled, common cause variation, and add the element of time. For the purpose of this text, it is enough to know that the Natural Process Limits represented by the dashed lines in Figure 6.2 are set at a distance of three-sigma above the central line and three-sigma below the central line. *Three-sigma* is a measure of dispersion for the individual values displayed in a chart (based on how the limits are calculated, sigma is not the same thing as standard deviation).[11]

This foundational premise of process behavior charts is illustrated in Figure 6.2. Once we differentiate between common cause and special cause variation, we then have a better understanding for a course of action. If the source of variation on some key measure is only due to common cause variation, and if you're not happy with the outcome, the appropriate corrective action is to change the process. If, on the other hand, the outcome is due to special cause variation, then the appropriate corrective action is to identify and remove the special cause.

Figure 6.2.
Foundation of the Process Behavior Chart

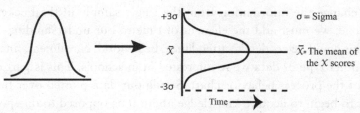

Note 6.2 *Source:* I first saw a version of this diagram in: James F. Leonard, *The New Philosophy for K-12 Education: A Deming Framework for Transforming America's Schools* (Milwaukee, WI: ASQ Quality Press, 1996), 129.

After viewing Figure 6.2, it is a good time to circle back to the idea that I brought up earlier in the chapter that knowledge has temporal spread. The normal distribution[12] on the left side of the diagram is a static snapshot of some piece of information from our system. It is analogous to taking a sample bucket of water from a mountain stream one time. The water sample in the bucket has some set of characteristics that are displayed in that normal distribution, but they may not be very representative of that mountain stream a week, a month, or a year later. Too often though, we are looking back at that original bucket of water weeks, months, or even years later as if it is helpful. This situation is represented in Figure 6.3.

Figure 6.3.

Normal Distribution as a Single Bucket from a Mountain Stream of Data

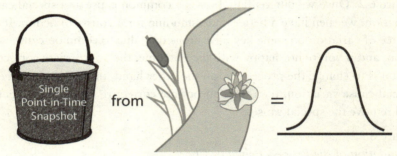

To change the information from the single sample in the bucket into knowledge, we must add the element of time to our understanding of the data. This could be academic, attendance, behavioral, enrollment, financial, or any other type of data we're interested in in schools. This is part of the power of the process behavior chart. Seeing our data plotted over time allows us to begin to acquire knowledge about it as opposed to one-point-in time snapshots of information. The data most helpful to system leaders in schools does not sit still like the water from the single bucket but rather rushes at us like a mountain stream. The process behavior chart allows us to display the mountain stream as it rushes by, so that we have a continuous sample of the water, as opposed to a point-in-time snapshot. Data displayed over time give us a much clearer picture of what is happening in our system as opposed to one or two data points. This is the basic idea underlying the premise that knowledge has temporal spread and is represented by the illustration in Figure 6.4.

UNDERSTANDING VARIATION

Figure 6.4.
Process Behavior Chart Captures Data that Streams in Continuously

Once we begin to plot our data over time and start to accumulate knowledge about how this data is performing, we can then begin to understand when to react to the data and, equally importantly, when not to tamper (i.e., overreact) with the data. This will be the focus of the next section.

Filtering Out the Noise

The process behavior chart can perform several important jobs because of how it takes the variation of any set of data into account. The chart defines the Voice of the Process by displaying the data as a time series. The *Voice of the Process* is the performance of a process over time, independent of the desired outcomes. Once you have enough baseline data (see Data Lesson #5 in Chapter 7), it gives you a way to understand if you can make predictions about the performance of future data. When the conditions are satisfied for making predictions about future performance, the chart will also define the range of values that you can reasonably expect to see in the near future, assuming nothing fundamental changes within your system. If something changes within your system, the chart will communicate this to you as well.

One of the primary flaws with the state testing data in Table 6.1 is the attempt in both the headline and the description to the left of the chart to attach meaning to each year of results. The process behavior chart approach instead focuses on the behavior of the state testing data over time. When it comes to filtering out the noise, Wheeler has the following critical advice:

> Variation is the random and miscellaneous component that undermines the simple and limited comparisons. The "noise" introduced by routine variation is what confuses and clouds all comparisons between single values. Until you can allow for the noise in a time series, you cannot fully under-

stand just what may be indicated by a single value. Is the current value a "signal" that something has changed, or does the current value differ from the historic average by nothing but "noise"? The answer to this question is the essence of making sense of any value from a time series.[13]

The whole point of the process behavior chart once you have a data set of historical values is to be able to differentiate between "noise" (common cause variation) and "signals" (special cause variation). Being able to make the distinction between noise and signals or between common cause and special cause variation is the foundation for properly analyzing and interpreting data. Remember Wheeler's first principle: "No data have meaning apart from their context." His second principle for understanding data is: "While every data set contains noise, some data sets contain signals. Therefore, before you can detect a signal within any given data set, you must filter out the noise."[14]

The power of the process behavior chart lies in its ability to filter out the noise, or common cause variation, through the construction of *Natural Process Limits*. There are several rules that can then be used to detect signals, or special cause variation, within the data set. Rule 1 for detecting a signal is indicated by any single data point that falls outside of either the Upper or Lower Natural Process Limit. Rule 2 for detecting a signal is indicated by a run of eight data points on the same side of the central line. Rule 3 for detecting a signal is indicated when three out of four consecutive data points are closer to the upper or lower limit than to the central line. The three rules are illustrated in Figure 6.5 on the next page.[15]

It's worth revisiting the idea of Mistake 1 (overreaction) and Mistake 2 (underreaction) introduced earlier in this chapter. Mistake 1 likely leads to the biggest source of wasted time and resources and occurs when routine, common cause variation is interpreted as meaningfully different from past performance. In other words, this is interpreting noise as if it were a signal. In organizations like schools, Mistake 1 leads to lots of tampering, which in turn typically leads to worse results. Much of this tampering in schools is perpetrated by state departments of education and other similar institutions as they attempt to improve schools with good intentions but without an understanding of the natural ups and downs of educational data. Mistake 2 is the opposite of Mistake 1. It occurs when a significant change has occurred

UNDERSTANDING VARIATION

Figure 6.5.
Rules for Finding Signals

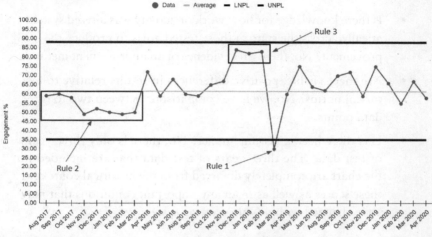

Note 6.5. *Source:* I first encountered the three rules for finding signals displayed in this way in: Mark Graban, *Measures of Success: React Less, Lead Better, Improve More* (Colleyville, TX: Constancy, Inc., 2019).

in a process or system, but it goes undetected. This could occur with any type of educational data but would be missed if you're not charting your data over time.

The process behavior chart allows the user to differentiate between the noise of common cause variation and the signals of special cause variation. The *Natural Process Limits* allow us to filter out the noise in order to identify the signals or special events in our data. This in turn allows us to chart a proper course of action for any improvement attempts that are made on our system.

Writing Fiction

Let's return now to the state testing data and the accompanying narrative that is displayed in Table 6.1. The overall claim accompanying the data is that "Ohio students continue to show improved achievement in academic content areas." Any claim of improvement must meet the three parts of the definition of improvement (changing how we work, positive results, lasting impact) outlined earlier in this chapter. Does the claim hold up to this scrutiny? I would say that is clearly not the case. Even in the grade levels and subjects where there was a single-year increase in the test data noted by the up arrows, none of the conditions of improvement are met.

- Is there knowledge for how work or activity was altered systematically across the state in those tested areas to produce the improvement? No, there isn't evidence of an improvement method.

- Are there visible, positive differences in results relative to historical norms? No, we have comparisons between two to three data points.

- Has there been a lasting impact? No, there is only three years of test data. The three years of test data that are included in the chart are completely divorced from the historical context of these scores as well as from any important conditions that may have changed within Ohio's testing system.

We'll narrow our focus from the full list of test scores and just look at what's happening in 3rd grade English language arts. In the second to last sentence in the paragraph to the left of Table 6.1 the report says, "Third grade saw decreases this year but has maintained higher proficiency than two years ago."

Table 6.2.

3rd Grade State Test Results

Grade	Subject	2015-2016	2016-2017	2017-2018	
3	English Language Arts	54.9%	63.8%	61.2%	↓
	Mathematics	65.8%	70.6%	67.0%	↓

During the 2015-16 school year, 54.9% of third graders were proficient on the ELA test. This increased to 63.8% during the following year, and then declined to 61.2% during the 2017-18 school year. Again, when the data is divorced from historical context there is no way to understand what is going on with 3rd grade ELA test scores with any confidence. Now that we have some understanding of variation, we also have to ask ourselves if the ups and downs in this data would show up as common cause variation in a process behavior chart or if there are indeed meaningful signals of a special cause present.

Much of the data we look at in the education sector is organized in tables just like those in Table 6.2 and, just like in this case, comparisons are

UNDERSTANDING VARIATION

most often being made between two and three data points. The only context that we have about what is going on with Ohio's third graders is that scores increased in 2016-17 from the previous school year and then declined in 2017-18. However, the story shifts completely when you look at this same data in context over time. We'll do this first by turning to viewing the data in the run chart in Figure 6.6. A *run chart* is a simple plot and display of data and trends over a specified time period, but unlike process behavior charts, do not include the Natural Process Limits.

Figure 6.6.
Run Chart: Ohio 3rd Grade ELA State Testing Proficiency Levels (2004-21)

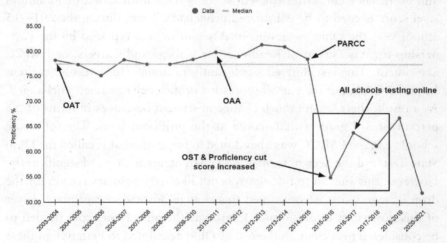

This particular chart displays the average proficiency levels on the 3rd grade ELA test between the spring of 2004 and 2021 (there is no data for Spring 2020 because of the pandemic). Spring 2004 was the first time Ohio administered a state-wide ELA test in 3rd grade, and Spring 2021 was the most recently available data. I've also noted several important annotations in this run chart in order to paint a more complete picture of what is happening over time in the world of Ohio's 3rd grade state ELA testing. Let's first turn to the run chart, and then we will dive into the annotations.

The three data points from Table 6.2 are in the black rectangle in Figure 6.6. When you add in the additional data going back to 2004 as well as the additional data points from the Spring 2019 and 2021 tests that followed the publishing of the state document, a completely different picture emerges.

Between spring testing in 2004 and spring testing in 2015, the data is bouncing around a consistent range of proficiency levels between a low of 75.1% proficiency in 2006 to a high of 81.4% in 2013. But then, the scores take a precipitous dive in the spring of 2016 and have been bouncing around a new lower median albeit with what appears to be more year-to-year variance than before this steep drop.

Before going any further with the analysis, let's look at the annotations. The Ohio Achievement Test, or OAT, was rolled out in spring 2004. Its name changed to the Ohio Achievement Assessment, or OAA, in spring 2011 but largely remained unchanged in terms of test design, test content, and proficiency cut scores (the cut score is the cut-off score, or minimum level score needed to be considered proficient). Then, during the 2014-15 school year the Ohio Achievement Assessment was replaced by the Partnership for Assessment of Readiness for College and Careers, or PARCC assessment. This test differed significantly in design, format, and content from the OAA, but the cut-off scores for proficiency remained unchanged. As a result, there wasn't much change in student outcomes in terms of the percent of 3rd graders that scored at the proficient level. The following school year, the PARCC was abandoned in favor of what is called the Ohio State Test and the design, format, and content again changed significantly. However, this shift in test design was not likely the primary reason for the drop in scores that accompanied this change. Instead, the primary driver of this downshift in proficiency levels was the higher cut score needed to be considered proficient on the test as Ohio attempted to better align these scores to college readiness. Then in 2016-17 all Ohio public schools had to administer the test in an online format. On the PARCC assessment and during the first year of the OST assessment, schools had the choice to administer the test using paper and pencil or online.

The run chart with the annotations is a useful visualization tool for the 17 years of state testing data. You can quickly get a sense for how the proficiency rates have changed over time in the 3rd grade ELA state testing system. However, there have been too many changes to the system to place all of this data on a process behavior chart. The context from which the data is produced matters; given the changes that have happened over time, the testing system from 2003-15 is not logically comparable to the system that has been in place since the 2015-16 school year. Given this, what we'll do next is return to the claims of improvement from Table 6.1 using the pro-

UNDERSTANDING VARIATION

cess behavior chart methodology for testing events that occurred from 2016 and beyond. The additional feature that the process behavior chart has that the run chart does not is the inclusion of the Natural Process Limits. These limits allow us to differentiate between common cause and special cause variation.

Goal Setting is Often an Act of Desperation

In my experience over the last two decades, we often choose goals in important areas out of thin air, build an accountability system around those goals, and then rate and rank schools based on how they perform within that system. In other words, "Goal setting is often an act of desperation."[16] The typical reaction to the quote is something like the following: "But I thought goal-setting was something highly effective people and organizations do?" I would argue however, that this is rarely the case, be it in organizations or accountability systems, and only can be true if several conditions are met during the goal-setting process. To be clear, I'm not advocating against setting goals. Rather, I am arguing against the typical goal setting that goes on in educational systems. A good example of this is the expectation in Ohio that 80% of 3rd-8th graders will score proficient on state tests. But, why not 50%? Or, 82.5%? Or, 75%? Or, 95%?

The point of this line of questioning is that the 80% rate was chosen arbitrarily and in the absence of some important considerations. Deming's philosophy helped me to understand that in the absence of these considerations, numerical goal setting is not only folly, but potentially harmful. Prior to setting goals, organizations should:

- understand the capability of the system or process under study.
- understand the variation within the system or process under study.
- understand if the system or process under study is stable.
- have a logical answer to the question, "By what method?"

Let's take a deeper look at the implications of each of these four conditions using the 3rd grade ELA state testing data. Proficiency rates since the 2015-16 school year are displayed in the process behavior chart in Figure 6.7 on the next page. This is the same data we've been examining throughout this chapter. The first three data points are from the state testing results document, and the last two data points are the more recent test results available after the document was published.[17]

Figure 6.7.
X Chart: Ohio 3rd Grade Reading State Testing Proficiency Levels

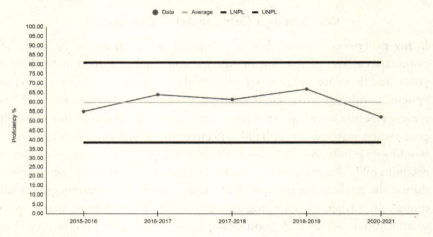

Understanding System Capability: As we saw in the annotated run chart, beginning with the Spring 2016 testing season, the Buckeye State began administering a version of assessments called the Ohio State Tests. To meet the state's benchmark, schools need at least 80% of their students to score proficient or higher in each tested area. Let's look at how Ohio's 3rd graders are performing on the state's test. In other words, we are going to figure out the capability of this system. Here, the system is defined as the third-grade students in Ohio public schools, their teachers, their reading curriculum, their schools, and any number of other in-school and out-of-school variables that impact the performance of a 3rd grader on the state test.

This capability is outlined in the process behavior chart above. For the five years for which we have testing data on the Ohio State Tests, the system of education in Ohio is likely incapable of hitting that 80% mark. Specifically, the Natural Process Limits tell us that we could expect this system to produce proficiency rates between 38% and 80%, which is why 80% is unlikely rather than impossible (based on how the limits are calculated, there is approximately a 3 in 1,000 chance of achieving the goal).[18] In other words,

UNDERSTANDING VARIATION 133

the 80% target is completely disconnected from the system's current 59.7% average proficiency rate over this time.

Understanding System Variation: The data in Figure 6.7 helps us to understand the variation in our system. In the case of the five data points displayed in the chart, we can see that it is bouncing around that aforementioned average of 59.7%. We have two points below the average, including the most recent test administration, and three points above the average. The year-to-year test results increase, then decrease, then increase, and then decrease across the five years. There are no signals in the chart to indicate that any of the increases or decreases are of significance. There are no data points outside the Natural Process Limits (Rule 1 signal), nor are there three out of four successive data points closer to one of the limits than the central line (Rule 3). There are only five data points, so there is no way to have a Rule 2 signal (eight consecutive points on one side of the central line). While five data points represent a limited amount of data, it is clear from what we have seen so far that setting the goal at 80% has had no impact on the outcomes of the 3rd grade reading system.

Understanding System Stability: A system that is producing predictable results is performing as consistently as it is capable of doing so. Ohio's 3rd grade reading system is a stable system. Based on the results thus far, we can reasonably expect that future results will continue to bounce around the current average. However, the results are clearly unsatisfactory. In our 3rd grade reading system, less than 60% of students are achieving proficiency on average over the last five years. So, we have a stable system that is producing less-than-desirable outcomes. Because this system only has common cause variation, it can only be improved by working on the design of the system, including the inputs and throughputs that are a part of it. This is a very different approach than setting a goal and then holding educators accountable to this goal.

By What Method?: As previously mentioned, the state's 80% goal is very likely beyond the capability of the system. Some schools within Ohio regularly surpass this benchmark and many others are nowhere near it. My *a priori* hunch is that, like the overall system, individual school's 3rd grade reading test results are stable. The low-scoring schools stay low-scoring, and the high-scoring schools stay high-scoring. The 80% target is a sorting mechanism rather than an improvement roadmap.

By What Method?

So, this brings us to the all-important question. I can almost hear Deming slowly standing as I've seen in his recorded training sessions and asking in his deep monotone, "By what method?" By this he meant, from where do these arbitrary goals come? And more importantly, what is the plan for achieving this new goal of 80% proficiency in every subject and grade level?

Instead of working together to improve the system of instruction and intervention for 3rd grade readers, there is a tremendous amount of time being wasted performing the mental gymnastics of trying to convince everyone that there is indeed improvement occurring throughout the system. These mental gymnastics, or fictional writings, trickle down to districts and schools as these various accountability reports are released every year. We perform these same exercises of writing fiction with our own test reports for various internal and external audiences. I want to be clear that I am not talking about anything nefarious here, but rather I am saying we waste a tremendous amount of time comparing year-to-year results. We either celebrate increases in year-to-year results that aren't meaningful or we attempt to explain away those same types of changes that happen to go in the other direction. Most of the time this fiction writing happens in the absence of acknowledging changes to the context of the testing system itself like those outlined in Figure 6.6. Almost no one remembers even just a year or two after those changes went into effect.

This is a perfect time to revisit the earlier idea that when people are pressured to meet a target value, there are three approaches that they can take: (1) they can work to improve the system; (2) they can distort the system; or (3) they can distort the data. In this case, almost all the reaction and explanation that I see at all levels of the education system in response to state testing results is focused on point two (distorting the system) or point three (distorting the data). Again, I want to reiterate that I am not talking about anything illegal here in most cases, but rather the idea of numerical naiveté. Most of what I see falls exactly along the lines of the claims made in the state document from Table 6.1. Statements such as "Ohio students continue to show improved achievement in academic content areas" and "Third grade saw decreases this year but has maintained higher proficiency than two years ago" are nothing more than writing fiction.

UNDERSTANDING VARIATION

Throughout my career, I've been just as guilty of this type of analysis and fiction writing as anyone, but once you understand the right way to interpret data, you want to scream from the mountain tops when you see it. Additionally, it's important to reiterate here that process behavior charts displaying common cause variation can and must be improved in many situations. This occurs by working to both decrease the variation present and raise the overall average in the system, while using methods that help continually improve the results. I'm making a point here to emphasize that systems that only contain noise are stable, but this doesn't mean their performance is satisfactory. In the current system, the results are stable, but two in five students can't read at a proficient level!

The early results indicate that the state's 80% goal is likely beyond the capability of the system. In order to meet this goal, the system would have to be improved in some fundamental way. Charting the proficiency rates will not give us insight into how to improve the system nor will it point out the problem spots. The state education department is not going to bring about improvement in the 3rd grade ELA test scores by setting goals for student proficiency rates. The only way to bring about this change is to work together to improve the process of K-3 reading instruction happening every day in classrooms throughout Ohio. Bringing about this improvement is a much more daunting task than simply admonishing schools who are not meeting the arbitrary 80% target.

The bottom line is that improvement will never be brought about through an accountability system, but rather will only come to fruition if educational leaders at all levels have methods for continual improvement, including understanding variation, in their tool kit. To me, the real win of moving in this direction is that working in schools would be much more fulfilling if we spent less time scurrying about writing fiction and more time working to improve the system. A necessary first step is Knowledge about Variation.

Endnotes

1. W. Edwards Deming, *The Essential Deming: Leadership Principles from the Father of Quality*, ed. Joyce Nilsson Orsini (New York: McGraw-Hill, 2013), 170.

2. W. Edwards Deming, *The New Economics for Industry, Government, Education*, 3rd ed. (Cambridge, MA: The MIT Press, 2018), 169.

3. James F. Leonard, *The New Philosophy for K-12 Education: A Deming Framework for Transforming America's Schools* (Milwaukee, WI: ASQ Quality Press, 1996), 117.

4. Ibid., 101.

5. Ibid., 104-108.

6. Donald J. Wheeler, *Understanding Variation: The Key to Managing Chaos,* 2nd ed. (Knoxville, TN: SPC Press, 2000), vi.

7. Ibid., 12.

8. Ibid., 13.

9. Ibid., 13.

10. Ohio Department of Education. Ohio School & District Results 2017-18, reportcardstorage.education.ohio.gov/archives-2018/2018-state.pdf.

11. A detailed description of the three-sigma value, including how it is calculated, can be found in: Donald J. Wheeler, *Making Sense of Data: SPC for the Service Sector* (Knoxville, TN: SPC Press, 2003).

12. Dr. Donald Wheeler, email message to author, December 17, 2021: The process behavior chart works with all kinds of histograms, and it is not necessary to have a bell-shaped curve before you place your data on such a chart. The normal curve is a worst-case situation, and that is why we use it in the drawings.

13. Donald J. Wheeler, *Understanding Variation: The Key to Managing Chaos,* 2nd ed. (Knoxville, TN: SPC Press, 2000), 29-30.

14. Ibid., 30.

15. There are other sets of detection rules such as the Western Electric Zone Tests and Nelson's Detection Rules. I've chosen to follow the advice of Dr. Donald Wheeler in terms of his recommended detection rules. These are found in: Donald J. Wheeler, *Making Sense of Data: SPC for the Service Sector* (Knoxville, TN: SPC Press, 2003), 112.

16. This concept comes from Dr. Donald Wheeler in: Donald J. Wheeler, *Understanding Variation: The Key to Managing Chaos,* 2nd ed. (Knoxville, TN: SPC Press, 2000), 84.

17. Useful limits can be computed with as few as five or six values. See Lesson 5 in the "10 Key Lessons for Data Analysis" in Chapter 7.

18. A run chart can be converted into a process behavior chart once we have enough data to construct the Natural Process Limits. In practice, limits based upon an average moving range will begin to solidify when 17 or more values are used in the computation of those limits (when using the median, moving range solidification begins when 23 or more values are used in the computation). But we often must work with fewer data points in real life, and useful limits can be computed with as few as five or six values.

CHAPTER SEVEN

Using Knowledge about Variation

"Confusion between common causes and special causes leads to frustration of everyone, and leads to greater variability and to higher costs, exactly contrary to what is needed."[1]

— *W. EDWARDS DEMING*

THINK ABOUT THIS: WHY do you collect data as a part of your role at your school or school system? When asked this question, I think most people would say something to the effect of, "I collect data so that I can understand where we are on X metric, and so that we can improve X." This means that data is collected as a basis for some type of action that we in turn hope leads to better performance. However, as we established in the last chapter, before we can use data as a basis for improvement efforts, it has to be interpreted. We would be wise here to follow Dr. Wheeler's two rules for understanding data outlined in Chapter 6. Remember that the first rule was to always present data in context. The second rule was that the analysis must filter out the noise within the data.

The most typical approach to using data in schools is the limited comparison of pairs of values often combined with a color-coded scale. Limited comparisons often occur between two time periods, such as last week and this week, last month and this month, or last year and this year. The typical color-coded scale is the red, yellow, and green stop light colors added to a spreadsheet or table of numbers, usually based on an arbitrary scale with a resemblance to a grading scale (e.g., 90% or higher is green, etc.). This observation is based on what I did myself as a school leader and what I've seen in my work visiting dozens of schools in the past two decades.

Figure 7.1.
Attendance Data Board

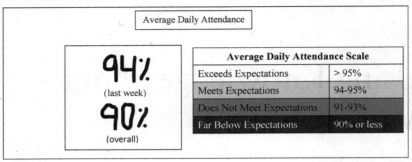

The attendance data board in Figure 7.1 is a very typical data display and happens to come from one of the middle schools within the United Schools Network. The label at the top reads "Average Daily Attendance" and then the handwritten numbers on the left read "94% (last week)" and below that "90% (overall)." The data point from last week "Meets Expectations" according to the Average Daily Attendance Scale posted next to the data values. The overall rate is "Far Below Expectations" on that same scale. As an aside, I'm not going to focus much on the attendance scale itself other than to say that after some study a few years ago, we realized that 95% attendance is nowhere near a worthy attendance goal. In a 180-day school year, missing 5% of the year equates to nine absences or almost two weeks of school. Rather, our focus is going to be on the 90% overall value and the 94% value from last week.

As presented, the attendance data may lead either to overreaction (tampering) or underreaction (not responding to a signal) given that the two values do not present enough context to point to a roadmap for improvement. Displayed in this way, we have no idea if the attendance rate from last week represents common or special cause variation. It is very possible that if we had more data available, the rate would only represent common cause variation.

There are other problems with the board. For one, as the board is currently set up, who remembers the value from the previous week or the previous month? Another issue is that the comparison to the scale is not helpful because it does not filter out any noise in the data. The only thing that this board really communicates is whether things are above, below, or meeting expectations as defined by the standard set by the scale. On any given week, if the school is in fact meeting expectations, there is no ability to make predictions about what will happen in the future. If things are below expectations,

USING KNOWLEDGE ABOUT VARIATION 139

there is no way to tell if the value of the week is meaningfully different nor does it give any indication about how to get out of trouble.

Later in this chapter, we're going to take this attendance data and go step-by-step into the thinking underlying a continual improvement approach. We'll start by displaying the information from the middle school data board over time, first using a run chart and then transition it to a process behavior chart once we have enough data. Time series graphs like these are the most powerful tools we have available for presenting our data in context. Along the way, I'll narrate the thinking needed to properly analyze the data. We'll answer questions such as the following: How much data do we need to construct a process behavior chart? How much baseline data do I need? How do I interpret the data in relation to the Natural Process Limits?

There are many powerful tools in the continual improvement toolbox, but like Dr. Wheeler, I believe that the process behavior chart may very well be the most important. For this reason, we'll spend the rest of the chapter studying how to think about the data displayed in these charts.

Aim of this Chapter

The purpose of this chapter is to outline the "10 Key Lessons for Data Analysis" that are critical to understanding variation and using process behavior chart methodology. Most of the lessons have been touched on at least briefly earlier in the book. However, I am going to list them in one place for easy reference. Then, we'll apply those lessons to the attendance case study, and I'll describe the way of thinking that goes along with these tools. As you'll come to see, the way of thinking is far more important than the tools themselves.

What is process behavior chart methodology?

Process behavior charts have been mentioned numerous times up to this point in *Win-Win*, but it will be helpful here to touch on some key points of the methodology. A *process behavior chart* is the pairing of two specialized and complementary run charts typically displayed stacked on top of each other. The top chart is called the *X-chart* or *Individuals Chart* and contains the data points from the metric under study. The second chart displayed below the X-chart is called a *Moving Range Chart*, or *mR Chart* for short. This chart displays the amount of point-to-point variation between each successive point in the data set. While the charts are designed to be used in concert, I'll focus on the X-chart throughout this chapter just as I've done thus far in the book (no mR will be included, with the exception of Appendix B). This will simplify the approach, since this is likely an introduction to these methods for most readers, while still giving exposure to the most important core concepts.

Process behavior charts start out as run charts on which we plot data for some metric over time. Then a series of simple calculations are used to add the central line (typically the average) as well as the Upper and Lower Natural Process Limits. The limits are the boundaries that describe where a predictable process is likely to vary over time unless something changes within the system. A key point is that the limits are not a goal, a specification, or a target set by management, but rather are determined by a mathematical formula. The calculations for both the central line and the limits are described in detail in Appendix B.

10 Key Lessons for Data Analysis

The ten data lessons that follow are derived from three primary sources: (1) *Making Sense of Data: SPC for the Service Sector*, (2) *Understanding Variation: The Key to Managing Chaos*, and (3) *Measures of Success: React Less, Lead Better, Improve More*.[2] I've taken what I've found most useful from all three books and made several modifications that I think will be helpful for users in education-based contexts to employ the process behavior chart methodology.

Lesson 1: Data has no meaning apart from its context.

Anyone looking at the data should be able to answer some basic questions such as: Who collected the data? How was the data collected? When was the data collected? Where was the data collected? What do these values represent? What is the operational definition of the concept being measured? How were the values of any computed data derived from the raw inputs? Have there been any changes made over time that impact the data set (i.e., change in the operational definition of the concept being measured, change in the formula being used to compute the data, etc.)?

USING KNOWLEDGE ABOUT VARIATION

Lesson 2: We don't manage or control the data; the data is the Voice of the Process.

However, we do manage the system and processes from which the data come. A key conception of the systems view of organizations is that improvement efforts require someone from the outside that has Profound Knowledge collaborating with the people working in the system (i.e., students) and the managers that have the authority to work on the system (i.e., teachers, school leaders). If we wish to make breakthrough improvements in our schools and school systems, we must make time to work on the system of learning and to continually improve it with the help of our students. The System of Profound Knowledge provides the theoretical foundation for the transformation of conventional classrooms to those guided by quality learning principles.

Lesson 3: Plot the dots for any data that occurs in time order.

The hashtag plot the dots (#plotthedots) was developed by the improvement team at the National Health Service in England.[3] The primary point of 'plot the dots' is that plotting data over time helps us understand variation in our data and leads us to take more appropriate action. As Dr. Donald Berwick put it, "Plotting measurements over time turns out, in my view, to be one of the most powerful things we have for systemic learning."[4] Plot the dots for any data that occurs across time. Plotting data on a run chart and connecting consecutive data points with a line makes analysis far more intuitive than data in a table. The run chart serves as the foundation for plotting the dots on a process behavior chart once you have enough data to do so (see Lessons 4 and 5). The bottom line is that both run charts and process behavior charts will always tell us more than a list or table of numbers.

Lesson 4: Two or three data points are not a trend.[5]

The plotting of dots should occur as soon as you have decided to collect some set of data which occurs over time. This encompasses almost all data we are interested in analyzing when the goal is to improve schools. Many of us will have relied on comparing two points from consecutive weeks, months, or years. However, the problem with looking at just two or three points of data is that it tells you nothing about trends nor anything regarding how much the data varies naturally.

Lesson 5: Show enough data in your baseline to illustrate the previous level of variation.

A run chart can be converted into a process behavior chart once we have enough data to construct the Natural Process Limits. In practice, limits based upon an average moving range will begin to solidify when 17 or more values are used in the computation of those limits (when using the median moving range, solidification begins when 23 or more values are used in the computation).[6] But we often must work with fewer data points in real life, and useful limits can be computed with as few as five or six values.[7]

Lesson 6: The goal of data analysis in schools is not just to look at past results but also and perhaps more importantly to look forward and predict what is likely to occur in the future.

Process behavior charts provide a better approach to the interpretation of data because they take the effects of variation on the data into account. These charts allow us to classify variation as either routine (common cause variation) or exceptional (special cause variation) and in turn allow us to focus on the behavior of the underlying system that produced the results. This focus on the system and its processes is the basis for working towards continual improvement.

Lesson 7: The improvement approach depends on the stability of the system under study.

A system that is producing predictable results is performing as consistently as possible. It is a waste of time to explain noise (common cause variation) in a stable system because there is no simple, single root cause for noise. Instead, if the results are unsatisfactory, the appropriate focus is working on improvements and changes to the system. Allow me to say this another way: we can improve a common cause process or system by working on the design of the system, including the inputs and throughputs that are a part of it. In contrast, in an unpredictable system, which displays special causes, it is a waste of time to attempt to improve or change the system until it is stable again. In this type of system, you must investigate, with the goal of identifying what causes the data points to be different. You then want to study and remove the special causes affecting the system to return it to a stable, predictable state. The inability to recognize these two different improvement roadmaps is the source of tremendous confusion and wasted effort in the education sector.

USING KNOWLEDGE ABOUT VARIATION 143

Lesson 8: More timely data is better for improvement purposes.

State testing data isn't very useful for improvement purposes because it is only available once per year and results often arrive after the end of the school year. It is better to have more frequent data, so that we can understand if an intervention is having its intended effect. Most importantly, the frequency of data collection needs to be in sync with the improvement context, and no matter the frequency of collection, we shouldn't overreact to any single data point. Ultimately, the data allows us to understand the variation and trends within our system, whether our system is stable or unstable, and what type of improvement effort would be most effective.

Lesson 9: Clearly label the start date for an intervention directly in the chart.

A change idea or intervention should be clearly marked in your process behavior chart. This can be done by inserting a dashed vertical line on the date the intervention is started and should include a simple label that captures the essence of the intervention. This allows the team to easily see the data prior to and after the implementation of the change idea. The three rules for finding signals (see also Figure 6.5) can then be used to see if the intervention is indeed bringing about the intended improvement.

- Rule 1: Any data point outside of the limits.
- Rule 2: Eight consecutive points on the same side of the central line.
- Rule 3: Three out of four consecutive data points that are closer to the same limit than they are to the central line.

Lesson 10: The purpose of data analysis is insight.

Dr. Wheeler tells us that the best analysis is the simplest analysis which provides the needed insight. Plotting the dots first on a run chart and then on a process behavior chart is the most straightforward method for understanding how our data is performing over time. This understanding is much more intuitive to understand than data stored in tables, and patterns in this data become much more apparent using time-sequenced charts.

Understanding Variation in Action: Attendance Case Study

With the "10 Key Lessons for Data Analysis" in hand, we are going to turn back to the attendance data board from Figure 7.1 to bring the learning from the chapters on variation alive. I think we would all agree that data is collected as a basis for some type of action. However, before we can act on data, we must properly interpret it, and this can only happen if the data is presented in context. Additionally, the technique we use for analysis must be able to differentiate between noise and signals, so that we know when and how to react. The snapshot represented by Figure 7.1 from the attendance data board was taken in January 2019, and includes a weekly rate from that month as well as a year-to-date rate. For the sake of this example, I am going to use monthly attendance rates for the past four years as opposed to weekly rates, so that we can better see the natural rhythms of the school year during these four years. The analysis will include the January 2019 period though, and in fact, the weekly rate displayed on the data board (94%) is a bit higher than the attendance rate for the full month (92.42%).

Let's start by looking at the graphical representation of the January 2019 data; basically, looking at the data available on the attendance board but at the level of a monthly rate as opposed to the weekly value. Graphs are the most powerful tool available for presenting data in context, but even with a graph, there is almost no analysis that can occur given limited comparisons of values. In many cases, our data tools include comparisons between a pair of values, such as when we compare two successive months, or two successive years of a given metric. In the case of the attendance data board, we don't even have that. Instead, we only have one data point to consider. If you visited the middle school and saw the data board, you may come away impressed that the data is posted for all staff to see. However, when putting this data into graphical form as I've done in Figure 7.2, it becomes readily apparent that the idea of trying to improve with a single data point is absurd.

There is no way to know what happened prior to January 2019 nor is there any way to predict what will happen next. There is no context on which to interpret the data. Let's say that the school took their data board a step further and displayed two data points instead of one. I'm sure we've all seen example data displays either on the wall or in electronic form like that in Table 7.1.

USING KNOWLEDGE ABOUT VARIATION

Figure 7.2.
January 2019 Attendance Rate

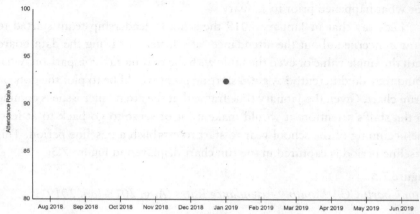

Table 7.1.
Revised Data Board

	Target	January 2019	February 2019
Attendance Rate	94%	92.42%	94.76%
Percentage Change			+2.34%

It is entirely possible that if the school displayed their data in this way, the staff might say, "Hooray, we saw an increase of more than 2% from last month!" That is nothing more than writing fiction. How do you know that the rate hadn't decreased by a similar amount in the preceding months of the school year? We're missing important context that lets us know if the difference between January and February 2019 is routine or exceptional. To interpret the increase properly, we'd want to know how much the rates normally change from month-to-month.

Comparing the two data points from January and February doesn't provide enough information to understand the school's attendance system nor does it allow staff to properly evaluate trends in performance. Think back to the definition of improvement last covered in Chapter 6. None of the three dimensions of improvement (changing how we work, positive results, lasting impact) have been met. We don't have any indication that an intervention has been implemented nor do we have any historical norms in the data board to indicate that the January-to-February increase is a sustained positive change. We also have no idea if the positive change will be sustained after February nor what happened prior to January.

Let's say that in January 2019 the school's leadership team started to grow concerned about the attendance rate. Instead of using the data board with the single value or even the table with the two-month comparison, what could they do differently? A good starting point would be to plot the dots on a run chart. Given the January time frame that the attendance issue is coming to the staff's attention, it would make a lot of sense to go back to at least the beginning of the school year to start to establish a baseline period. This baseline period is captured in the run chart displayed in Figure 7.3.

Figure 7.3.
Run Chart: CCA Monthly Attendance Rates (Aug. 2018-Jan. 2019)

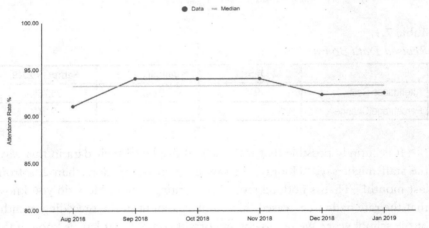

The first six months of the school year start to paint a picture of how the attendance rate is changing from month-to-month. If we continue to add to the run chart by adding the data from the rest of the school year as in Figure 7.4, that picture becomes even clearer.

When we look at the entire school year, we can see that the August attendance rate was low, and then during the fall there was a sustained increase for three months from September through November. Then there is a two month decline in the rates including the month of January prior to a one-month bump in February. Clearly, if the staff had celebrated that February increase, concerns would have quickly returned because there was a steady

USING KNOWLEDGE ABOUT VARIATION

Figure 7.4.
Run Chart: CCA Monthly Attendance Rates (2018-19 School Year)

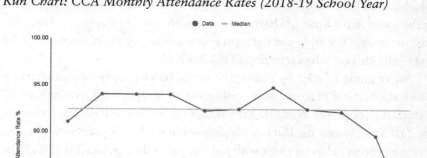

decline in attendance rates across the rest of the school year. This includes a rate in the low 80s in June 2019. It is important to note that the school year ended on June 5th and the month of June only included three school days. However, I left it in the chart because it is important for the staff to know this data and think about why students attended at such a low rate at the very end of the year.

The main point is that the run chart is a better way to look at the attendance rates than simply posting a single month's worth of data on the board or storing the data in a table. However, without the Natural Process Limits, the run chart does not allow us to filter out the noise and identify signals in our data. While the run chart does allow us to see the month-to-month variance in our data more intuitively, it doesn't allow us to know if the ups and downs we are seeing are meaningful. Without the ability to differentiate between common and special cause variation, we also don't know what type of improvement approach to take. For this, we need to view the attendance data in a process behavior chart.

Process Behavior Chart Analysis: Attendance Case Study

There are several different types of process behavior charts (e.g., p-charts, c-charts, u-charts, np-charts, XmR charts, etc.) that can be used in different situations. For our purposes, we are going to stick to one type of chart called the *Individuals with Moving Range Chart*, often abbreviated as XmR Chart, which can be used with many different types of data. Think of the XmR Chart as the Swiss Army knife of charts; it works with almost all types of data.[8] For our purposes, I'll simply use the term process behavior chart throughout the rest of the chapter when referring to the XmR chart.

We're going to start by getting the initial baseline data for our chart on which the Natural Process Limits will be based. Ideally, we'd have at least 17 historical data points available for calculating the initial baseline. However, the "10 Key Lessons for Data Analysis" taught us that, if necessary, you can create a process behavior chart with just five or six data points if that is all the data you have at the start, but the limits won't be as statistically valid until you have 17 or more points. The main idea here though is that even a small number of data points plotted in time series is better than the color-coded approach or the limited two-point comparisons that are so common. If you do start with a smaller number of data points, the limits can be recalculated when you've gathered more data down the road.

One of the keys in the calculation of the limits in the baseline period is that the historical data you are using for this purpose is a part of the same system as data that will be collected in the future. The idea is to improve the process being displayed in the process behavior chart, so we shouldn't be arbitrarily choosing timeframes for our charts for the purpose of telling a certain preferred story. In the case of the attendance example, we have monthly attendance rates going back over a decade. As a result, I'm going to add the monthly rates from the 2017-18 school year to my data set, which already includes the 2018-19 school year. That way, I will have a baseline period established by using the data points from August 2017 through June 2019, which is 22 points across those two school years.

After establishing the baseline period, the next step in the process is to calculate the central line for my chart. The central line for the attendance process behavior chart will be the arithmetic mean, or average, of the monthly data points.[9] The data should be collected in a spreadsheet program such as Microsoft Excel or Google Sheets and stored in columns, so that the formulas available in those programs can be utilized.

All process behavior charts start as run charts with the data points and the center line. I've gotten in the habit of using a template that uses blue for the data, green for the central line, and red for the limits, although black and shades of grey have been used in the book. I've stuck to these colors for con-

USING KNOWLEDGE ABOUT VARIATION

sistency's sake and to make analysis easier. If you're using a program such as Excel or Google Sheets, you'll choose "line chart" and use this as the starting point to build your run chart in just a few steps. The run chart for our baseline data is in the figure that follows.

Figure 7.5.
Run Chart: CCA Attendance Rate Baseline Period (Aug. 2017-June 2019)

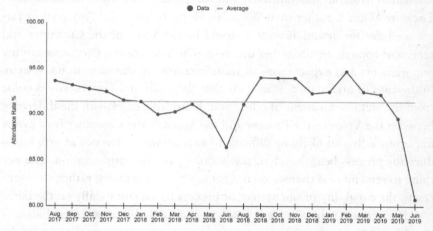

We don't know for sure if we have a predictable system until we get to the point of constructing the limits, which are not a part of the run chart. If the system is predictable as the data moves up and down across time, we'd expect about half the points to be above the average and half the points to be below the average. However, given that the process behavior chart methodology doesn't require normally distributed data, it's possible, as an example, that 75% of the data are below the central line. In the baseline data above, 13 of the points (59%) are above the average and 9 of the points (41%) are below the average. Process behavior charts work with many different statistical distributions, hence my earlier reference that they are the Swiss Army knife of charts.

Building a run chart allows us to take an initial look at our data prior to having enough points with which to construct the full process behavior chart. We won't be able to filter the noise from the signals with just the run chart because we cannot yet assess for Rule 1 (single point outside either limit) or Rule 3 (3 of 4 successive data points closer to a limit than the central line), but we can look for Rule 2. Remember that Rule 2 is a trend of eight consecutive points on either side of the central line, and we do see a run of eight between September 2018 and April 2019. Now that we have the full set of baseline data in run chart format, we can move to make the calculations necessary to add the Natural Process Limits (see Appendix B for the process and formulas for these calculations). This in turn will allow us to look for those other signals within our data.

The most important thing to remember is that the process limits are calculated from our baseline data, and so, represent the Voice of the Process. They are What Is rather than What We Hope Them to Be. Any goal or target we have for attendance rates would be the Voice of the Customer and represent something altogether different. The *Voice of the Customer* are the requirements and expectations of some customer of the educational system. In the case of attendance, it is likely that the goals and targets would come from the state department of education. Being able to explain the difference between the Voice of the Process and the Voice of the Customer is of prime importance. It will likely be difficult to explain this difference as you introduce the process behavior chart methodology to your organization. The key thing to remember is that we do not get to choose the limits; rather, they represent the capability of our system or process based empirically on the data.

The process behavior chart limits are calculated in a way that balances the risk of Mistake 1 (missing a signal of a change in our system) and Mistake 2 (thinking there is a signal when there hasn't been a change to the system). The limits filter out between 99% and 100% of the routine, common-cause variation which in turn is the filter for most of the noise in the metric.[10] With the addition of the limits, we have now turned the run chart from Figure 7.5 into the process behavior chart in Figure 7.6.

Figure 7.6.
Baseline Period X-Chart: CCA Attendance Rates (Aug 2017-June 2019)

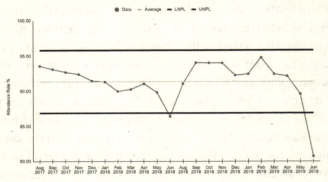

USING KNOWLEDGE ABOUT VARIATION

The Lower Natural Process Limit is 86.85% and the Upper Natural Process Limit is 95.81%. This means that if we have a predictable attendance system then most of our future data points will likely fall between 86.85% and 95.81%. Remember that the limits were calculated based on the 22 data points within our baseline period which includes the monthly attendance rates for both the 2017-18 and the 2018-19 school years. We can now check our baseline period for any signals that might be in our process behavior chart. Take a moment to look back at the baseline period chart. Do you see any signals?

Sometimes the initial process behavior chart does not represent a predictable system, as is the case with our baseline period. There are four signals in the baseline data. In June 2018 there is a Rule 1 signal because the point is below the lower limit. Beginning in September 2018 through April 2019 we see eight consecutive points above the central line which is a Rule 2 signal. The first three of the eight points in that run is also a Rule 3 signal because there are three out of four that are closer to the limit than the central line. In June 2019, we see another Rule 1 signal because the point is again below the lower limit. All four signals are highlighted in Figure 7.7.

Figure 7.7.
Baseline Period X-Chart with Signals Highlighted

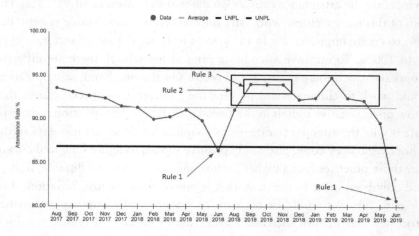

In the case of an initial process behavior chart that includes signals in the baseline period, we can keep the data that represents the signals. The limits are not goals, but rather part of the story that is being told by our data. It's most helpful to keep the signals in our baseline data, recognize that they are a part of the attendance system, and try to understand the special causes underlying those signals. Over time, as we continue to track the monthly attendance data, we can see if any action we are taking on the system brings about a predictable system or if we still see those same signals over time.

Given that the historical data does contain those signals, we cannot predict future attendance rates with confidence. One item the school leaders of Columbus Collegiate Academy might investigate is why attendance drops so much at the end of the year in June. There are significantly fewer school days in June, but there is no reason why attendance should be lower on any given day at the very end of the year. Similarly, it would be helpful to investigate why there was a sustained increase in attendance rates illustrated by the Rule 2 and Rule 3 signals in the data. As a part of this investigation, we might also want to look at monthly data for more than two years to see if there is in fact a seasonality aspect of the increases and decreases.

With the data now displayed in the process behavior chart, Columbus Collegiate Academy's leaders can begin to ask targeted questions in an effort to increase the attendance rate above the two-year average of 91.33%. The aim of this improvement work isn't only to create a predictable system, but also to create improvement in the system to bring the attendance rate closer to 100%. To improve attendance rates at the school, there are different fronts on which these efforts could focus. On the one hand, school leaders could work to eliminate and prevent the recurrence of special causes that show up as negative signals in the attendance data. A key question to investigate is why the attendance rate drops so much for those last few days of the school year. They could also study positive signals to figure how to incorporate those practices into a higher-performing system. On the flip side, if there had only been noise in the data, that is only common cause variation, then the path forward would be to work to systematically improve attendance processes that in turn increase average performance and reduce variation around this improved average.

The main purpose of the process behavior chart is to help us improve our organizations. It can help us know when to react and, just as importantly, when not to react to our data, which saves us time and resources. The tool

USING KNOWLEDGE ABOUT VARIATION

can also help us systematically determine if an intervention is bringing about improvement, helping us to decide if we should adopt the idea or abandon it. Even in the absence of a signal, we can still work to improve the system if it is not meeting our expectations.

Returning to the attendance data in Figure 7.7, as time goes on, we would continue to add data points to the chart each month. You could choose to show the most recent three (33 points), four (44 points), or even five (55 points) school years while allowing older data points to drop off the chart as time moves forward, although you shouldn't delete the data for the points that are dropping off.

There also may be times when you need to calculate a new central line and limits to reflect a changed system that is performing differently than it had been previously. The most likely signal of a sustained shift is a Rule 2 signal where there are eight consecutive points on either side of the central line. The important thing to remember here is that there is no hard-and-fast rule for when to shift the central line and the upper and lower limit. Instead, the chart should be used to help tell the story that you are seeing in the data. In the case of the attendance charts, I didn't shift the limits due to the eight points from September 2018 to April 2019 because there was nothing the school team was doing to change the system at the time. In other words, there was no intervention implemented in the August or September 2018 time frame that was put in place that in turn brought about the improved rates over the next eight months. Similarly, I didn't shift the limits for June 2018 and June 2019. It is more likely that we are seeing some type of seasonality in our data rather than changes to the attendance system itself.

Shifting the Limits: Attendance Case Study

When I started using process behavior charts in my work, I was very uncertain about when to shift the Natural Process Limits. This uncertainty has not fully gone away with experience, but something I heard during a workshop on the methodology with Dr. Donald Wheeler certainly helped. In reference to the limits, he said, "The objective is not to get the right limits, but rather to tell the right story." In this final section of Chapter 7, we'll continue the attendance example, but we'll add two more school years of data to the charts that have been built previously. This will allow us to examine if and when to shift the limits with the 44 data points available from those four school years.

Process behavior charts help us to tell the story of our data, and just as with any story, there can be plot twists. A plot twist in a process behavior chart occurs when a signal indicates that something has changed in the system or process under study, in this case the attendance data at Columbus Collegiate Academy. However, the presence of a signal doesn't necessarily mean that you should shift the limits. You should also consider if the data displays a distinctly different kind of behavior from the past and if you know the reason for this change in behavior. If you have all three of those pieces of information, a shift in the limits is likely warranted.[11]

In Figure 7.8, I've added the data for the 2019-20 and 2020-21 school years, an additional 22 points, to the process behavior chart from Figure 7.7. We'll look for signals and determine if a shift has occurred, and, if so, I'll revise the limits.

Figure 7.8.
X-Chart: CCA Attendance Rates (Aug 2017-June 2021)

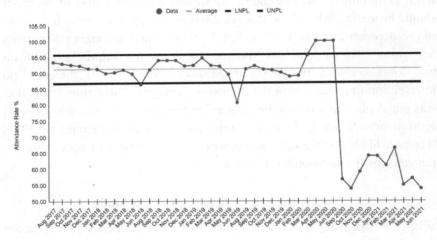

It's clear from looking at the chart that some pretty wild things are going on with Columbus Collegiate Academy's attendance system. As you look at the dates when most of the signals are popping off the page on the right side of the chart, you probably have surmised that you are seeing the impact of the pandemic on the school's attendance rates. Besides the end-of-year signals in June 2018 and June 2019 already touched upon earlier in the chapter, all the other Rule 1 signals indeed coincide with this disruption.

USING KNOWLEDGE ABOUT VARIATION

The governor ordered the shutdown of Ohio's public schools beginning on March 16, 2020. This means that for the first half of the month, Columbus Collegiate Academy had normal in-person classes, and then the school transitioned to remote learning for the rest of the month. At this point, all students were counted as in attendance across the state from March 16th and into April, May, and June. Therefore, you start to see artificially inflated attendance rates in March, and then for the rest of the year the school had 100% attendance. I chose to leave those months in the data set for now because they are a part of the attendance story.

This story shifts entirely as the 2020-21 school year kicks off, again with students attending school remotely beginning with a later than usual start date in September. For the first three months of the school year, students had to complete the daily practice set in each class to be counted as in attendance. This policy was modified, and a new policy went into effect on November 30th whereby families had to fill out a form to say that their student was in attendance for the day. A final major event was that the school transitioned from a remote learning model to a hybrid model beginning on February 1, 2021. Now that we have some background on pandemic-related events, we'll look at this attendance data through the lens of the process behavior chart.

When schools started taking attendance again with the start of the 2020-21 school year, we see that Columbus Collegiate Academy kicks off the year with eight consecutive points not only below the baseline average but also below the Lower Natural Process Limit. This suggests that student attendance in a remote learning model is a very different system from student attendance in a normal, in-person learning system. It is important to keep in mind here that a process behavior chart will tell us that *something* has changed; however, it won't necessarily tell us *what* has changed. In the case of the pandemic though, the data is so dramatically different at exactly the point you'd expect, given how it unfolded and impacted schools, that we can point to this cause with confidence. This is evidenced by both the Rule 1 and Rule 2 signals starting in September 2020.

Given the signals beginning in September 2020, we could calculate a new central line and limits from the eight points that represent the newly changed system. This trend extends from the eight original points from September 2020 to April 2021 and on to the entire 2020-21 school year, so we'll use those additional two points in our new limits and average as well. Once we adjust the limits and central line, it will be important to keep in mind that the limits based on these ten points won't be as statistically valid as the initial limits that were based on the 22 data points from the 2017-18 and 2018-19 school years. One other important item of note before we look at the new process behavior chart is that I chose to take out the data for March, April, May, and June 2020 prior to shifting the limits. I chose to do this because the story I am most interested in understanding is the difference between in-person attendance and remote learning attendance. Those four removed data points represent a non-existent system whereby 100% of students were counted as in attendance.

The new central line and limits from the 10 most recent points are 59.11% (average), 40.3% (Lower Natural Process Limit), and 77.92% (Upper Natural Process Limit). The chart with the newly shifted limits is displayed in Figure 7.9.

Figure 7.9.
X-Chart with Shifted Limits: CCA Attendance Rates (Aug 2017-June 2021)

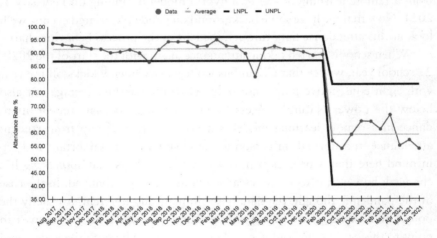

The process behavior chart indicates that we have a new system that is predictable around a lower average. Part of the power of this methodology is the visual cues that jump off the page without having to read every bit of data. Notice the significant drop in average attendance as well as the much wider spread between the upper and lower limits because of the pandemic.

USING KNOWLEDGE ABOUT VARIATION 157

With some confidence, we could predict that if remote learning continued to be the educational delivery model into the 2021-22 school year, we'd see attendance rates much lower than were previously the case at Columbus Collegiate Academy. However, our prediction for remote learning attendance would be on less solid ground than the prediction of pre-pandemic rates for in-person learning. This is because the in-person prediction would be based on the 29 points prior to the shift in the limits in Figure 7.9 whereas the remote and hybrid learning shift is only based on 10 points.

In either case, be it the 91% average attendance rate from the baseline school years or the 59% average attendance rate during the pandemic, neither system is where we want it to be. Understanding the variation of our attendance rates as illustrated by the process behavior chart allows us to clearly see the story being told by our data. Attendance was low prior to the pandemic and in need of improvement. It dropped off a cliff during remote learning, which should serve as a stark indicator that this type of system is not serving students well. In both cases, the chart and the way of thinking that goes along with understanding variation are powerful tools that we can utilize for school improvement efforts. We often talk about a better way. The more that I've studied the System of Profound Knowledge the more convinced I've become that these methods of continual improvement are that better way.

Endnotes

1. W. Edwards Deming, *Out of the Crisis* (Cambridge, MA: MIT, Center for Advanced Engineering Study, 1986), 315.

2. "Summary of Key Points from Measures of Success," Measures of Success book, https://www.measuresofsuccessbook.com/extras/.

3. England, National Health Service. *Making Data Count*, December 23, 2019, www.england.nhs.uk/publication/making-data-count/.

4. Donald M. Berwick, *Escape Fire: Designs for the Future of Health Care* (San Francisco: Jossey-Bass, 2004).

5. You can compute limits for as few as four data points based on the work of: Donald J. Wheeler, *Making Sense of Data: SPC for the Service Sector* (Knoxville, TN: SPC Press, 2003), 104. However, when only four values are used to compute the limits, those four values will always fall within the limits.

6. Ibid., 164.

7. Ibid., 129.

8. To view a technical description of chart selection and why XmR Charts are the Swiss Army knives of charts see Chapter 14 in: Donald J. Wheeler, *Making Sense of Data: SPC for the Service Sector* (Knoxville, TN: SPC Press, 2003).

9. The average is generally used in charts but there are some cases where the median is a better choice. For an excellent description of such cases see Chapter 6 in: Donald J. Wheeler, *Making Sense of Data: SPC for the Service Sector* (Knoxville, TN: SPC Press, 2003).

10. Ibid., 97.

11. Donald J. Wheeler, *Twenty Things You Need to Know* (Knoxville, TN: SPC Press, 2008), 59.

CHAPTER EIGHT

Building Knowledge in Context

The accuracy of prediction is an observable measure of knowledge. Prediction, which can take the form of a plan, a strategy, a decision, or any statement about the future, requires a theory. Accuracy of prediction depends on the extent to which a theory is aligned with the world to which the prediction refers.[1]

—*EDWARD MARTIN BAKER*

IN THE LAST TWO chapters, we've spent significant time studying a method for displaying and interpreting different types of data that occur in our system over time. It is with the third component of the System of Profound Knowledge, Theory of Knowledge, that two powerful ideas come together. The first idea is that knowledge has temporal spread, a concept introduced in Chapter 1 and expanded upon in Chapter 6. This means that our best understanding for how the processes and systems in our organizations are performing can only be interpreted after we view the variation of this data over time. The second idea is one that was mentioned in Chapters 2, 5, and 6. This is the idea that when people are pressured to meet a target value, there are three ways they can proceed: (1) they can work to improve the system; (2) they can distort the system; or (3) they can distort the data. The big question is: How do you use an understanding of variation to build knowledge in our local context and improve our educational systems while avoiding illusions of improvement through system or data distortions?

The answer lies in W. Edwards Deming's approach to continual improvement; he defined quality in terms of a never-ending cycle of improvement. Dr. Donald Wheeler characterized the Deming approach to continual improvement this way:

This is why Continual Improvement is different from all other approaches to quality . . . It is not a quick fix-"do this and you will get that." It is, instead, a way of thinking, a way of acting, and a way of understanding the data generated by your processes, that will collectively result in improved quality, increased productivity, and an advantageous competitive position.[2]

This way of thinking must underlie all approaches to improvement in the real world. Utilizing the theory of systems and variation as the basis for improvement represents a very different way of thinking at United Schools Network, and I'm guessing it would be completely new at your school or district as well. Continual improvement as a method uses these theories and has as its primary tool the process behavior chart. Fully grasping this approach allows us to differentiate between common and special cause variation, to know the difference between reacting to noise and understanding signals, and ultimately to have the ability to understand messages contained in our data. If we want to see breakthrough improvements in schools, then teachers must come to understand these methods over time and with guidance for how to employ them at the classroom level with their students. Absent this understanding and support, no amount of money or education reform is going to move the needle on student outcomes that have been the focus of so many efforts over the last three decades. Taking this approach to school improvement would represent a completely new way of thinking.

Combining systems thinking and understanding variation with the Plan-Do-Study-Act cycle give us one more piece of the Deming approach. Thus far, we've discussed Appreciation for a System and Knowledge about Variation. We'll now turn our attention to Theory of Knowledge, for which the PDSA cycle lies at the heart.

Aim of this Chapter

The purpose of this chapter is to build on the definition and overview of the *Theory of Knowledge* first introduced in Chapter 1. Most of the focus will be on Deming's *Plan-Do-Study-Act* (PDSA) cycle as a method for generating and building knowledge about how to improve our educational systems in the actual context in which it is situated. This is of critical importance to systems leaders who are not just concerned with "What works?" in our schools,

BUILDING KNOWLEDGE IN CONTEXT

but rather "What works, for whom, and under what conditions?" The latter question is the type of knowledge generated by the PDSA cycle.

What is the Plan-Do-Study-Act cycle?

The PDSA cycle is shorthand for testing a change by developing a plan to test the change (Plan), carrying out the test (Do), observing and learning from the consequences (Study), and determining what modifications should be made to the test (Act). Each cycle is a mini-experiment in which observed outcomes in the Study phase are compared to predictions from the Plan phase, and differences between the two become a major source of learning.[3] In improvement work, PDSA cycles offer a supporting mechanism for iterative development and scientific testing of change ideas in complex systems.[4]

Theory of Knowledge Revisited

The Theory of Knowledge was first introduced in Chapter 1, but it is worth revisiting this component of the System of Profound Knowledge. In that early chapter I defined Theory of Knowledge as the study of how what we think we know and claim to know actually is the way we claim it is. It is also known as epistemology, which comes from the Greek *episteme*, meaning knowledge, and *logos*, meaning study of. Dr. Deming closely studied the work of philosopher C.I. Lewis in this area, especially his book *Mind and the World Order*, where Lewis described his theory of knowledge. Deming translated these ideas into a more easily understood version for management audiences, although full disclosure, this can be a difficult area of the System of Profound Knowledge to comprehend. However, it is very much worthy of our study, and as such, this chapter will be focused on translating the Theory of Knowledge for use by education systems leaders.

The purpose of knowledge is to improve the future. Given that one of our most important responsibilities as systems leaders is the continual improvement of our schools, it would follow that the quality of this knowledge is of prime importance. There are some core ideas to keep in mind as we think about how to ensure that the knowledge we are relying on to make important decisions is sound. The numbered list that follows captures the core ideas of the Theory of Knowledge, some of which have been touched upon in other parts of *Win-Win*.

1. Nearly every decision in school and school district leadership requires prediction. Any rational plan, no matter the complexity, requires prediction concerning what we think is going to happen after we implement the plan.

2. Knowledge is built through the systematic revision and extension of theory by comparing prediction with observation. The difference between our prediction for what is going to happen upon implementation and what actually happens is the learning on which the revisions and extensions are developed. In the absence of theory, there can be no learning, and, without prediction, experience and examples are unable to teach us anything.

3. By definition, prediction is impossible in an unstable system. Prediction is only possible in a stable system, as determined by the Natural Process Limits, but this prediction can only occur with a high degree of belief in the immediate future.

4. The interpretation of data from a PDSA cycle or experiment is also prediction. It's a prediction because you must determine how to act on the results from the cycle or experiment. This interpretation will require both Profound Knowledge as well as subject-matter knowledge in the area under study.

5. Experience and examples are no help to leaders unless they are studied with the aid of theory. To copy an example of success may lead to disastrous results because of an underappreciation of the contextual factors that differ between your organization and the organization in which the example was originally developed.

6. No number of examples establishes a theory. However, a single unexplained failure of a theory requires revision or possibly even abandonment of the theory.

7. There is no true value of any characteristic, state, or condition that is defined in terms of observation or measurement. The value comes from our definition. When the definition of proficiency changed in Ohio's testing system, 3rd grade read scores dropped nearly 24% (Figure 6.6). There was nothing different

BUILDING KNOWLEDGE IN CONTEXT

between the cohort of 3rd grade test takers in 2014-15 (78.5% proficiency) and the cohort from 2015-16 (54.9% proficiency) other than the definition of proficiency.

8. Operational definitions put communicable meaning into a concept and include a method of measurement or test as well as a set of criteria for judgment. Concepts that are important to schools, such as proficiency, have no communicable value until they are expressed in operational terms. To be useful, we need to know precisely what procedure to use to measure or judge concepts like proficiency, and we need an unambiguous decision-rule that communicates how to act on the results.

9. Information that arrives on our desk, no matter how complete it is or how fast it came to us or how often we receive it, is not knowledge. Knowledge has temporal spread and comes from theory. Without a theoretical underpinning, there is no way to use the stream of information that comes to us in our roles as educational leaders.

10. There are common practices in schools and school systems that purport to be knowledge-building activities. These include teachers training other teachers, working with best efforts to create policy, and enlarging committees, thinking that the bigger group will generate better ideas. Without the guidance of Profound Knowledge, all of these activities have the very real potential to make things worse, not better.

There are important questions that follow from the application of the Theory of Knowledge such as, "How do I know what I know?," "What degree of belief do I have in this knowledge?," and "Why do we do things the way we do them?" If you reflect on those questions in your own work, you may be surprised at where those answers lead, even as you examine well-established policies, processes, and practices within your organization. For example, consider the instructional methods at your school. What is the underlying theory for those methods? Does the theory align with the best of what we know about memory and cognitive psychology? Is there a book or perhaps a pedagogical expert that helped inform those practices? It's very possible that no one in the organization has clear answers for these types of questions. Nonetheless, they are important questions to ask, even if the answers cause anxiety at the onset, because those questions are the first step on a journey to grounding your work in better theory.

When we do evaluate our ideas, it is not always based on the straight-forward logic we may like to believe it is. There is a danger here that very little thinking or evaluation is going on at all in schools as we see many education leaders hop from fad to fad in their attempt to find silver-bullet improvement ideas. Assuming this is not the case in your organization, there are still biases we must overcome. For example, we often evaluate ideas from people we like more favorably than those with whom we don't like, rather than evaluating the idea on merit alone. As decision makers, we are also very susceptible to confirmation bias, which means that we tend to latch onto evidence that supports our beliefs and ignore evidence that contradicts those same beliefs. To more effectively adjust our beliefs to reality, we are well-served to question whether we are falling for these biases.

Plan-Do-Study-Act Cycle

One of the most powerful tools that sits at the heart of Deming's Theory of Knowledge is the *Plan-Do-Study-Act* (PDSA) cycle. *Deductive learning*, moving from a theory to the test of the theory, is combined with *inductive learning*, using results from a test to revise the theory, in rapid succession during the cycle. This is a key differentiator of PDSAs as a learning process as contrasted with using ideas generated through traditional research methods, even gold standard methods such as randomized controlled trials. By their very design, studies that result in evidence-based practices discount externalities instead of solving for them. In other words, evidence-based practices have been tested under specific conditions and those conditions often don't match our contexts in important ways. The idea that many interventions are effective in some places but almost none of them work everywhere is such a common idea in the education research sector that this phenomenon has its own name—*effects heterogeneity*.

Beyond the concern of effects heterogeneity, there are several other reasons the PDSA is an effective tool. People learn better when they make predictions as a part of the learning process because making a prediction during the planning phase of the PDSA forces us to think ahead about the outcomes. In my experience, we are often overly optimistic in terms of both the speed

BUILDING KNOWLEDGE IN CONTEXT

and magnitude at which we think improvement will occur. But, because making a prediction causes us to examine the system, question, or theory under study closely, we are forced to think deeply about what it will take to bring about meaningful improvement. By predicting, we also get to see the thinking process of our team members. Learning about your own ability to predict, in addition to your team members' ability to predict, gives insight into how closely connected your organization's theories are to its reality.

The Plan-Do-Study-Act Cycle, in Deming's words, "is a flow diagram for learning, and for improvement of a product or of a process."[5] In our organizations, theory must be the basis of all investigation, and the basis for any action we take to improve systems within our organizations has to include testing the theory. This is why the PDSA cycle begins with the Plan; it is our theory for how to bring about improvement. The cycle is a process through which to gain empirical knowledge by applying and evaluating our theories to learn and improve. The invisible world of theory (Plan) and the observation of the visible world (Do) work hand-in-hand to generate this learning.

The PDSA is where theory and practice come together. As we plan the learning cycle for any given situation, we bring a theory to that planning. When I say theory, I don't necessarily mean a high-brow academic theory from a scientific journal, although it could be that. The theory could be formal or informal, or even simply a hunch. In the first stage of the cycle, the Plan, you are describing your theory for how to bring about improvement. My experience has been that this Plan more often resembles a hunch than a formal academic theory.

PDSA Cycle Template

To bring the concept of the Plan-Do-Study-Act cycle alive, it will be useful to provide an overview of the template I use in my own improvement work. First, I'll show you the full template, and then I will zoom in and provide a snapshot and brief description of each section. Then, I will do the same thing with an actual PDSA cycle that I designed and implemented through an improvement project. Through the PDSA process, a team tested specific change ideas within a broader improvement project effort (see Appendix A for how the PDSA fits into the larger improvement context).

The PDSA template I use originated at the Institute for Healthcare Improvement (IHI). Over the years, I've made minor modifications, such as including headers as well as a space for operational definitions, but this by and large is the template in use at IHI.[6] Figure 8.1 is the full template. Following that full template is a snapshot of each section accompanied by a brief description of each step in the PDSA process.

Figure 8.1.
Plan-Do-Study-Act Template

PDSA Tracker [INSERT LINK]

Project: [TITLE]
Test Start Date: XX/XX/XXXX
Test End Date: XX/XX/XXXX

UNITED SCHOOLS NETWORK
UNITE TODAY, CHANGE TOMORROW

PDSA [#]: [INSERT TITLE]

Objective:

1. **Plan:** Plan the test, including a plan for collecting data.

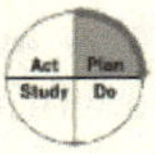

Questions and predictions:

Who, what, where, when:

Operational Definitions:

Plan for collecting data:

2. **Do:** Run the test on a small scale.

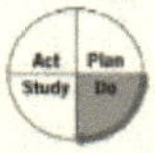

Describe what happened. What data did you collect? What observations did you make?

3. **Study:** Analyze the results and compare them to your predictions.

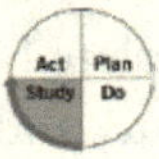

Summarize and reflect on what you learned:

4. **Act:** Based on what you learned from the test, make a plan for your next step.

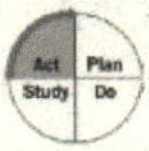

Determine what modifications you should make - adapt, adopt, or abandon:

Probably wrong, definitely incomplete

PDSA Template: Header & Title

In the header of the document displayed in Figure 8.2, there are three components to my PDSA template. The top left corner includes the title of the improvement project as well as the PDSA cycle start and end dates. These are the dates for this testing cycle rather than the start and end dates for the entire project. An improvement project can have many PDSA testing cycles; I've found testing cycles that are two to four weeks long to be a good rule of thumb for length. This length strikes a balance between having enough time to gather useful data with a short enough cycle that it can be useful in practical terms. The top right corner includes the label PDSA Tracker and is hyperlinked to a spreadsheet in which I track all the testing cycles for a particular improvement project. The middle of the header includes a logo for our school network, which is helpful in case this document is shared with an external school or district or perhaps through a conference presentation.

Figure 8.2.
PDSA Template: Header, Title, and Objective

Below the actual header, there is a place to record the title of the change idea that is being tested, as well as the cycle number. For example, during the pandemic I ran an improvement project called *Distant but Engaged* with the aim of improving student engagement rates. Because so much remote teaching was asynchronous, we tested the idea of providing synchronous reading intervention sessions to 7th graders. The title of the third testing cycle for this change idea read "PDSA 3: How do you like me live?" Right below the title is a place to record the objective or purpose for the testing cycle.

PDSA Template: Plan

Planning is prediction, and the further you look out into the future, the more that you must rely on theory to support your ideas. Dr. Deming suggested that a theory be tested first on a limited basis in a practical way in case the theory does not produce the type of improvement that was hypothesized at the outset. It is important here to remember Deming's admonishment that experience in and of itself teaches nothing. Experience can only teach us something useful if it is framed in the testing of a theory. The Plan section of the PDSA cycle includes both the details of the test as well as the plan for collecting data during the test cycle. The components of the Plan phase can be found in Figure 8.3.

Figure 8.3.
PDSA Template: Plan

1. **Plan:** Plan the test, including a plan for collecting data.

Questions and predictions:

Who, what, where, when:

Operational Definitions:

Plan for collecting data:

I've broken the plan for the test and the plan for collecting data into four sections. In the first box, the questions you are trying to answer during the testing cycle are listed, as well as the explicit predictions of each improvement team member. My preference for the prediction is to have everyone make their own independently, list those predictions separately in a bulleted list, and then discuss how each person came up with their prediction. Doing so allows you to get a sense for how team members are thinking about the

BUILDING KNOWLEDGE IN CONTEXT

problem, as well as their confidence in the change idea. In the next section, the Who, What, Where, and When of the Plan is outlined in detail. This box should include the logistics of the test, so it is very clear who is doing what as well as where and when those tasks are going to take place. It is critical to be specific so everyone knows their job in the testing cycle, and there should be enough detail so that others could replicate the test in the future if so desired.

The importance of operational definitions was noted earlier in this chapter, as well as in Chapter 1; however, it is worth repeating that the core concepts under study should be defined in a way that allows everyone to understand how measurement will occur. The definitions listed should include the criterion (What do you want to improve?), the test procedure (What methodology will be used for improvement?), and the decision rule (How will you know when things have improved?).[7]

Similar to the Who, What, Where, and When section, the Plan for collecting data should be detailed and specific. Name the person(s) that will be responsible for data collection and include how often and where this data will be stored. My preference has been to add a table for storing the data right under the Plan for collecting data section, so that everything is in one easy-to-access place.

PDSA Template: Do

The Do phase is straightforward. The team runs the test on a small scale or, in other words, the Plan is implemented. In this section of the template, displayed in Figure 8.4, the team records what actually happened, the data that was collected, and the observations that were made.

Figure 8.4.
PDSA Template: Do

2. **Do:** Run the test on a small scale.

Describe what happened. What data did you collect? What observations did you make?

At first, I was a bit confused with how the information in this section was different from what is captured in the Study section. The important distinction here is that in the Do section, you simply record information about the implementation of the Plan without analysis or interpretation. In many cases, this will likely include details regarding how the implementation differed from the Plan. For example, perhaps an inclement weather day or other unanticipated aberration occurred during plan implementation. Any aberrations from the Plan should be noted in the Do section.

PDSA Template: Study

A key revelation of the PDSA process occurred when I realized that the power of the testing cycle lies in the comparison of the prediction to the outcomes. Each PDSA cycle is a mini-experiment designed to test a change idea. Observed outcomes are compared to predictions and the differences between the two become the learning that drives decisions about next steps with the change idea. This learning is summarized in the section outlined in Figure 8.5.

Figure 8.5.
PDSA Template: Study

3. **Study:** Analyze the results and compare them to your predictions.

Summarize and reflect on what you learned:

Again, the purpose of the Study section is to analyze the results of the test and compare them to your predictions. In the Study phase, you are not only summarizing the results, you are interpreting those results and reflecting on what you learned. The learning gleaned from the experiment will serve as the basis for how the team decides to Act in the final stage of the PDSA process.

PDSA Template: Act

After the test has been completed and analyzed, the final step in the PDSA cycle is the Act stage. In this stage, the team must decide how to react to the test results that were studied. No matter what happens, even if the test results

BUILDING KNOWLEDGE IN CONTEXT

were completely different from what was expected, learning occurred. Instead of fretting about a "failed" test, the team should instead focus on what was learned. Additionally, if the concept of the "start small, fail fast" approach was adopted in the PDSA cycle, then the team can also be thankful that the learning occurred prior to a significant investment of time, effort, and resources. In the Act step, the team uses the learning from the Do and Study steps to make plans for what to do next. The immediate decision falls into one of three buckets, or what I call the 3 A's—abandon, adapt, or adopt—as noted in Figure 8.6.

Figure 8.6.
PDSA Template: Act

4. **Act:** Based on what you learned from the test, make a plan for your next step.

Determine what modifications you should make - adapt, adopt, or abandon:

The team might choose to abandon a change idea if the results didn't indicate that the idea was effective in bringing about the intended outcome. This typically won't happen after only one testing cycle, but if the change idea has been run through several cycles without success, then this might be a prudent choice. A second option is to adapt a change idea based on the learning from the previous cycle. It may be that the test didn't go perfectly as planned, but some component may have worked to the extent that the team chooses to build on it in subsequent iterations. The final choice is to adopt and standardize the change idea in your organization. This typically would occur after the idea has been tested under various conditions through multiple testing cycles.

PDSA Template: Footer

It's worth mentioning that the PDSA template, like all the documents I design for my improvement work, have the same phrase in the footer. The footer like the one in Figure 8.7 always reads "Probably wrong, definitely incomplete," which I picked up from an improvement conference led by the Carnegie Foundation for the Advancement of Teaching.

Figure 8.7.
PDSA Template: Footer

Probably wrong, definitely incomplete

1

I thought the idea was so important that I not only include it in the footer, but also inculcate improvement team members to that way of thinking. On its face, "Probably wrong, definitely incomplete" doesn't inspire confidence; however, it is a core ethos of both improvement work and the PDSA cycle. It's a foundational idea for the culture of improvement that is absolutely critical when trying to improve complex problems in schools. It's not that we don't have confidence in our ability to improve tough-to-solve problems. It's just that if you don't humble yourself at the beginning of these types of projects, I believe you are setting yourself up for failure and that you likely know far less about the road to improvement than you think. If you charge ahead without this mindset, your improvement project is doomed from the start. The PDSA tool, and the Theory of Knowledge more broadly, are powerful ways to gain knowledge. It is also worth noting here that you may get some early results by using the PDSA cycle along with other quality tools like the process behavior chart that have been described elsewhere in the book. However, the real power for change comes not from any one tool, but rather through using all four components of the System of Profound Knowledge together and the way of thinking that comes from this powerful map of theory.

The PDSA Cycle in Action

Now that I've outlined the basic idea of the PDSA cycle, it will be helpful to turn to a real PDSA that I ran in my work at United Schools Network. This in fact was the first PDSA I ever designed, so it is by no means being held up as perfect. However, I think it is useful as an introductory point to the concept because this example is so simple. I'm also happy to report that for a first attempt, this PDSA cycle was successful.

By way of introduction, it will be helpful to understand the context in which this PDSA cycle was designed. During the 2018-19 school year, I had launched and was leading an improvement project we called 8th Grade On-Track. I had been exposed to on-track work through a grant application to the Bill & Melinda Gates Foundation. Through this application process, I

BUILDING KNOWLEDGE IN CONTEXT

had learned of the on-track indicator systems being developed by various education organizations across the country. One such system predicted the 8th graders who went on to graduate from high school with 96% accuracy. It included a combination of indicators including GPA, grades in core classes, attendance rate, and discipline events, and each indicator had a threshold students had to meet to be considered on-track. The indicators are displayed in Table 8.1.

Table 8.1.

8th Grade On-Track Indicator Minimum Thresholds

GPA	Reading	Writing	Math	Attendance	Behavior
≥ 2.5	≥ C	≥ C	≥ C	≥ 96%	= 0 OSS Events

As a part of our project work, the team had adopted an on-track system, and we were studying how our 8th grade students were performing through the lens of these indicators. The on-track data had been collected for each indicator for all 8th grade students dating back to their 6th grade year and was updated each grading period. It was through this study that we noticed that James' reading grade dropped from a B in 7th grade to a D during the first trimester of his 8th grade year.[8] The rest of his grades were a C or higher, his attendance rate was above 96%, and he had never been in serious trouble. Most people would look at James' academic, attendance, and behavior stats and not see a student that needs intervention, but the improvement team felt otherwise. At the very moment that his reading grade dropped, James needed extra support. What we had learned through our research is that off-track 8th graders become off-track 9th graders, and this is especially problematic because freshman year is the make-or-break year for high school graduation.[9] In most schools, a student like James probably wouldn't get much attention, but research suggests that his grade drop is a leading indicator of things to come. Grades tend to drop in high school, compared to middle school, by about half a GPA point, and students receiving Ds in the middle grades are likely to receive Fs in high school.[10]

When viewed through this lens, there was urgency to get James back on-track. However, even though we now had a definition of on-track for high school readiness, we didn't initially have an answer for the important question of: How do we get off-track students like James back on-track?

174   *Win-Win*

While I hadn't yet completed a deep study of Deming's improvement theory, I had been exposed to several improvement science tools and techniques, including the PDSA cycle. What we developed was a simple but profound innovation by which we combined a technique called the Five Whys with an empathy interview to figure out the root cause for why each student was off-track.[11] From there, we took that root cause and used the PDSA tool for the iterative testing of interventions. James was in fact the first student with whom we worked after the development of this protocol.

Let's first look at James' on-track indicators, Five Whys, and empathy interview, as shown in Table 8.2, before turning to his PDSA. It's worth noting that all of the following snapshots of the on-track system, Five Whys, and empathy interview for James were originally captured on a large sheet of Post It chart paper, so we could put the information on the wall for the improvement team to see. This arrangement became a protocol as we used the same formula with other students as the project progressed. However, for now we'll just focus on how these tools were used with James and led directly to the design of his PDSA cycle.

Table 8.2.
James' On-Track Data & Layers 1-2 of the Five Whys

Five Whys: James							
	GPA	Reading	Writing	Math	Attend.	OSS	On-Track
7th Gr EOY	2.4	B	C	B	97.0%	0	No
8th Gr Tri 1	2.0	D	C	C	96.4%	0	No

Problem: James was on-track in 6th grade, just under on-track in 7th grade, and off-track in Trimester 1 of 8th grade.		
1st Layer	Question:	Why was James off-track in Trimester 1 of 8th grade?
	Answer:	His reading grade dropped from a B in 7th grade to a D in Trimester 1 of 8th grade.
2nd Layer	Question:	Why did James' Trimester 1 reading grade drop from a B to a D?
	Answer	Despite high reading test scores, he has a low homework grade in reading class.

The very top of the Five Whys included the six on-track indicators for James' 7th grade year as well as the first trimester of 8th grade. In 7th grade, James was doing relatively well, but was considered off-track because his

BUILDING KNOWLEDGE IN CONTEXT

175

2.4 GPA fell just below the on-track standard of 2.5. He was on-track in all other areas. At the start of his 8th grade year, his GPA dropped to 2.0 because of the two-letter grade drop in reading. To transition from the on-track indicators to the Five Whys, we first drafted an explicit problem statement as it was currently understood. In this case, the problem statement was as follows: "James was on-track in 6th grade, just under on-track in 7th grade, and off-track in Trimester 1 of 8th grade."

James' reading teacher (Dr. Brennan) and I then began the Five Whys process, in which a question is asked five times, each why question in response to the prior answer.[12] We based our inquiry in the 1st layer of the tool on the problem statement, then the 2nd layer question was based on the answer from the 1st layer. So, in the 1st layer the question was "Why was James off-track in Trimester 1 of 8th grade?", and our answer was "His reading grade dropped from a B in 7th grade to a D in Trimester 1 of 8th grade." The question in the 2nd layer then was "Why did James' Trimester 1 reading grade drop from a B to a D?" As we dug into his grade data, we framed our answer to this question as, "Despite high reading test scores, he has a low homework grade in reading class." The next logical question in this sequence was "Why does James have a low homework grade in reading?" At this point in the Five Whys, James was invited to participate in the process because the most important information for why James' reading grade dropped was in his head. The continuation of Why questions with James is shown in Table 8.3.

Table 8.3.
James' Five Whys Layers 3-5

James is invited to participate in the Five Whys activity from this point on, including the design of the intervention (Empathy Interview).		
3rd Layer	Question:	Why do you have a low homework grade in reading?
	Answer:	I do the easy/less time-consuming homework (M, Sci, H) first during Focus period.
4th Layer	Question:	Why do you do your reading homework last?
	Answer:	I don't like doing my reading homework.
5th Layer	Question:	Why do you dislike your reading homework?
	Answer:	It is too much work, so I put off doing it until the last possible moment.
Root Cause:	James dislikes doing his reading homework, and as a result does it last, often on the bus ride to school in the morning.	

The 3rd layer question was modified to read "Why do you have a low homework grade in reading?" You'll also see that the highlighted portion of Table 8.3 notes that it is at this point that the Five Whys includes an empathy interview component because James has joined Dr. Brennan and me in the inquiry, problem-solving, and intervention design process. James' answer to the 3rd layer question was, "I do the easy/less time-consuming homework (math, science, history) first during Focus period at the end of the day (Focus was a structured homework support period at the school). Based on this answer, the 4th layer question was, "Why do you do your reading homework last?" In response to this question, James shared that "I don't like doing my reading homework." In turn, we asked the following in the 5th layer, "Why do you dislike your reading homework?" to which he said, "It is too much work, so I put off doing it until the last possible moment." It isn't captured in James' 5th layer answer, but he also shared that the last possible moment typically meant that he was hurriedly doing his homework on the bus ride to school in the morning. Dr. Brennan, James, and I then took all the information from our conversation and framed the root cause of James' reading grade drop as follows: "James dislikes doing his reading homework, and as a result does it last, often on the bus ride to school in the morning."

With the insight provided through the Five Whys and the empathy interview, we could now design a PDSA cycle targeted at this root cause. The rest of this chapter will include snapshots of each component of the PDSA, along with a brief description. Like the Five Whys, the PDSA was designed by Dr. Brennan, James, and me. The Plan phase of his PDSA is shown in Figure 8.8.

The objective of the PDSA was fairly simple, based on the root cause of the reading homework issues James identified. As you can in Figure 8.8, the objective of the PDSA was to have James do his reading homework first as opposed to last over the course of the next five school days. We went with this short time frame for two reasons. For one, we would then get back data very quickly to see if our intervention was working. The other reason we went with this short time frame was because James was not very fond of the idea. However, he did commit to trying the intervention for one week to see how it worked.

The basic question that the PDSA was designed around was, "Will doing his reading homework first be enough to raise James' homework grade to 70% or higher during the five-day intervention?" Similarly, the predic-

BUILDING KNOWLEDGE IN CONTEXT

Figure 8.8.
James' PDSA Objective & Plan

PDSA 1: James's Reading Homework

Objective: Through a Five Whys root cause analysis and an empathy interview, it was discovered that James dislikes doing his reading homework, and as a result does it last, often on the thirty minute bus ride to school in the morning. Low homework grades caused his Trimester 1 reading grade to drop to a D after earning a B in 7th grade, despite the fact that he earned an 85% on the Trimester 1 Comprehensive Exam. The objective of the PDSA is to have James do his reading homework first as opposed to last over the course of the next five school days.

1. **Plan:** Plan the test, including a plan for collecting data.

Questions and predictions:

Question: Will doing his reading homework first be enough to raise his homework grade to a 70% or higher during the five-day intervention?

Prediction: James will score a 70% or higher on each of his reading homework assignments during the PDSA Cycle.

Who, what, where, when:

On 3/22(Th), 3/23 (F), 3/26 (M), 3/27 (T), and 3/28 (W), James has committed to working on his reading homework first during Focus at the back kidney table in the Drew classroom. Ms. Kramer will monitor Focus and ensure James is in fact working on his reading homework first during the five-day intervention.

Plan for collecting data:

Dr. Brennan will enter the dates and scores for his five reading homework assignments prior to the intervention (baseline) and for his five reading homework assignments during the intervention. Grey cells were pre-intervention.

tion was that he would in fact score 70% or higher on each of his reading assignments during the cycle. To accomplish this, James committed to working on his reading homework first on March 22, 23, 26, 27, and 28. He did ask for a special seating assignment at the back kidney table during Focus, which was accommodated. The plan was also communicated to Ms. Kramer, who was the teacher assigned to monitor students in Focus. Throughout the cycle, Dr. Brennan committed to recording each homework grade in a simple table within the PDSA template. The data table included five pre-intervention assignments for the purpose of serving as a baseline. These baseline data points are displayed in grey in Table 8.4 on the following page. Homework assigned after the PDSA commenced are in the white rows in the data table.

Table 8.4.
James' PDSA Data Table

Date	Homework Assignment	Score
3/11/2019	5.1 Rhetorical Appeals	6/10
3/13/2019	5.3 Parts of an Argument 2	3/5
3/15/2019	5.4 Author's Purpose	3/5
3/18/2019	5.6 Purpose Annotations	3/5
3/19/2019	5.7 POV	1/5
3/22/2019	5.10 Drawing Connections	5/5
3/26/2019	5.12 Counterclaims 1	3/5
3/27/2019	5.13 Counterclaims 2	6.75/10
3/28/2019	5.14 Evaluating Arguments 1	5/5
3/29/2019	5.15 Evaluating Arguments 2	4/5

The data table was included in the Plan because this section includes a *Plan for collecting data*, but the data is actually collected after transitioning from the Plan to the Do section of the PDSA cycle. The Do section of the PDSA is displayed in Figure 8.9.

Figure 8.9.
James' PDSA Do

2. **Do:** Run the test on a small scale.

Describe what happened. What data did you collect? What observations did you make?

For the past week, Dr. Brennan has collected and graded James's homework assignments to see if the "Reading Homework First" intervention is working. First, James's Focus teacher reported that he did indeed work on his reading homework first as called for in the intervention. He did this during the school's end-of-day homework period called Focus. In addition to working on his least favorite homework first, James had asked for a seating assignment in the back of the room at a kidney table so he could concentrate. This request was accommodated throughout the intervention period. Five homework assignment grades were collected prior to the start of the intervention, and five additional assignments were collected after the start of the intervention.

After initial reservations, James showed enthusiasm for the change in homework routine and the success he found by completing his reading homework first.

The Do section includes a description of what happened while the intervention was being tested. As noted in the snapshot, the Do unfolded just as planned. Ms. Kramer reported that James did in fact work on his reading homework first during Focus, and Dr. Brennan recorded the scores in the data table. One other item that is noted was that after initial reservations, James went from hesitance to showing enthusiasm for the idea after experiencing

BUILDING KNOWLEDGE IN CONTEXT

some early success. We'll get into the Psychology component of the System of Profound Knowledge in the next chapter, but it is worth mentioning that there is probably something to be said about the agency activated in James as an active participant in this process. This may be at the root of James' change of attitude during the cycle. After running the five-day test, we learned some interesting things, which are described in Figure 8.10.

Figure 8.10.
James' PDSA Study

3. **Study:** Analyze the results and compare them to your predictions.

Summarize and reflect on what you learned:

James earned 16 out of 30 points (53%) on the five homework assignments immediately prior to the start of the intervention which reflects his typical homework scores throughout his 8th grade year. All five of these were failing homeworks. After the intervention began on March 22nd, five additional homework assignments were collected and graded in reading class. James passed four out of five assignments and earned 23.75 out of 30 points (79%) during the intervention period. This was 9% higher than the predicted increase in homework grades.

If you look back to the specific language in our prediction, we had said that James would earn a 70% or higher on each assignment. He earned the predicted score on three out of five assignments, but if you look at all five assignments combined, he earned 79% of the points. This was 9% higher than predicted and was 26% higher than he had earned on the baseline assignments. We then had to take this information and consider how we would act on what had been learned during the cycle. This decision is detailed in Figure 8.11.

Figure 8.11.
James' PDSA Act

4. **Act:** Based on what you learned from the test, make a plan for your next step.

Determine what modifications you should make - adapt, adopt, or abandon:

Given the initial success of the "Reading Homework First" intervention, we are going to keep the same design in place. For PDSA Cycle 2, we are going to check-in with James to see how he is feeling about the intervention. If he is on-board with committing to extending the intervention, we will collect data on his next ten homework assignments as well as check-in with him on his overall trimester reading grade when he receives his next progress report on April 16th.

The point of the Act stage is to decide what to do next based on the learning from this PDSA Cycle. If the change idea is going to be adapted or adopted, then the Act in Cycle 1 becomes the foundation for the Plan in Cycle 2. In this case, Dr. Brennan, James, and I decided to extend the testing of this intervention over the course of an additional ten homework assignments. This probably best falls into the *Adapt* category because we were now going to modify the time-period under which the change idea was tested. It is not *Abandon* because the change idea is continuing to be tested. It is also not *Adopt* because we are not going as far as to say that the change idea will be a permanent part of James' learning system.

In thinking about James in relation to Appreciation for a System, it is also worth mentioning something else that is not noted in the PDSA. With all of this attention paid to his reading grade, how were James' grades in other subject areas impacted? As the PDSA unfolded during this final marking period, I'm happy to report that he maintained his grades in writing, math, science, and social studies while raising his reading grade. This goes back to the idea we covered earlier from Dr. Ackoff that improving one part of the system has the potential to degrade the system as a whole. If I had it to do over again, I would have incorporated this whole-system thinking more explicitly into the design of the PDSA.

Nonetheless, James' PDSA is an illustration of just how powerful this process can be in bringing about improvement. It brings the invisible world of theory and observation of the visible world together. We had a theory (in James' case, it was the Reading Homework First change idea) and then we observed what happened in the real world. The PDSA cycle gives us a disciplined framework by which to test our theories in real classrooms and schools and gives agency to the very people charged with implementing improvement ideas. This is a radical and hopefully refreshing departure from typical approaches to school improvement.

We'll add to this approach by discussing the final component of the System of Profound Knowledge, Psychology, in Chapter 9.

Endnotes

1. Edward Martin Baker, *The Symphony of Profound Knowledge: W. Edwards Deming's Score for Leading, Performing, and Living in Concert* (Bloomington, IN: iUniverse, 2017), 38.

2. Donald J. Wheeler, *Making Sense of Data: SPC for the Service Sector* (Knoxville, TN: SPC Press, 2003), 4.

3. Anthony S. Bryk, Louis M, Gomez, Alicia Grunow, and Paul G. LeMahieu, *Learning to Improve: How America's Schools Can Get Better at Getting Better* (Cambridge, MA: Harvard Education Press, 2015), 200.

4. Michael J. Taylor, Chris McNicholas, Chris Nicolay, Ara Darzi, Derek Bell, and Julie E. Reed, "Systematic review of the application of the plan-do-study-act method to improve quality in healthcare," *BMJ Quality & Safety* 23, (2014): 290-298, https://qualitysafety.bmj.com/content/23/4/290.

5. W. Edwards Deming, *The New Economics for Industry, Government, Education,* 3rd ed. (Cambridge, MA: The MIT Press, 2018), 91.

6. Institute for Healthcare Improvement. "QI Essentials Toolkit," 2017, 33-38, www.ihi.org/resources/Pages/Tools/Quality-Improvement-Essentials-Toolkit.aspx.

7. Donald J. Wheeler, *Making Sense of Data: SPC for the Service Sector* (Knoxville, TN: SPC Press, 2003), 345.

8. James is a pseudonym.

9. Emily Krone Phillips, *The Make or Break Year: Solving the Dropout Crisis One Ninth Grader at a Time* (New York & London: The New Press, 2019).

10. Todd Rosenkranz, Marisa de la Torre, and Elaine Allensworth, "Free to Fail or On-Track to College: Why Grades Drop When Students Enter High School and What Adults Can Do About It" (The University of Chicago Urban Education Institute, UChicago Consortium on School Research, September 2014), consortium.uchicago.edu/publications/free-fail-or-track-college.

11. John A. Dues, "A Formula for Improvement," *In Schools, On Schools* (blog), *School Performance Institute,* March 30, 2019, www.schoolperformanceinstitute.org/blog/2019/3/29/a-formula-for-improvement.

12. The Five Whys questioning technique was developed by Shakichi Toyoda. Five whys (or 5 whys) is an iterative interrogative technique used to explore the cause-and-effect relationships underlying a particular problem. The primary goal of the technique is to determine the root cause of a defect or problem by repeating the question "Why?". Each answer forms the basis of the next question. The "five" in the name derives from an anecdotal observation on the number of iterations needed to arrive at the root cause of the problem under question.

CHAPTER NINE

Psychology's Role in Improvement

"Our schools must preserve and nurture the yearning for learning that everyone is born with."[1]

—W. EDWARDS DEMING

THINK ABOUT THE ENERGY, joy, and pride you experience in a preferred hobby, leisure activity, or side hustle. Now think about the energy, joy, and pride you and your close family and friends experience in your educational and professional lives. While I count myself among the privileged who find at least as much joy in their professional work as they do in their personal passions, I believe this to be more exception than the rule. Now, think about the underlying cause of this dynamic in the United States.

Unfortunately, many school and work systems in the United States have inadvertently eliminated joy in work and learning, intrinsic motivation, and people's willingness to cooperate with each other. W. Edwards Deming noted that people are born with intrinsic motivation, self-esteem, dignity, cooperation, curiosity, and joy in learning, but that these characteristics are gradually crushed by what he called the *forces of destruction*. It is important here to clearly list these destructive forces; those that Deming identified as working directly against the optimization of our educational and work systems. The purpose of the System of Profound Knowledge is to combine the methods and tools for improving quality with a management philosophy that created not only better quality, but also better effectiveness, efficiency, productivity, and joy in learning and work.

The problem is that many of the management and leadership practices we employ in our educational and work systems are not only ineffective, but also run directly counter to better quality, effectiveness, productivity, and joy in learning and work.

Many of these practices are so ingrained in the way we run our organizations that we don't even question them. Even when we recognize the destructive nature of these practices, we often don't know what would be more effective. At United Schools Network, we are in the process of evaluating many of our practices through the lens of Profound Knowledge and thinking about how to employ Deming's theory in designing replacements. Table 9.1 outlines several practices that schools and other organizations regularly use that suboptimize the system.

Table 9.1.

Forces of Destruction

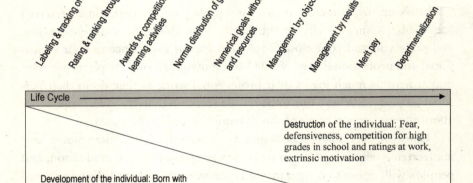

Note 9.1. *Source:* Adapted from W. Edwards Deming, *The New Economics for Industry, Government, Education,* 3rd ed. (Cambridge, MA: The MIT Press, 2018), 84.

It is worth pointing out the unifying theme of all the items in Table 9.1. That is, extrinsic motivators do not work or improve performance in most of the situations that we are most concerned with in schools and work. This is a key problem for us to solve; be it carrot or stick, we employ many practices that simply do not improve school and work systems.

PSYCHOLOGY'S ROLE IN IMPROVEMENT

Aim of this Chapter

The purpose of this chapter is to build on the overview of the Psychology component of the System of Profound Knowledge first introduced in Chapter 1. Returning to an oft-repeated theme of *Win-Win* is the idea that improvement efforts require someone from the outside that has Profound Knowledge collaborating with the people working in the system (i.e., students) and the managers that have the authority to work on the system (i.e., teachers, school leaders). It's also worth repeating the idea that if we wish to make breakthrough improvements in our schools and school systems, we must make time to work on the system of learning and to continually improve it with the help of our students. To be able to work effectively on these types of teams, it is imperative that systems leaders have some understanding of Psychology.

What is Psychology's role in organizational improvement?

W. Edwards Deming did not focus on any single psychological theory when he described its role in creating Profound Knowledge. Instead, his insights were based on decades of experience working with organizations in industry, government, and education, where he often saw the talents of human beings suppressed. For example, a leader with some knowledge about variation, who combines that knowledge with the psychology of management, can no longer subscribe to methods of rating and ranking people. He took this broad view of the field while incorporating its application to important concepts which include transformation, the psychological effects of management systems, joy in work, motivation, and cooperation. These concepts will be the focus of Chapter 9, beginning with the idea of the psychological transformation of the individual who subscribes to the System of Profound Knowledge.

Individual Transformation

In Chapter 2, I introduced the idea of transformation as a change in state from the prevailing system of management to one guided by Profound Knowledge. However, individual transformation precedes organizational transformation, meaning that a systems leader must undergo this change in state individually prior to it being able to occur across an organization. W. Edwards Deming described individual transformation in *The New Economics*:

> The first step is transformation of the individual. This transformation is discontinuous. It comes from understanding of the system of profound knowledge. The individual, transformed, will perceive new meaning to his life, to events, to numbers, to interactions between people.[2]

The idea of transformation can be difficult to wrap your head around; this was certainly the case for me. Frankly, the idea of individual transformation seems strange on its face. However, this is exactly what happened the more and more I began to understand the theory. In the quote above, Deming states that the transformation is "discontinuous," meaning that the transformation process happens in stages with intervals between them. For me, that meant an initial introduction followed by a two-year hiatus driven both by dissonance and a lack of understanding. This was then followed by a voracious period of study, but even that study wasn't without fits and starts. Overcoming those obstacles usually involved reaching out to someone well-versed in the Deming approach to ask clarifying questions; this occurred most often in areas where I experienced significant dissonance, such as when I was studying the theory of variation or the idea that educators should work toward the abolishment of grading.

Time and again though, the theory held up under my scrutiny as I tried to poke holes in it and find errors in its logic. That introspection has in turn caused me to think deeply about the practices I use as an educator and to share this thinking with colleagues. This sharing marks a shift that occurs from individual study and transformation to organizational transformation. As I've mapped Deming's theory to concrete practices, I've realized that there is a litany of shifts in mindset and practice that we need to make.

One example I encountered when first studying Deming's philosophy was his admonishment of performance reviews (i.e., teacher evaluations) on the job. When I first heard this, it was antithetical to everything I had ever learned about school management. The idea of the performance review and by extension, the rating and ranking of teachers, was central to President Obama's Race to the Top program designed and implemented during his first term. Putting a teacher evaluation system in place was, in fact, a prerequisite for receiving these federal funds. However, when I first read Deming's perspective on the issue, I began to reflect a bit more on this practice. Two key thoughts came from this reflection. First, the performance reviews I've received never mapped to a method for improving my own practice. Second,

PSYCHOLOGY'S ROLE IN IMPROVEMENT

there was nothing motivating about the review, even though the reviews I've received have been overwhelmingly positive throughout my career. By this I mean that the hours and dedication I've put into my work over the last two decades have had nothing to do with the reviews. This is just one example of many practices that take inordinate amounts of time that at best have no value, and at worst, work to demotivate educators.

The transformative idea in this example is as follows: my experience receiving performance reviews is no different from my colleagues' or our students' experience with performance reviews. I want to be clear here by what I mean by this: I am not special. That is, it is not my exceptionalism that makes performance reviews unnecessary, but rather that they are built on faulty assumptions. Those faulty assumptions include:

- Evaluations will improve an individual's performance.
- The individual has control over the results.
- The individual's contribution to the results can be accurately differentiated from other educators in the system as well as from the system itself.
- The standards of the evaluation system are aligned to factors important to the school system and its customers.
- The standards are within the capability of the system.
- The system within which the individual works is stable.
- The evaluation is representative of the time period for which it covers as opposed to a period in recent memory.
- The evaluation is representative of the time period for which it covers as opposed to a snapshot within that time period (e.g., observing 1-2 lessons as if they are representative of performance over a semester or school year).
- There is consistency between different evaluators.
- Each evaluator is consistent and fair with each individual's evaluation. [3]

There are many practices in our organizations that are akin to the performance review with all its faulty assumptions, in that it can be a bit overwhelming as the transformative veil drops. One question that quickly comes to mind as a systems leader is: How do I know which practices fall into this category? It takes significant practice, but the System of Profound Knowledge equips us with the theoretical framework for just such an informed evaluation. In fact, once I had a basic understanding of Deming's theory, I found myself applying the lessons to my professional role. Within this role, I now had a sound set of principles from which to make decisions and to use in the organizational transformation process. I now had a sound management philosophy.

Management Philosophy and Psychology

What is your management philosophy?

For the first time in my career, I have an answer to this question, which has been posed to me repeatedly over the last two decades. In the past, I'd mumble some nonsensical jargon I had picked up from business and leadership books. My own inability to articulate a coherent philosophy may in part give some insight to the constantly changing ideas on leadership in the broader society. In education systems, we seem to have an almost insatiable appetite for the latest fads in our sector, an interest in the new and the shiny, as opposed to what works.

I kicked off my teaching career in 2001 and was thrust into a grade-level chair role the following year, and have held some type of formal teacher or school leadership role since then. I sometimes ask myself how I could be a leader for nearly twenty years without being able to clearly articulate a management philosophy. Despite being a lifelong learner, it bothered me immensely that I couldn't answer this question.

With my study of the System of Profound Knowledge, this has changed. I suppose here, I can also be comforted by Deming's words when he noted, "I make no apologies for learning." While I understand and appreciate the sentiment, I feel as if I owe apologies to the teachers and students I have worked with prior to having the leadership principles that underlie Deming's theory. The *mea culpa* aside, after a leader has adopted the new philosophy, a key realization is that the individual components of the system, be it divisions in a business or departments in a school, are not competitive but, rather, must reinforce each other through cooperation. The job of the leader then is to accomplish the transformation of their organization by helping everyone to understand that they must work in cooperation to optimize the

PSYCHOLOGY'S ROLE IN IMPROVEMENT

system. The System of Profound Knowledge is the theory or lens through which one begins to understand why the transformation would bring gains to the organization.

Deming said that once leaders understand the System of Profound Knowledge, there is a compulsion to accomplish transformation as an obligation to themselves and the organization. This certainly rings true from my experience as I began to understand the theory, making me realize that there was a far better way by which to lead my organization. Almost immediately I started viewing United Schools Network in a different way and gained this drive to spread Deming's ideas.

Of course, this is easier said than done. Deming called for transformation leaders to be practical, to have a step-by-step plan, and to explain it in simple terms. This all makes perfect sense, but for someone in the first stages of both individual and organizational transformation, this is no small task. It is especially difficult to explain the System of Profound Knowledge because of its complexity as you are trying to understand it yourself. For me, after about three months of intense study of the theory I put together a presentation that included a handful of slides on each of the four components of the System of Profound Knowledge and began presenting it to one to three people at a time. These presentations lasted about an hour and took place with people I knew well from both inside and outside of my organization. Each time I gave the presentation, I was able to sharpen my knowledge of the theory and improve the presentation.

This was a small way to get started with the theory as well as a way to spread it to others who could serve as thought partners in my study of the System of Profound Knowledge. This individual transformation really picked up speed when I entered into a more formal coaching relationship with David Langford, one of the pre-eminent Deming practitioners in the field of education. The self-study, combined with the coaching, gave me the confidence to spread these ideas across my organization, one of the most important ideas being that everyone is entitled to Joy in Work.

Joy in Work

W. Edwards Deming taught us much about Joy in Work. In Chapter 1, we studied the difference between a traditional organizational chart (Figure 1.2) and the systems view of an organization (Figure 1.3). He proposed posting employee names on the systems view of an organization: you work here; Jennifer works there; Trevor works there; Jessica works there; Catie works there; Ashley works there; I work here. By placing individuals on the systems map, everybody in the organization can see clearly what his or her job is— whom do I depend on and who depends on me? In doing so, everyone will then understand how their work fits in with the work of their colleagues. By seeing the system, individuals can better understand two important components regarding their role in the school system. First, the system's view makes it clear who is depending on them and how others are depending on them. Second, they can clearly see the implications of doing good work. All this is to say that the individual now understands what is meant by doing a good job and may now take joy in his or her work.

The systems model viewed as an organizational chart is far more useful than the traditional hierarchical model. The traditional organizational chart only shows the titles of the people that work there, the reporting structure of those people, and in turn the accountability system within the organization. In other words, it shows who reports to whom. The hierarchical organizational structure may serve some useful purposes, but it most certainly does not describe the system that produces high-quality learning. It is also very possible that the traditional organizational chart in isolation may contribute to several issues. For one, it doesn't communicate to anyone how their work fits into the work of other people in the school district. As Deming notes, organizational charts convey that the primary concern of the worker is to satisfy their boss to attain a good rating. There is no place for the customer within the traditional chart, so taking this perspective is likely to destroy the system. Moreover, the organizational chart can also contribute to the creation of silos throughout the district or even within a single school building. By silos I mean that academic departments, grade levels, or business units seek to optimize individually, which has the potential to destroy the system as a whole. There are no silos in the systems view because cooperation across the system is a critical component to optimization.

While I am a bit of a natural cynic, I don't believe anyone started out with the goal of killing off joy in work. However, some of the detrimental aspects that persist in organizations today have roots in the scientific management methods of early 20th century production facilities. This is not to say that the mistreatment of workers began at this point in world history,

PSYCHOLOGY'S ROLE IN IMPROVEMENT

but rather that at this point offices, factories, and schools began to look like and operate in a way that is recognizable to us as workers in 21st century organizations.

The factories and offices that began to proliferate across the United States in the late 1800s and into the early 1900s function in very different ways from the most typical work settings of the previous 500 years. The family farm and cottage industries where most people worked prior to the Industrial Revolution differed dramatically from modern factories and offices. On the farm, or perhaps in the blacksmith or cobbler's shop, you can almost picture in your mind a very different approach to work. I am by no means a historian of work, but you can imagine the satisfaction and pride in workmanship that one would have in being able to sell the fruits of your labor to support your family. At the very least, the farmer, the blacksmith, and the cobbler would have had a very clear picture of the system of production on their farm or in their workshop even if they never thought about it in this way. The connection from your labor to the end product would be very clear because you were involved in every aspect of the process. This is not the case in the early 20th century factory, where so-called scientific management practices led to division of labor practices that, while highly efficient, probably did not bring the same type of psychological satisfaction as those pre-Industrial Age work settings mentioned above (I also recognize that there is wide variation in these work settings by time, place, and circumstance, some of which were far worse than the factories of the early 1900s).

During the summers of 1925 and 1926 while in graduate school, Deming worked on telephone transmitters in the AT&T Western Electric Hawthorne manufacturing plant in Chicago.[4] He was dismayed by the hot and dirty work conditions within the facility and observed that employees couldn't wait for their monotonous shifts to end each day. The management at Hawthorne, as well as in many factories, were heavily influenced by Frederick Taylor and other efficiency experts of the time. The basic gist of the idea, what came to be known as "Taylorism," was that workers on the floor did not have the education or mental capacity to make important decisions regarding how their work should be done. Instead, engineers planned the work, established work standards, and divided jobs so that they only required simple, repetitive tasks. Workers and foremen had very little discretion in how to perform their jobs and instead were simply required to execute the plans from management.

Deming was born on a farm in Iowa and later moved to the Wyoming frontier as a young boy. His family participated in barn-raisings and quilting bees that embodied the sense of community and cooperation necessary for survival, and this included innumerable jobs he undertook both as a young boy and as a man in support of his family. Fast forward to his observations at Hawthorne where instead people were laboring exclusively for their wages rather than finding pride in their work. In this setting and as reported by Edward Baker:

> Cooperation meant that every worker followed the standard. The decoupling of human beings at work from their wholeness as human beings was institutionalized by Taylor's management methods. In order to maximize the speed and efficiency of production, work was broken into simple repetitive tasks. Parts of people produced parts of products. People did not understand how they fit into the larger picture. Some people who screwed parts together all day long may have gotten the idea that the company was in the screw-tightening business. Being able to see the big picture could have helped them see the value of what they were doing.[5]

Much of the focus of the Taylor method was piece-rate payment that was thought to be needed to motivate workers. This form of extrinsic motivation was hypothesized to be necessary to reach the mind of workers which, in turn, controlled their efficiency. Rather than promoting cooperation, allowing workers to see how they fit into the larger system, and facilitating pride in workmanship, the incentive pay scheme was seen as a necessary component to prod "lazy" and "unmotivated" workers. The reader will very likely see parallels in this behaviorally-focused incentive system not only in their work experience but also in their school experience. I know that these systems have existed in every school that I attended and for those in which I've worked. I in fact have been a designer in these incentive systems as both a teacher and school administrator.

But what do these systems communicate? It seems to me that this is clear. The schoolwork itself, like the work in those early factories, is not engaging or worth attention except under conditions of extrinsic rewards or punishments. While this surely doesn't apply to every classroom and school, I am willing to stake a fairly large amount that some version of this is a common experience for most people educated in the United States. Deming in fact

PSYCHOLOGY'S ROLE IN IMPROVEMENT

discussed the destruction of schools through suboptimization of systems and through reliance on extrinsic motivators in *The New Economics*. In his chapter entitled *Introduction to a System,* he put it this way:

> A public school in the United States is not operated as a component of a system. Optimization is obstructed by a city superintendent, a county superintendent, a school board (elected, shifting over time, no constancy of purpose), district board, local government, county government, state board of education, federal government, assessment by standardized tests of pupils, comparisons between districts and states.[6]

This synopsis is as true today as it was when Deming published *The New Economics* in 1994. It is in fact feasible that optimization is even more obstructed today compared to 1994 with the addition of public charter schools and the increased role of the federal and state bureaucracy in the education ecosystem. After serving as a charter school and network leader in Columbus for the last decade and a half, I can tell you that I've never heard anyone talking about optimizing the system of education in Columbus. Think of the possibilities to such an approach—instead of bickering about this or that, we'd be working to optimize the system of education in Columbus and beyond to the benefit of students (Joy in Learning) and educators (Joy in Work).

Grading Systems, Motivation, & Psychology

Let's start with three suppositions about motivation. First, there are intrinsic and extrinsic sources of motivation. Second, total submission to extrinsic motivation leads to destruction of the individual. Third, all people are motivated to a different degree both extrinsically and intrinsically. Earlier in this chapter, when I re-introduced the psychological component of the System of Profound Knowledge, I included a table with the forces of destruction. We are born with a desire to learn, self-esteem, curiosity, intrinsic motivation, and dignity that lead to optimization. Then, we increasingly encounter those forces of destruction across the life cycle that suboptimize joy in learning, self-esteem, intrinsic motivation, cooperation with others, and self-worth. These same items in turn work to suboptimize both work and school systems. I've discussed a number of these suboptimizing mechanisms such as merit pay and performance reviews. Other items on this list are numerous and include: labeling and tracking of children; rating and ranking through grading; awards for competition in learning activities; normal distribution of grades; numerical goals without methods and resources; management by objectives; management by results; and departmentalization. I am going to pick one item on this list—rating and ranking children through grading—and provide an analysis for how suboptimization of intrinsic motivation and joy in learning is killed through this practice. Selfishly, I am choosing to focus here because it is the hardest practice for me to wrap my head around. Grading systems are so entrenched in the K-12 *modus operandi*, it is hard to imagine schools without them.

In Chapter 3, when introducing the "14 Principles for Educational Systems Transformation," I first explained the idea of working to abolish grading and the harmful effects of rating people. The main reason for abolishing grading and rating is because of the resulting displacement of priority from the learning to the grade. In the explication of Principle 3, I also outlined three robust differences between students who were graded and those who were not including:

- Students who are graded tend to become less interested in whatever topic they were studying.

- Students who are graded, when they have a choice to pick, pick the easiest possible task.

- Students who are graded are more likely to think in a superficial or shallow fashion, more likely to ask questions like, "Do we have to know this?" as opposed to more thoughtful questions about the content itself.

I'm still pondering these points, but the argument is compelling and serves as a jumping off point for my own thoughts on grading practices. To begin with, I want to mention two things. First, traditional grading practices are still the norm at United Schools Network. Second, I've found it helpful when introducing this idea to ask people for a personal anecdote where grading practices went awry. We shouldn't necessarily draw conclusions from these stories, but I do think it is a good place to start the thinking process.

For me, I go back to a decision I made in my senior year of high school that was completely driven by the consequences of the grading system, rather than by what was best for learning's sake and for my long-term academic

PSYCHOLOGY'S ROLE IN IMPROVEMENT

success. During the last twice-a-day football practice of the summer, I dislocated my elbow, and the injury required surgery. This occurred just about a week prior to the start of the school year, and as I started the year, my calculus class was especially challenging. In addition to the ongoing pain from the injury, I was also dealing with the mental fog that came from the pain medication I was taking. Math had long been the most challenging subject in school for me, and with the added challenge of the injury, I decided to drop the class three weeks into the school year. The primary reason for doing so was because I feared getting a B or lower in the class and that this in turn would lower my GPA, taking me out of the running to become the class valedictorian. Without question, this was the wrong decision and most definitely a decision made for the wrong reasons. The decision was completely driven by extrinsic motivators. It in fact impacted my course selection decisions the following year as a freshman in college and ultimately my choosing of a major. This all came at the expense of where the focus should have been, that is, the benefits to learning calculus in one's life. This fundamental displacement of priority from the learning to the grade is at the heart of this issue.

Deming held a deep concern for education in the United States and held the belief that no notable improvement would come until schools abolish merit ratings of teachers and abolish comparison of schools based on scores. In relation to grades, he said:

> Abolish grades (A, B, C, D) in school, from toddlers on up through the university. When graded, pupils put emphasis on the grade, not on learning. Cooperation on a project may be considered cheating (W.W. Scherkenbach, The Deming Route, p. 128). The greatest evil from grades is forced ranking-only (e.g.,) 20 percent of pupils may receive A. Ridiculous. There is no shortage of good pupils...Our schools must preserve and nurture the yearning for learning that everyone is born with. Joy in learning comes not so much from what is learned, but from learning. Joy on the job comes not so much from the result, the product, but from contribution to optimization of the system in which everybody wins.[7]

Albeit anecdotal, I've given one reason why we should at least do some thinking about traditional grading systems in schools. That is, they can cause us to make myopic decisions focused on short-term rather than long-term benefits especially if the decision-making is heavily influenced by extrinsic forces. A second reason to do some thinking about grading practices is well-captured by a question from frequent Deming collaborator William Scherkenbach when he asked: Certainly we see differences in performance, but are those differences due to the system or the individual?[8]

This question encapsulates what is perhaps the most radical challenge put forth by Deming and the systems perspective. This challenge is the idea, outlined in previous chapters, that outputs at school (or work) are the result of more than an individual's skills and efforts. There is a third powerful factor, which is the effect of the system on those outputs. Systems thinking assigns most of the differences in student performance that are represented by a grade to the system and not the students. This is one of those ideas that underlies the transformation, or change of state, which Deming advocated. I outlined a very similar example focused on school performance data in Chapter 3. The theory underlying this radical perspective in both examples can be represented by the following math equation:

If $A + B + C + D + E + F = 71$ (student's grade), what is the numerical value of F?

Obviously, the equation cannot be solved without knowing the values of A through E, or at least their sum. However, the grading system suggests that we can assign a value to F (the student) with no knowledge of the values or effects of the other variables. The grading system accomplishes this impossible task as follows:

Table 9.2.

An Impossible Equation Revisited

A + B + C + D + E + ...	+ F	= 71
State standards, curriculum, assignment design,	+ Student	= Grade
grading scale, teaching methods, classroom technology,		
support services, school funding, facility quality,		
community resources, neighborhood safety, household income,		
household wealth, home environment, access to healthcare,		
access to healthy food, housing stability,		
and many (if not countless) other variables . . .		

PSYCHOLOGY'S ROLE IN IMPROVEMENT

The basic idea with traditional grading practices is to take the myriad variables of the teaching and learning process, add the student to the mix, and then assign the sum of these variables in the form of a grade to the student. If you closely examine the list of variables on the left of the table above, it is evident that the variation in grades comes from many sources and not simply from the student.

I can imagine that many people reading this are having feelings of significant cognitive dissonance about now. I had those very same feelings when initially introduced to Deming's philosophy on grading, and frankly, I am still working through the dissonance as I write this chapter. In addition to the anecdote I shared above from my high school experience, I'd ask you to think of two other things that may at least cause you to continue the critical thinking process in this area. First, if you're a parent, think about what you hear when you ask your child how they did on a recent assignment, test, or project. If your kids are anything like mine, my hunch is that their first instinct is to report the grade they received on the assignment, test, or project. Many conversations end there. But, if you take it a step further and ask what they learned by completing the assignment, test, or project, you often get a blank look even if you continue this line of questioning. Second, think about what you actually know after reviewing your child's grade report. If it is mostly As and Bs, then most people are probably satisfied. However, reflect on what you really know if your 5th grader's report card has a B listed for reading class. The B communicates somewhere between little to nothing about the quality of work that was required for your child to receive this grade. On the flip side but still within the same vein, what if your child received a D instead of a B in reading. Many parents would likely go to the school to figure out what is going wrong. However, figuring out what exactly a D means in 5th grade reading would not be easy. The B or D grade in and of itself tells you very little about the quality of work that led to those grades.

To reiterate, I am still wrestling with the idea of abolishing grading. Upon a close read of my Principle 3, the exact text is: ". . . work to abolish grading and the harmful effects of rating people." This implies that there should be a deliberative process to go from a traditional grading system to one without grades. As you consider any type of significant change to your school system following the Deming philosophy, it would be wise to heed the words of practitioners that have made the shift.

198   *Win-Win*

One such person is Dr. Henry Neave, who was a close collaborator with Dr. Deming and is one of the foremost experts on the System of Profound Knowledge in England. In his seminal work, *The Deming Dimension,* he gave this prescient advice to those working to implement Deming' ideas:

> The 14 Points are a substantial aid to teaching and to learning. But, although the 14 Points are an extremely helpful guide to important parts of the philosophy, they may also increase the danger of people trying to take action in order to obey words before developing understanding. That can be a fatal mistake. The context of the 14 Points is a commitment to continual improvement in quality, in its widest sense and interpretation, and what is needed to fulfill that commitment. That certainly involves a lot of action-but it also involves a lot of education and understanding of why that action is needed, and of the pathways that need to be cleared before some of the action becomes appropriate.
>
> Hasty action . . . and the general tendency to jump to conclusions based on insufficient understanding, can harm the reputation and credibility of the Deming philosophy itself.[9]

In *The Deming Dimension,* Dr. Neave relates a story that he heard from Deming that makes concrete the warning to think prior to doing. Deming spoke of a manager from Ford, who after attending a four-day seminar, went back to work the following Monday and fired all his inspectors. The reason the manager did this was because he thought Point 3 from Deming's 14 Points was telling him to do so. Point 3 is: "Cease dependence on inspection to achieve quality. Eliminate the need for inspection on a mass basis by building quality into the product in the first place." Clearly, the manager didn't think at all prior to firing the inspectors. The14 Points are not a checklist to be completed, but rather, they provide guidance on how to make a shift over a period of time.

Deming's 14 Points are meant to open our minds to a new philosophy, a new approach to running our organizations. The "14 Principles for Educational Systems Transformation" (see Chapter 3 for full descriptions and Table 5.1 for an overview of the 14 Principles) translate these key points that he authored for industry and government leaders to those that lead our education systems. In both cases, the point is to navigate from prevailing management

PSYCHOLOGY'S ROLE IN IMPROVEMENT

practices to this new philosophy. Author and consultant James Leonard stated this new philosophy for education in a way that is well worth repeating:

> Learning and applying the system of profound knowledge in order to (1) understand the statistical nature of work and learning; and (2) view work and learning as dynamic processes; then take appropriate action to accomplish improvement because wherever children and their future are concerned, there can be no such thing as good enough in our schools.[10]

This synopsis sounds right to me and is the underlying rationale for this learning journey. I hope people heed my advice to really think about any of these ideas before trying them in their own school systems. It is critical that before trying anything in practice that there is a deep understanding for why the new processes or systems being proposed are better than those currently in place. This rationale for change should be well understood and articulated prior to moving forward with their adoption.

In reviewing the two ideas embedded in Leonard's definition of the new philosophy as applied to education, there are some questions that arise that would be a good starting point for this thinking. First, as we seek to understand the statistical nature of work and learning when it comes to students, the question, "Are these students different?" would be replaced with the question, "Are these students significantly different?" Traditional practices such as the grading system do not consider this understanding of variation. Second, if we view learning as a part of an education production system with dynamic processes, we may ask, "How do we define the student's contribution to the equation $A + B + C + D + E + F = 71$?" Grading is only valid if the student, as represented in the equation by the variable F, always equals 71, which we know is not the case.

Deming's call for the abolishment of grades is grounded in the theory of systems, variation, and psychology, and in the idea that in the traditional grading system, students put emphasis on the grades and not the learning.

I have not gone so far as to propose an alternative grading system. While I have some initial ideas, they are not developed enough to outline here. Instead, I'll leave you with a series of questions you can ask as you are reviewing your own system:

- Do students, parents, and teachers understand the grading system?

- Does the grading system cause students to focus on grades or on the learning?

- Does the grading system cause students to become more or less focused on the topics they are studying?

- Does the grading system cause students to take on more or less challenging tasks?

- Does the grading system cause students to ask deeper or more superficial questions?

- Do students regularly receive timely and meaningful feedback on their assignments?

- How does the grading system facilitate or impede timely and meaningful feedback?

- Does the grading system cause students to make decisions that are in their long-term best interests?

I've spent much of this chapter on the psychological component of the System of Profound Knowledge discussing traditional grading systems. I focused on grading because it is a ubiquitous feature of the American education system and something nearly everyone can relate to. The goal of this chapter was to get you thinking about how this system impacts students from a psychological perspective and to start asking questions like those listed above, which can serve as a starting point for conversations regarding the impact of your grading system on students and other stakeholders. In addition to the questions about grading, one might also begin to think more deeply about individual transformation, your management philosophy, intrinsic and extrinsic motivation, and joy in work and learning. These questions can put us on the path to transformation and a better educational system for all. On this front, let's give Deming the last word:

> The result [of educational transformation] will in time be greater innovation and reward for everyone. There will be joy in work; joy in learning. Anyone who enjoys his work is a pleasure to work with. Everyone will win; no losers.[11]

Endnotes

1. W. Edwards Deming, *The Essential Deming: Leadership Principles from the Father of Quality*, ed. Joyce Nilsson Orsini. (New York: McGraw-Hill, 2013).

2. W. Edwards Deming, *The New Economics for Industry, Government, Education,* 3rd ed. (Cambridge, MA: The MIT Press, 2018), 63.

3. Peter Scholtes, *The Leader's Handbook: A Guided to Inspiring Your People and Managing the Daily Workflow* (New York: McGraw-Hill, 1998), 295.

4. "Deming the Man Timeline," The W. Edwards Deming Institute, accessed August 9, 2021, deming.org/timeline.

5. Edward Martin Baker, *The Symphony of Profound Knowledge: W. Edwards Deming's Score for Leading, Performing, and Living in Concert* (Bloomington, IN: iUniverse, 2017), 233.

6. W. Edwards Deming, *The New Economics for Industry, Government, Education,* 3rd ed. (Cambridge, MA: The MIT Press, 2018), 50-51.

7. W. Edwards Deming, *The New Economics for Industry, Government, Education,* 3rd ed. (Cambridge, MA: The MIT Press, 2018), 100.

8. William W. Scherkenbach, *The Deming Route to Quality and Productivity: Road Maps and Roadblocks* (Rockville, Maryland: Mercury Press, 1988), 55.

9. Henry Neave, *The Deming Dimension* (Knoxville, Tennessee: SPC Press, 1990), 283-284.

10. James F. Leonard, *The New Philosophy for K-12 Education: A Deming Framework for Transforming America's Schools* (Milwaukee, WI: ASQ Quality Press, 1996), 175.

11. Ron Warwick, *Beyond Piecemeal Improvements: How to Transform Your School Using Deming's Quality Principles* (Bloomington, IN: National Educational Service, 1995), 46.

CHAPTER TEN

A Win-Win for You

"Joy on the job comes not so much from the result, the product, but from contribution to optimization of the system in which everybody wins."[1]

—W. EDWARDS DEMING

WIN-WIN SEEMS LIKE A fitting place to end this book. The idea of Win-Win was a refreshing concept when I first discovered it as I studied the Deming philosophy and the System of Profound Knowledge. It is what Dr. Henry Neave called the "backbone of the new philosophy." When we think of industry, government, and education, aren't there supposed to be winners and losers? Doesn't someone have to be at the top of the class or on top of a dog-eat-dog corporate world? The answer in short is no. There is a better way, and this better way is what Deming referred to as Win-Win. The call to action is the restoration of the individual within industry, government, and educational organizations as well as throughout society more generally.

My hope is that this idea has come through in the book, specifically in the restoration of the individual within the complexity of 21st century school districts in the United States. We all have a role to play in this restoration, be it the restoration of students or educators, and Deming and his System of Profound Knowledge provide the map of theory for this transformation. The overall transformation must be guided by the System of Profound Knowledge. As systems leaders learn and apply the theory to organizations, they will exhibit certain behaviors that in turn lead people and those organizations toward continual improvement of teaching and learning processes. A key part of this process is in the management of people, with leadership behaviors guided by an appreciation for a system, rational theories of variation and knowledge, and an understanding of motivation.

Aim of this Chapter

The purpose of this chapter is two-fold. First, I'll tie all of the major themes of the text back to the Win-Win philosophy. Second, I'll give you some concrete ideas to get you started on your own continual improvement journey aligned with this philosophy.

What is the Win-Win philosophy?

In Chapter 2, I introduced the idea of transformation, and the route to this transformation is in the adoption of the Deming philosophy. Win-Win is a core part of the "backbone" of the new philosophy for industry, government, and education, which is grounded in the idea of cooperation and Win-Win, so that everybody wins. The old system was based on conflict and competition and Win-Lose, by which either you win and I lose, or I win and you lose. Ultimately, the goal of Win-Win and transformation is the optimization of systems within which we live and work, making it possible to realize the full potential of these systems and everyone working within them.

Win-Win & Transformation

Think back to Chapter 4 when I discussed the system of education in Columbus, Ohio where I serve as an educator. It seems to me that we are still stuck in the Win-Lose system where traditional school districts, public charter schools, and private schools view themselves as competitors rather than cooperators. It's probably fair to say that this same Win-Lose approach is also apparent within the charter sector itself where individual schools are viewed as competitors. This means that we have no chance of optimizing the system of education within the city of Columbus because it is being suboptimized through the separation of components of the system of education in the form of individual district and school fiefdoms. In the absence of this city-wide system of cooperation, a system of competition will be the default. So entrenched is this idea of competition, it is very likely that few have even considered the possibility of a system of education in Columbus. It is just as likely that without a system of cooperation across private schools, public charter schools, and traditional public schools for the benefits of the students that live in the city, there is little chance of a Win-Win system where all students have access to an excellent education.

A WIN-WIN FOR YOU

W. Edwards Deming was a visionary leader, part statistician and improvement leader and part moral philosopher. The world-changing nature of his new philosophy, what he eventually dubbed the System of Profound Knowledge, was what landed him on the list of nine lesser-known historical turning points introduced in Table 1.1 in Chapter 1. The idea of Win-Win that is so central to Deming's philosophy should not be taken to mean that he conceived of a world without competition. There is no question that we will face competition of various types on a regional, national, and/or global scale. The question is, how will we handle this competition?

At United Schools Network, we've long worked diligently to create a system of schools working cooperatively toward a common mission of providing an excellent education to students in Franklinton, the Near East Side, and surrounding communities. Even prior to going on my Deming learning journey, I had a strong appreciation for USN as a system. For example, we've never pitted teachers against one another based on value-added test results or through the administration of a merit pay system like many school systems did through the federal Race to the Top legislation. Similarly, at the school level, there has never been any competition to get the highest rating on the state department of education report cards. With my study of Deming's System of Profound Knowledge, I now have an even deeper appreciation for and an understanding of the theory underlying the Win-Win philosophy. As our network grew from six employees in 2008 to more than 130 in 2022, I now have a framework for sharing this philosophy in a concrete way both with USN staff as well as with my colleagues across the city, state, and country.

At the city level, consider again the idea of a system of education in Columbus that aims to provide excellent educational and social support from birth through higher education to residents of the city and the surrounding areas. How can we attain such an aim? I would posit that it is not by creating more competition internally within this system of education in Columbus. At this scale, with the city of Columbus defined as the core system, the supra system is nearby cities and states in the Midwest. Or we may even consider a larger supra system that includes the United States. In either case, to optimize this system of education, we'd need to ensure cooperation between its components rather than internal competition and strife. The same could be said if we enlarged the core system from the system of education in the city of Columbus to instead be the system of education in the United States. Think here of President Kennedy's proclamation on May 25,

1961, "that this Nation should commit itself to achieving the goal, before this decade is out, of landing a man on the moon and returning him safely to earth."[2] This aim led to a serious investment in education at both the K-12 and university levels, especially in the areas of science, technology, engineering, and math. The goal not only inspired a nation and provided a clear aim, but it also helped focus and align the efforts of many individuals. This is a good example of Win-Win in action.

Deming's Win-Win idea doesn't imply that everybody's outcomes will be the same. Rather I take Win-Win to mean that opportunity will be more equally distributed across society, and even though it is inevitable that some will win less than others, there will be far less losing. Deming's overarching thesis is that rather than a society divided into winners and losers, we all win. This is a much-needed message of hope for industry, government, and education.

Getting Started with the Deming Philosophy

I've spent a significant amount of time outlining the System of Profound Knowledge as a theory for organizational improvement. The theory has been accompanied by a number of applied examples, including the 8th grade math engagement data from Chapter 1, the attendance case study from Chapter 7, and the Plan-Do-Study-Act cycle example from Chapter 8. However, I recognize that knowing that the Deming theory is important is not the same thing as knowing how to get started with it in your own school system. As helpful resources I've also included Appendix A, which outlines United Schools Network's ten-step improvement process, as well as Appendix B, which takes you through the creation of a process behavior chart. The improvement process operationalizes the System of Profound Knowledge in a step-by-step fashion for use with an improvement team. The process behavior chart instructions were included because of the central importance of this tool in continual improvement work. While the examples and appendices will no doubt be useful to you in this learning process, what will be most helpful is to leave you with a description of an improvement project guided by the System of Profound Knowledge. For that, we'll turn to a project completed during the 2021-22 school year.

A WIN-WIN FOR YOU

A Case Study in the Science of Improvement

Our case study focuses on an improvement project completed by 4th grade teacher Jessica Cutler as a part of her participation in United School Network's Continual Improvement Fellowship. The aim of the fellowship is to learn Deming's improvement theory along with a number of tools, techniques, and processes to support the transformation of conventional classrooms to those guided by continual improvement methods. In Jessica's case, she was attempting to improve the joy in learning of students in her science class. As you read the case study you will notice both elements of the improvement process outlined in Appendix A, as well as elements from the "10 Key Lessons for Data Analysis" from Chapter 7.

As previously discussed, students, as well as someone from outside the System with Profound Knowledge (or someone internally that taps into outside knowledge gained through the System of Profound Knowledge), are the substantially underutilized secret weapons of continual improvement efforts in schools. Students working in the system can help identify the waste and inefficiency in the system. They must be paired with teachers and principals who have technical knowledge and the authority to change the system. Both must be guided by someone from outside the system with an understanding of the System of Profound Knowledge. In Jessica's project, she served as the subject-matter expert with the authority to change her science class. I served as a resource with expertise in the System of Profound Knowledge. Students from her science class were the third component of the improvement team that helped identify obstacles to their Joy in Learning.

Step 1: See the System

The first thing that Jessica had to figure out was the largest system within her sphere of influence that she could improve. She decided that system was her 4th grade science class and from there, worked with her students to write a clear purpose or aim for 4th grade science. The aim that she and her class settled on was: "The purpose of this class is to create a love of learning science." It was really important to establish a clear, well-defined aim because all of the subsequent work flows from this statement.

Step 2: Define the Problem

Early on, she and her students also had to create a problem statement that clearly outlined the problem they were going to work to improve. The problem statement they outlined had three parts including the current state, its impact on the class, and the desired state. The current state was: "Students have a difficult time staying focused and sitting still through their science block after they complete social studies." The impact on the class was: "Their science comprehension is inconsistent, students begin talking, and the ability to stay still and complete work becomes more difficult." The desired future state was: "Students are able to stay focused through both science and social studies, enjoy science class, and remain engaged." The class then came up with an operational definition for Joy in Learning which was: "To have fun learning, finding things we like to learn, and have fun completing classwork and activities."

Step 3: Understand the Current Situation

After Jessica and her students had the operational definition of Joy in Learning in science, she then designed a simple survey to collect student feedback several times each week. The first question on the survey was: "On a scale of 1-10 how much did you ENJOY science class today?" The second question, "What made you enjoy/not enjoy class today?," was open-ended. As Jessica started to administer the Joy in Learning survey, she immediately began "plotting the dots" on a run chart. The run chart in Figure 10.1 helped her and her students to see variation in the survey data over time.

Figure 10.1.
Run Chart: Joy in Science

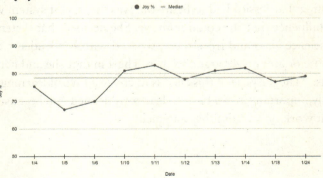

A WIN-WIN FOR YOU

The run chart has data from the first 10 surveys Jessica administered to her 4th grade science class. Even with only 10 data points plotted over time, we are beginning to learn a lot about the Joy in Learning concept, and we're certainly learning much more than we would with just two or three points, or even with 10 points stored in a spreadsheet. She continued to collect data from the Joy in Learning survey through February and March. At this point, I turned the run chart into a process behavior chart with upper and lower limits, and then we collected an additional 20 points to include in our baseline data. The process behavior chart for this data is displayed in Figure 10.2.

As of March 22nd, Jessica and her students had collected 30 Joy in Science data points, which works out to two to three data points for most of the weeks during that period. Most importantly, they were not overreacting to any single data point; rather, they worked to understand the variation and trends within the 4th grade science system. The Lower Natural Process Limit during the baseline period was 66%, the Upper Natural Process Limit was 95%, and the average was 81%. This means that if nothing changes within the 4th grade science system, we can expect the data to bounce around the 81% average and stay within the bounds of the limits in the near future. We do see one signal in the data, which is a run of nine points between February 17th and March 16th. However, we chose not to shift the limits because

Figure 10.2.
Baseline Period X Chart: Joy in Science

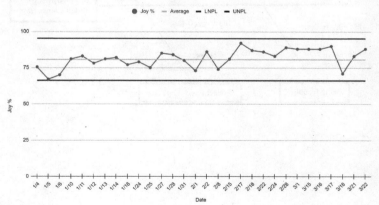

there was nothing we could point to that was a change that we had made to the system that would bring about this shift. Besides that signal, we only see common cause variation present.

Step 4: Study the Causes

The 4th grade Joy in Science data indicate that this is mostly a predictable, stable system. This means that the way to improve is to work on changes to the system itself. There were no negative special causes to study and remove, but the team wasn't happy with the 81% Joy in Science average. The class used the fishbone diagram displayed in Figure 10.3 to map the obstacles to enjoyment. A *fishbone diagram* is a tool for analyzing process dispersion. The diagram illustrates the main causes and sub causes leading to an effect. Within the various causes, the students identified distracting noises as the dominant obstacle to increasing joy.

Figure 10.3.
Fishbone Diagram

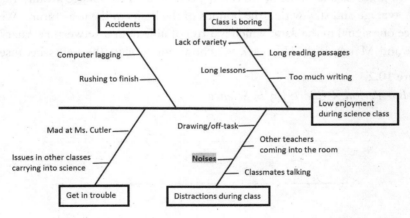

A WIN-WIN FOR YOU

Step 5: Determine Measures of Success

A change idea or intervention should be clearly marked in your process behavior chart. This can be done by inserting a dashed vertical line on the date the intervention is started and should include a simple label that captures the essence of the intervention. This allowed Jessica and her students to easily see the data prior to and after the implementation of the change idea. They then used the three rules for finding signals to see if the intervention is indeed bringing about the intended improvement. As we learned in Chapter 6, those rules include:

- Rule 1: Any data point outside of the limits.
- Rule 2: Eight consecutive points on the same side of the central line.
- Rule 3: Three out of four consecutive data points that are closer to the same limit than they are to the central line.

Step 6-7: Design and Test a Theory for Improvement

Jessica and her class developed a change idea around reducing distracting noises during science class. Specifically, students said, "If we get automatic deductions for making noises, then there will be less noises." Deductions are the equivalent of a demerit in the school's management system, but the key point here is that students developed this idea, and as a result, will be much more likely to be invested in the system. Their basic theory is, "If there is less noise, then we will be able to enjoy science class." Keep in mind that all of this is being created by 9- and 10-year-olds with guidance from their teacher! The class rolled out this change idea on March 19th as marked by the dashed vertical line and label in the process behavior chart in Figure 10.4.

Figure 10.4.
X Chart with Change Idea

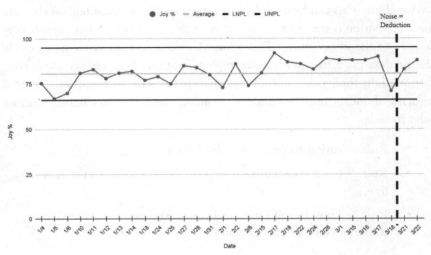

Jessica continued to gather the Joy in Science data to see if the team's theory was correct. The prediction was that reducing noises during science would lead to more joy in the class. If their theory is effective, they should see signals to that effect after the change idea is implemented. If it is not, they'll have learned this through a very low-stakes experiment and will then try another approach.

Step 8: Study the Results

There were two signals that indicated that the class's theory led to improvement of the problem. The data point for March 23rd showed a Rule 1 signal because it was outside the upper limit. Additionally, the 11 data points after the change idea was implemented show a Rule 2 signal because there are eight or more consecutive points on the same side of the central line. As a result, the limits of the Joy in Science process behavior chart were shifted to reflect this new and improved system! This is illustrated in Figure 10.5.

A WIN-WIN FOR YOU

Figure 10.5.
X Chart with Shifted Limits

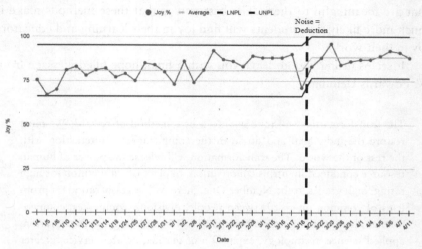

Step 9: Reflect and Establish Future Plans

After reviewing the results of the experiment, the class decided that they would continue to implement the change idea for the rest of the 2021-22 school year. Jessica also added a positive component to the plan where students who were consistently meeting expectations earned shout outs. She reported that students enjoyed the positive praise and an environment that is quiet, so that everyone could enjoy what they were learning without disruptions in class. Moreover, she planned to bring this process into social studies as well.

Improvement with Joy

Jessica's project illustrates a very different approach to school improvement, one guided by sound continual improvement methods. Instead of setting an arbitrary improvement goal at the outset of the project, she and her 4th graders avoided this "act of desperation" and studied their system. Too often in our attempts to improve schools, we go fast, learn slowly, and fail to appreciate what it actually takes to make some promising idea work in practice. Left in the never-ending wake of good intentions are teachers with initiative fatigue. However, Jessica and her 4th graders demonstrate that there is a better way to work toward improvement where everyone wins. In this example, Jessica and her students are developing and testing the ideas that are meaningful to them. The best part is that these methods make it much more likely that students will find joy in their learning and educators joy in their work.

It seems fitting here to leave you with a final, hope-filled message from W. Edwards Deming:

> The transformation will take us into a new method of reward. We must restore the individual and do so in the complexities of interaction with the rest of the world. The transformation will release the power of human resource contained in intrinsic motivation. In place of competition for high rating, high grades, to be Number One, there will be cooperation on problems of common interest between people, divisions, companies, competitors, governments, countries. The result will in time be greater innovation, applied science, technology, expansion of market, greater service, greater material reward for everyone. There will be joy in work, joy in learning.[3]

In other words, a Win-Win for everyone.

Endnotes

1. Ron Warwick, *Beyond Piecemeal Improvements: How to Transform Your School Using Deming's Quality Principles* (Bloomington, IN: National Educational Service, 1995), 123.

2. NASA, "President Kennedy Challenges NASA to Go to the Moon." YouTube, May 20, 2013, www.youtube.com/watch?v=GmN1wO_24Ao&ab_channel=NASA Video.

3. W. Edwards Deming, *The New Economics for Industry, Government, Education,* 3rd ed. (Cambridge, MA: The MIT Press, 2018), 85.

GLOSSARY

aim (of a system): A qualitative statement with methods included that details a system's long-term constancy of purpose. Deming said, "A system must have an aim. Without an aim, there is no system. The aim of the system must be clear to everyone in the system. The aim must include plans for the future. The aim is a value judgment. The secret is cooperation between components toward the aim of the organization. We cannot afford the destructive effect of competition."[1]

Appreciation for a System: One of the components of W. Edwards Deming's System of Profound Knowledge. Taking a systems approach results in management viewing the organization in terms of many internal and external interrelated connections and interactions, as opposed to discrete and independent departments or processes governed by various chains of command. When all the connections and interactions are working together to accomplish a shared aim, an organization can achieve tremendous results—from improving the quality of its products and services, to improving the entire esprit de corps of the organization.[2]

common cause variation: When a process displays predictable variation, that variation may be thought of as the result of many different cause-and-effect relationships where no one cause is dominant over the others. While every process is subject to many different cause-and-effect relationships, predictable processes are those in which the net effect of the multiple causes is a sort of static equilibrium. Deming's terminology for this condition was common cause variation, while Walter Shewhart called it "controlled variation."[3]

deductive learning: In the context of the Plan-Do-Study-Act cycle, deductive learning involves moving from a theory to the test of the theory. From Plan to Do is a deductive approach where a theory is tested with the aid of a prediction. In the Do phase, observations are made and differences from the prediction are noted.[4]

effects heterogeneity: Over the last fifty years, educational studies have found that many interventions can be made to work in some places but that virtually none work everywhere. This finding has become so common with education-related Randomized-Controlled Trials that it has taken on its own technical name: effects heterogeneity.[5]

elements (of a system): Elements are the visible, tangible parts of the system but also include intangible parts of a system. The system called a school is made up of tangible parts such as buildings, students, teachers, administrators, books, computers, etc., but elements also can be intangible parts such as school pride and academic prowess.[6]

extrinsic motivation: Refers to external processes applied to individuals or organizations, such as rewards and punishments used to influence people to improve performance. (e.g., merit pay, grades, etc.). When motivation is extrinsic, the satisfaction people get from a learning or work activity comes from outside the activity itself.[7]

fishbone diagram: A tool for analyzing process dispersion. It is also referred to as the "Ishikawa diagram," because Kaoru Ishikawa developed it, and the "fishbone diagram," because the complete diagram resembles a fish skeleton. The diagram illustrates the main causes and sub-causes leading to an effect (symptom). The cause-and-effect diagram is one of the "seven tools of quality."[8]

function (of a nonhuman system): Where purpose is used to describe the reason for a human system's existence, function is used for nonhuman systems. A system's function or purpose is not necessarily spoken, written, or expressed explicitly, except through the operation of the system; it is deduced by watching how the system behaves. While function is generally used for a nonhuman system and purpose for a human one, the distinction is not absolute since so many systems have both human and nonhuman elements.[9]

Fundamental Attribution Error: We make this error when we explain our behavior in terms of the situation or environment while holding other people accountable for their own behavior. It is often easier to blame people than to take a hard look at how the system affects behavior.[10]

improvement: Improvement results from fundamental changes that alter how work or activity is done or the make-up of a tool; produce visible, positive differences in results relative to historical norms; and have a lasting impact.[11]

GLOSSARY

inductive learning: In the context of the Plan-Do-Study-Act cycle, inductive learning involves using results from a test to revise the theory. From Do to Study is an inductive approach where gaps or anomalies to the prediction are studied and the theory is updated accordingly. Action is then taken on the new learning.[12]

interconnections (of a system): The relationships that hold the elements of a system together. Some interconnections in systems are physical flows, many others are flows of information. These information flows are often signals that go to decision points or actions points within a system.[13]

intrinsic motivation: The natural form of positive motivation which comes from within the individual. When motivation is intrinsic, satisfaction comes from the activity itself.[14]

Joy in Learning: See Joy in Work. Joy in Learning is a similar concept, but applied to students in schools.

Joy in Work: W. Edwards Deming said, "People are entitled to joy in work".[15] Only by creating a management system that supports and respects people working in that system can an organization reach its potential. The Institute for Healthcare Improvement, which was founded using Deming's System of Profound Knowledge as the underlying philosophy, outlines the following characteristics for joy in work: The most joyful, productive, engaged staff feel both physically and psychologically safe, appreciate the meaning and purpose of their work, have some choice and control over their time, experience camaraderie with others at work, and perceive their work life to be fair and equitable.[16]

Knowledge about Variation: One of the components of W. Edwards Deming's System of Profound Knowledge. A way of statistical thinking that allows us to distinguish between common cause variation and special cause variation, understand its causes, and predict behavior, all of which is key to management's ability to remove barriers and problems within a system.[17]

Mistake 1: Interpreting the routine variation of noise (i.e., common cause variation) as if it amounted to a signal of a change (i.e., special cause variation) in the underlying process, thereby sounding a false alarm (see also tampering).[18]

Mistake 2: Thinking that a signal of a change (i.e., special cause variation) in the underlying process is merely the noise of routine variation (i.e., common cause variation), thereby missing a signal.[19]

moving Range (mR): The differences between successive values in a set of data needed to measure routine variation and compute the limits in a process behavior chart (specifically the chart for individual values and a moving range or XmR Chart).[20]

Natural Process Limits: The limits for a process behavior chart (Chart for Individual Values or X Chart) are commonly called the Natural Process Limits. The Upper and Lower Natural Process Limits are centered on the central line. The distance from the central line to either of these limits is computed by multiplying the Average Moving Range by a second scaling factor which is the value required to convert the Average Moving Range into the appropriate amount of spread for the running record of individual values. The Natural Process Limits are plotted on the X Chart portion of an XmR Chart and serve as the Voice of the Process. They define what the process will deliver as long as it continues to operate as consistently as possible.[21]

operational definition: An operational definition puts communicable meaning into a concept and includes a method of measurement or test as well as a set of criteria for judgment. Concepts that are important to schools such as attendance, engagement, graduation, and learning have no communicable value until they are expressed in operational terms.

optimization (of a system): Optimization is orchestrating efforts of all components in the system to the achievement of an aim.[22]

Plan-Do-Study-Act (PDSA) cycle: The PDSA cycle is shorthand for testing a change by developing a plan to test the change (Plan), carrying out the test (Do), observing and learning from the consequences (Study), and determining what modifications should be made to the test (Act). Each cycle is a mini-experiment in which observed outcomes in the Study phase are compared to predictions from the Plan phase and differences between the two become a major source of learning and know-how.[23] In improvement work, PDSA cycles offer a supporting mechanism for iterative development and scientific testing of change ideas in complex systems.[24]

GLOSSARY

process behavior chart: Process behavior charts are time-sequenced charts with Upper and Lower Natural Process Limits on which values of some statistical measure for a series of samples or subgroups are plotted. The chart frequently shows a central line to help detect a trend of plotted values toward either limit. The purpose of a process behavior chart is to separate variation into common and special causes.

Profound Knowledge: See System of Profound Knowledge.

Psychology: One of the components of W. Edwards Deming's System of Profound Knowledge. Psychology involves understanding the actions and reactions of people in everyday circumstances.[25]

quality: Minimal variation around some target or optimum value.

quality improvement: Reduced variation around the target or optimum value.

run chart: A simple plot and display of data and trends within observation points over a specified period of time. It is used to monitor progress, check averages for change, and to show variation in process.[26]

special cause variation: Those causes that are not part of the process (or system) all the time, or do not affect everyone, but arise because of specific circumstances.[27]

subject-matter knowledge: Professional knowledge within a field (e.g., education, healthcare) acquired through formal and informal learning and reinforced with experiences that are vital for developing changes that result in improvement.[28]

system: A system is an interdependent group of items, people, or processes working together toward a common purpose.[29]

System of Profound Knowledge: W. Edwards Deming proposed a framework called a "System of Profound Knowledge" which is the interplay of the theories of systems, variation, knowledge, and psychology. The word "profound" denotes the deep insight this knowledge provides into how to make beneficial changes in a variety of settings.[31]

systems thinking: Systems thinking is a way of thinking that focuses on recognizing the interconnections between the parts of a system and synthesizing them into a unified view of the whole.[30]

tampering: Action taken to compensate for variation within the control limits of a stable system; tampering increases rather than decreases variation.[32]

theory: Any system of assumptions that you use to predict what's going to happen in the future.[33]

Theory of Knowledge: One of the components of W. Edwards Deming's System of Profound Knowledge. A theory is a belief or hypothesis about how and why things work. Theories help management predict. Without a theory, nothing can be predicted. The Theory of Knowledge then is the study of how what we think we know and claim to know actually is the way we claim it is.[34]

three-sigma: Process behavior chart methodology uses three-sigma as the measure of dispersion for the individual values displayed in the chart. The Natural Process Limits are set at a distance of three-sigma above and below the central line. The Average Moving Range of the individual values is used in the calculation of the limits; thus sigma is not the same thing as standard variation.[35]

transformation: In Deming's view, transformation is a process guided by an understanding of the System of Profound Knowledge that helps people to pull away from the prevailing system of management and move into the new philosophy.[36]

Voice of the Customer: Plans, goals, budgets, and targets are the Voice of the Customer and help to separate the acceptable outcomes from the unacceptable outcomes after the fact. It defines what you want from a system and will tell you when you are in trouble, but it will not tell you why you are in trouble or how to get out of it. The Voice of the Customer is often little more than wishes and hopes.[37,38]

Voice of the Process: The Voice of the Process is the performance of a process over time, independent of the desired outcomes. The process behavior chart is the Voice of the Process, and it defines what you will get from a system.[39,40]

Endnotes

1. W. Edwards Deming, *The New Economics for Industry, Government, Education,* 3rd ed. (Cambridge, MA: The MIT Press, 2018), 29, 36.

2. "Appreciation for a System," The W. Edwards Deming Institute, accessed August 25, 2022, https://deming.org/appreciation-for-a-system/.

GLOSSARY

3. Donald J. Wheeler, *Making Sense of Data: SPC for the Service Sector* (Knoxville, TN: SPC Press, 2003), 97.

4. Gerald J. Langley, Ronald D. Moen, Kevin M. Nolan, Thomas W. Nolan, Clifford L. Norman, and Lloyd P. Provost, *The Improvement Guide: A Practical Approach to Enhancing Organizational Performance,* 2nd Ed. (San Francisco: Jossey-Bass, 2009), 82.

5. Anthony S. Bryk, Louis M, Gomez, Alicia Grunow, and Paul G. LeMahieu, *Learning to Improve: How America's Schools Can Get Better at Getting Better* (Cambridge, MA: Harvard Education Press, 2015), 207.

6. Donella H. Meadows, *Thinking in Systems: A Primer* (White River Junction, Vermont: Chelsea Green Publishing, 2008), 12-13.

7. David Langford, *Quality Learning Training Manual,* Version 12.0 (Langford International, 2008), Reference Material – 8.

8. "Quality Glossary," ASQ, https://asq.org/quality-resources/quality-glossary.

9. Donella H. Meadows, *Thinking in Systems: A Primer* (White River Junction, Vermont: Chelsea Green Publishing, 2008), 14-15.

10. Gerald J. Langley, Ronald D. Moen, Kevin M. Nolan, Thomas W. Nolan, Clifford L. Norman, and Lloyd P. Provost, *The Improvement Guide: A Practical Approach to Enhancing Organizational Performance,* 2nd Ed. (San Francisco: Jossey-Bass, 2009), 84.

11. Ibid., 16.

12. Ibid., 82.

13. Donella H. Meadows, *Thinking in Systems: A Primer* (White River Junction, Vermont: Chelsea Green Publishing, 2008), 14.

14. David Langford, *Quality Learning Training Manual,* Version 12.0 (Langford International, 2008), Reference Material – 9.

15. "Quotes," The W. Edwards Deming Institute, accessed August 25, 2022, https://deming.org/quotes/people-are-entitled-to-joy-in-work/.

16. Jessica Perlo, Barbara Balik, Stephen Swensen, Andrea Kabcenell, Julie Landsman, and Derek Feeley, "IHI Framework for Improving Joy in Work" (Cambridge, Massachusetts: Institute for Healthcare Improvement, 2017), available at ihi.org.

17. "Knowledge of Variation," The W. Edwards Deming Institute, accessed August 25, 2022, https://deming.org/knowledge-of-variation/.

18. Donald J. Wheeler, *Twenty Things You Need to Know* (Knoxville, TN: SPC Press, 2008), 2.

19. Ibid.

20. Donald J. Wheeler, *Making Sense of Data: SPC for the Service Sector* (Knoxville, TN: SPC Press, 2003), 99.

21. Donald J. Wheeler, *Understanding Variation: The Key to Managing Chaos,* 2nd ed. (Knoxville, TN: SPC Press, 2000), 40-43.

22. W. Edwards Deming, *The Essential Deming: Leadership Principles from the Father of Quality,* ed. Joyce Nilsson Orsini. (New York: McGraw-Hill, 2013), 58.

23. Anthony S. Bryk, Louis M, Gomez, Alicia Grunow, and Paul G. LeMahieu, *Learning to Improve: How America's Schools Can Get Better at Getting Better* (Cambridge, MA: Harvard Education Press, 2015), 200.

24. Michael J. Taylor, Chris McNicholas, Chris Nicolay, Ara Darzi, Derek Bell, and Julie E. Reed, "Systematic review of the application of the plan-do-study-act method to improve quality in healthcare," *BMJ Quality & Safety* 23, (2014): 290-298, https://qualitysafety.bmj.com/content/23/4/290.

25. *The Deming Library*, Volume 27, "A Study in Continual Improvement, Part II," licensed to The W. Edwards Deming Institute, produced by Clare Crawford-Mason, narrated by Lloyd Dobbins (1989; Wooten Productions, Inc., 1994; CC-M Productions), DemingNEXT.

26. David P. Langford, *Tool Time for Education: Choosing and Implementing Quality Improvement Tools* Version 15.0 (Molt, Montana: Langford International, Inc.), 124.

27. Gerald J. Langley, Ronald D. Moen, Kevin M. Nolan, Thomas W. Nolan, Clifford L. Norman, and Lloyd P. Provost, *The Improvement Guide: A Practical Approach to Enhancing Organizational Performance*, 2nd Ed. (San Francisco: Jossey-Bass, 2009), 90.

28. Ibid., 75.

29. Ibid., 77.

30. Donella H. Meadows, *Thinking in Systems: A Primer* (White River Junction, Vermont: Chelsea Green Publishing, 2008).

31. Ronald D. Moen, Thomas W. Nolan, and Lloyd P. Provost, *Quality Improvement through Planned Experimentation* 3rd ed. (New York: McGraw-Hill, 2012), 2.

32. "Quality Glossary," ASQ, https://asq.org/quality-resources/quality-glossary.

33. *The Deming Library*, Volume 19, "Profound Knowledge for Leadership," licensed to The W. Edwards Deming Institute, produced by Clare Crawford-Mason, narrated by Lloyd Dobbins (Wooten Productions, Inc., 1991; CC-M Productions), DemingNEXT.

34. *The Deming Library*, Volume 27, "A Study in Continual Improvement, Part II," licensed to The W. Edwards Deming Institute, produced by Clare Crawford-Mason, narrated by Lloyd Dobbins (1989; Wooten Productions, Inc., 1994; CC-M Productions), DemingNEXT.

35. Donald J. Wheeler, *Making Sense of Data: SPC for the Service Sector* (Knoxville, TN: SPC Press, 2003), 165, 383, 389.

36. Edward Martin Baker, *The Symphony of Profound Knowledge: W. Edwards Deming's Score for Leading, Performing, and Living in Concert* (Bloomington, IN: iUniverse, 2017), 103.

37. Donald J. Wheeler, *Making Sense of Data: SPC for the Service Sector* (Knoxville, TN: SPC Press, 2003), 115-116.

38. Donald J. Wheeler, *Understanding Variation: The Key to Managing Chaos,* 2nd ed. (Knoxville, TN: SPC Press, 2000), 79.

39. Donald J. Wheeler, *Making Sense of Data: SPC for the Service Sector* (Knoxville, TN: SPC Press, 2003), 116.

GLOSSARY

40. Donald J. Wheeler, *Understanding Variation: The Key to Managing Chaos,* 2nd ed. (Knoxville, TN: SPC Press, 2000), 79.

APPENDIX A

Improvement Process

#	Step	Primary Tool	Secondary Tool
	What are we trying to accomplish?		
1	**See the System**		
1a	What is the largest system to improve?	System Map	
1b	What is the aim of this system?	System Map	
1c	What are the opportunities for improvement within the target system?	Affinity Diagram	
1d	How will the opportunities for improvement be prioritized?	Interrelationship Digraph	Pareto Chart
1e	How will the project be chartered?	Project Charter	
2	**Define the Problem**		
2a	How is the project being funneled from a general to more specific problem?	PS Readiness Check	
2b	What is the precise problem statement?	Problem Statement	
2c	What are the key operational definitions?	Operational Definitions	
2d	Who will benefit most from the improvement effort and what are their needs?	Perception Analysis	
2e	What is the vision for excellence?	Imagineering	
	How will we know a change is an improvement?		
3	**Understand the Current System**		
3a	What is the current approach or process?	Process Map	
3b	What data or information is needed to measure baseline performance?	Run Chart	Pareto Chart
3c	What is the current system capability, variability, and stability?	Process Behavior Chart	
4	**Study the Causes**		
4a	What are possible causes of variation of current performance?	Fishbone Diagram	
4b	What is the dominant cause?	Interrelationship Digraph	Pareto Chart
5	**Determine Measures of Success**		
5a	What outcome measure linked to your system aim will indicate how the system is performing?	Outcome Measure (1-2)	Family of Measures
5b	What process measures will provide an early indication of improvement?	Process Measure (3-5)	Family of Measures
5c	What balancing measure will alert you to unintended consequences in other parts of the system?	Balancing Measure (1-2)	Family of Measures
	What change can we make that will result in improvement?		
6	**Design a Theory for Improvement**		
6a	What are the possible improvements or redesigns?	Driver Diagram	
6b	Which improvement or redesign has potential for the greatest result?	Logic Testing	Sentence Prompt Check
6c	What could cause this theory for improvement to fail?	Pre-Mortem	
7	**Run PDSA Cycles**		
7a	Plan: What is your plan for testing a change idea and for collecting data?	PDSA Template	
7b	Do: What happened when you ran the test on a small scale?	PDSA Template	
7c	Study: How did the results compare to your predictions from the plan phase?	PDSA Template	
7d	Act: Based on what you learned from the test, what will you do next?	PDSA Template	
8	**Study the Results**		
8a	To what degree has the improvement project been successful?	Family of Measures	
8b	Will any of the improvements be incorporated into the system as standard work?	Standard Work	
9	**Reflect and Establish Future Plans**		
9a	What was learned?	After-Action Report	Retrospective
9b	What will happen next?	After-Action Report	Retrospective
9c	Have the learning and plans for next steps been carefully documented and shared with stakeholders?	After-Action Report	Retrospective
9d	How will the project be stored for future use and knowledge-sharing?	Knowledge Management	
10	**Hold the Gains**		
10a	How will the team assess if the improvement was maintained over time?	Family of Measures	

APPENDIX B

Creating a Process Behavior Chart

WE'VE PRACTICED THE WAY of thinking that goes along with interpreting process behavior charts. Appendix B will focus on the procedure and formulas used to create these charts. Most typically, people use various software programs to generate their process behavior charts and perform the underlying calculations. If you choose to use one of these programs, it is important to understand the methodology embedded in the software and to ensure that it allows you to use the correct form of charting and the correct method for calculating the limits. It is also possible to create process behavior charts in a spreadsheet program such as Microsoft Excel or Google Sheets. In this tutorial, I utilize Google Sheets because it is becoming such a popular tool in schools, but the same set of procedures would also work in Excel.

Throughout the book, I utilized one type of chart called the Individual with Moving Range Chart (XmR Chart), which includes two charts. In all of the examples, I only displayed one of the two charts, that is the X chart. Typically, the XmR chart also includes a second chart below the X chart called the Moving Range (mR) chart that plots the variance or moving ranges of the data. The tutorial will include the procedures for creating the full XmR chart.

Step 1: Collect the Baseline Data

We're going to start by getting the initial baseline data for our chart on which the Natural Process Limits will be based. Ideally, we'd have at least 17 historical data points available for calculating the initial baseline. If necessary, you can create a process behavior chart with just five or six data points if that is all the data you have at the start, but the limits won't be as valid statistically until you have 17 or more points. The main idea here though is that even a small number of data points plotted in time series is better than the color-coded approach or the limited two-point comparisons that are so common.

One of the keys in the calculation of the limits in the baseline period is that the historical data is all part of the same system. The idea is to improve the process being displayed in the process behavior chart, so we shouldn't arbitrarily choose timeframes for our charts for the purpose of telling a certain preferred story. For the tutorial, I'm using the data from the attendance case study from Chapter 7. The baseline period is the 22 points from the two school years from August 2017 through June 2019.

Step 2: Calculate the Central Line for the X Chart

After establishing the baseline period, the next step in the process is to calculate the central line for my X Chart. It provides a visual reference to use in looking for trends in the plotted values. The central line for the X chart is generally the mean (arithmetic average) although there are some situations when it makes sense to use the median for this purpose.[1] In this example we'll use the average. Calculating the average of the attendance baseline data is simple. In Figure B.1, the spreadsheet formula in Cell C2 for the data displayed is =AVERAGE(B2:B23) for our 22 baseline points. We'll input the formula =C2 in Cell C3, and then copy that formula down through Cell C23 (the formula in C23 then is =C22). This average will serve as the center line in our baseline period. Additionally, we'll shade in the cells that represent the baseline period in our spreadsheet, so it is easy to see which data makes up the baseline. At this point, we have three columns within our spreadsheet which now looks like Figure B.1.

Step 3: Create a Run Chart

All process behavior charts start as run charts with the lines for the data and the average. I've gotten in the habit of using a template that uses blue for the data, green for the central line, and red for the limits (black, white, and shades of gray are used in the book because of the expense of color printing). I've stuck to these colors for consistency's sake and to make analysis easier. If you're using a program such as Excel or Google Sheets, you'll choose line chart and use this as the starting point of building your run chart in just a few steps. The run chart for our baseline data is in Figure B.2.

APPENDIX B

Figure B.1.
Baseline Period and Average Spreadsheet

	A	B	C
1	**Date**	**Data**	**Average**
2	Aug 2017	93.55	91.33
3	Sep 2017	93.09	91.33
4	Oct 2017	92.67	91.33
5	Nov 2017	92.38	91.33
6	Dec 2017	91.47	91.33
7	Jan 2018	91.31	91.33
8	Feb 2018	89.96	91.33
9	Mar 2018	90.24	91.33
10	Apr 2018	91.05	91.33
11	May 2018	89.82	91.33
12	Jun 2018	86.37	91.33
13	Aug 2018	91.05	91.33
14	Sep 2018	94.02	91.33
15	Oct 2018	93.99	91.33
16	Nov 2018	93.99	91.33
17	Dec 2018	92.24	91.33
18	Jan 2019	92.42	91.33
19	Feb 2019	94.76	91.33
20	Mar 2019	92.42	91.33
21	Apr 2019	92.13	91.33
22	May 2019	89.57	91.33
23	Jun 2019	80.70	91.33

Figure B.2.
Run Chart: CCA Attendance Rate Baseline Period (Aug. 2017-June 2019)

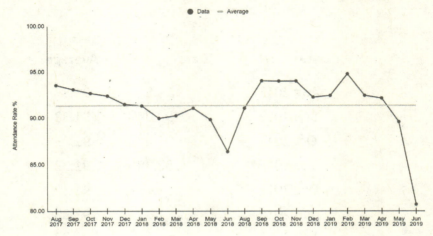

Building a run chart allows us to take an initial look at the data prior to having enough points with which to construct the full process behavior chart. With the full set of baseline data in run chart format, we can move to calculate the moving ranges, the average moving range, and the Natural Process Limits. This in turn will allow us to look for signals within our data.

Step 4: Calculate the Moving Ranges and the Average Moving Range

The process behavior chart method determines variation using a concept called Moving Ranges. A *Moving Range (mR)* is the absolute difference between each of two successive data points in the X chart. It allows us to compute limits appropriate for this data by providing a measure of routine variation. When we construct our spreadsheet, in Figure B.3, the first row of data (Row 2 in Figure B.3) does not have a Moving Range because there is no previous data with which to compare it. The second data point (Row 3 in Figure B.3) is the absolute value of the second data point minus the first data point. In our spreadsheet, the formula we'd enter in cell D3 is =ABS(B3-B2). You can then drag that formula down the column for the rest of the data points so that cell D4 has the formula =ABS(B4-B3) and so forth and so on down the column. It is worth noting here that after calculating all the Moving Ranges, you should do a quick check for any negative values in the column.

APPENDIX B

There shouldn't be any negative values since we are using the formula for absolute values.

In the case of the attendance example, we're using two school years' worth of data, or 22 months as our baseline period. This means we'll calculate the Average Moving Range for the first 21 moving ranges (remember the first data point doesn't have a moving range). We enter the formula =AVERAGE(D3:D23) in cell E2. The Average Moving Range for our baseline data is 1.68, and our spreadsheet now looks like this.

Figure B.3.

Baseline Period with Moving Range and Average Moving Range (mR Bar)

	A	B	C	D	E
	Date	Data	Average	Moving Range (MR)	mR Bar
1					
2	Aug 2017	93.55	91.33		1.68
3	Sep 2017	93.09	91.33	0.46	1.68
4	Oct 2017	92.67	91.33	0.42	1.68
5	Nov 2017	92.38	91.33	0.29	1.68
6	Dec 2017	91.47	91.33	0.91	1.68
7	Jan 2018	91.31	91.33	0.16	1.68
8	Feb 2018	89.96	91.33	1.35	1.68
9	Mar 2018	90.24	91.33	0.28	1.68
10	Apr 2018	91.05	91.33	0.81	1.68
11	May 2018	89.82	91.33	1.23	1.68
12	Jun 2018	86.37	91.33	3.45	1.68
13	Aug 2018	91.05	91.33	4.68	1.68
14	Sep 2018	94.02	91.33	2.97	1.68
15	Oct 2018	93.99	91.33	0.03	1.68
16	Nov 2018	93.99	91.33	0.00	1.68
17	Dec 2018	92.24	91.33	1.75	1.68
18	Jan 2019	92.42	91.33	0.18	1.68
19	Feb 2019	94.76	91.33	2.34	1.68
20	Mar 2019	92.42	91.33	2.34	1.68
21	Apr 2019	92.13	91.33	0.29	1.68
22	May 2019	89.57	91.33	2.56	1.68
23	Jun 2019	80.70	91.33	8.87	1.68

Step 5: Calculate the Natural Process Limits

The limits for the X Chart are called Natural Process Limits. They are centered on the central line; the distance from the central line to either of these limits is computed by multiplying the Average Moving Range by a second scaling factor. This scaling factor is the value required to convert the Average Moving Range into the appropriate amount of spread for the running record of individual values. The Upper Natural Process Limit is found by multiplying the Average Moving Range by 2.66, and then adding the product to the average represented by the central line. Similarly, the Lower Natural Process Limit follows the same process except the product of the Average Moving Range and the 2.66 scaling factor[2] is subtracted from the average represented by the central line. Use the data from the spreadsheet in Figure B.3, our spreadsheet formulas for the limits would be as follows:

Upper Natural Process Limit = C2 + (2.66 * E2)
Lower Natural Process Limit = C2 − (2.66 * E2)

The most important thing to remember is that the Natural Process Limits are calculated from our baseline values, and so, represent the Voice of the Process. They are what is rather than what we hope for them to be. Any goal or target we have for attendance rates would represent the Voice of the Customer and represent something altogether different. Being able to explain the difference between the Voice of the Process and the Voice of the Customer is of prime importance. It will probably be difficult to explain this difference as you introduce the process behavior chart methodology to your organization. The key thing to remember is that we do not get to choose the limits. Rather they represent the capability of our system or process based empirically on the data.

Returning to our attendance example, the Lower Natural Process Limit is 86.85% and the Upper Natural Process Limit is 95.81%.

Upper Natural Process Limit = 91.33 + (2.66 * 1.68) = 95.81
Lower Natural Process Limit = 91.33 − (2.66 * 1.68) = 86.85

This means that if we have a predictable attendance system then most of our future data points will likely fall between 86.85% and 95.81%. Our spreadsheet now looks like the top table in the figure below, and the bottom table includes the formulas that sit behind the data within the spreadsheet.

APPENDIX B

Figure B.4.
X Chart Spreadsheet & X Chart Spreadsheet Formulas

	A	B	C	D	E	F	G
1	Date	Data	Average	Moving Range (MR)	mR Bar	LNPL	UNPL
2	Aug 2017	93.55	91.33		1.68	86.85	95.81
3	Sep 2017	93.09	91.33	0.46	1.68	86.85	95.81
4	Oct 2017	92.67	91.33	0.42	1.68	86.85	95.81
5	Nov 2017	92.38	91.33	0.29	1.68	86.85	95.81
6	Dec 2017	91.47	91.33	0.91	1.68	86.85	95.81
7	Jan 2018	91.31	91.33	0.16	1.68	86.85	95.81
8	Feb 2018	89.96	91.33	1.35	1.68	86.85	95.81

	A	B	C	D	E	F	G
1	Date	Data	Average	Moving Range (MR)	mR Bar	LNPL	UNPL
2	Aug 2017	93.55	=AVERAGE(B2:B23)		=average(D3:D23)	=C3-(2.66*E3)	=C3+(2.66*E3)
3	Sep 2017	93.09	=C2	=ABS(B3-B2)	=E2	=F2	=G2
4	Oct 2017	92.67	=C3	=ABS(B4-B3)	=E3	=F3	=G3
5	Nov 2017	92.38	=C4	=ABS(B5-B4)	=E4	=F4	=G4
6	Dec 2017	91.47	=C5	=ABS(B6-B5)	=E5	=F5	=G5
7	Jan 2018	91.31	=C6	=ABS(B7-B6)	=E6	=F6	=G6
8	Feb 2018	89.96	=C7	=ABS(B8-B7)	=E7	=F7	=G7

Step 6: Create the X Chart

Now that the Upper and Lower Natural Limits have been calculated, we can transition the run chart from Figure B.2 into the X Chart in Figure B.5.

Figure B.5.
Baseline Period X Chart: CCA Attendance Rates (Aug. 2017-June 2019)

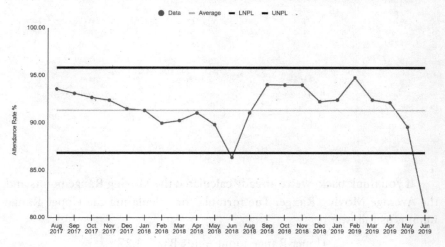

Step 7: Create the Moving Range Chart

The bottom chart in the XmR Chart combination is called the Moving Range Chart (mR Chart). The purpose of the Moving Range Chart is to help us to see if the point-to-point variation is consistent over time. There are times when the X Chart is free from signals, but a data point in the Moving Range Chart indicates special cause variation, even though the X Chart does not. There is only one indication of special cause in a Moving Range Chart, that is a single data point that is above what is called the Upper Range Limit. The *Upper Range Limit* is the equivalent of the Natural Process Limits from the X Chart. However, because the Moving Range values are never negative, the Moving Range Chart only has an Upper Range Limit and does not have a lower limit. Plotting the Moving Ranges gives us an additional opportunity to notice a signal that indicates a change of significance.

To create the Moving Range Chart, we need to add a column to our spreadsheet in Column H where we can calculate the Upper Range Limit, which we do in Figure B.6.

Figure B.6.
XmR Chart Spreadsheet and XmR Chart Spreadsheet Formulas

A	B	C	D	E	F	G	H
Date	Data	Average	Moving Range (MR)	mR Bar	LNPL	UNPL	URL
Aug 2017	93.55	91.33		1.68	86.85	95.81	5.51
Sep 2017	93.09	91.33	0.46	1.68	86.85	95.81	5.51
Oct 2017	92.67	91.33	0.42	1.68	86.85	95.81	5.51
Nov 2017	92.38	91.33	0.29	1.68	86.85	95.81	5.51
Dec 2017	91.47	91.33	0.91	1.68	86.85	95.81	5.51
Jan 2018	91.31	91.33	0.16	1.68	86.85	95.81	5.51
Feb 2018	89.96	91.33	1.35	1.68	86.85	95.81	5.51

A	B	C	D	E	F	G	H
Date	Data	Average	Moving Range (MR)	mR Bar	LNPL	UNPL	URL
Aug 2017	93.55	=AVERAGE(B2:B23)		=Average(D3:D23)	=C3-(2.66*E3)	=C3+(2.66*E3)	=E3*3.27
Sep 2017	93.09	=C2	=ABS(B3-B2)	=E2	=F2	=G2	=H2
Oct 2017	92.67	=C3	=ABS(B4-B3)	=E3	=F3	=G3	=H3
Nov 2017	92.38	=C4	=ABS(B5-B4)	=E4	=F4	=G4	=H4
Dec 2017	91.47	=C5	=ABS(B6-B5)	=E5	=F5	=G5	=H5
Jan 2018	91.31	=C6	=ABS(B7-B6)	=E6	=F6	=G6	=H6
Feb 2018	89.96	=C7	=ABS(B8-B7)	=E7	=F7	=G7	=H7

If you think back, we've already calculated the Moving Range points and the Average Moving Range. The formula for calculating the Upper Range Limit is as follows:

$$Upper\ Range\ Limit = mR\ Bar * 3.27$$

APPENDIX B

Like the 2.66 scaling factor used to calculate the limits in the X Chart, the 3.27 scaling factor[3] converts the Average Moving Range into an estimate of the distance between the central line and the upper limit on the mR Chart.[4] Figure B.6 displays the calculations in our updated spreadsheet on top and then the underlying formulas for the complete spreadsheet right underneath it. Returning to our attendance example, the Upper Range Limit is 5.51%.

Upper Range Limit = 1.68 * 3.27 = 5.51

Once we've calculated the Upper Range Limit, we're now ready to display the X Chart and mR Chart together as I've done in Figure B.7.

Figure B.7.
Baseline Period XmR Chart CCA Attendance Rates (Aug. 2017-June 2019)

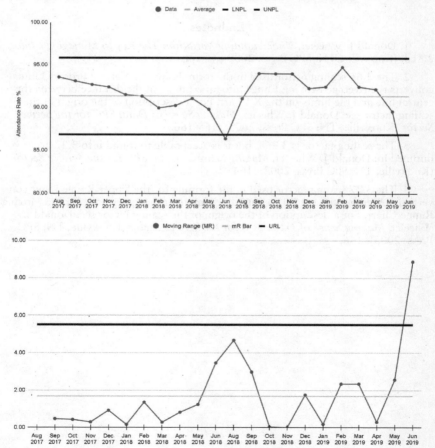

With the charts constructed, we can now look for signals. The signals for the X Chart were explained in Chapter 7. In the Moving Range Chart, there is only one signal to look for, that is a Rule 1 signal. A Rule 1 signal in a Moving Range Chart is a single point above the Upper Range Limit. The attendance Moving Range Chart in Figure B.7 says that any point-to-point variation above 5.51 is a signal that something changed in our system. There is one point in June 2019 where we see a Rule 1 signal in the moving ranges. In this case, the June data point is also a signal in the X Chart, but in other cases the Moving Range Chart will pick up signals that the X Chart doesn't. Therefore, it is best to use the two charts together when working to interpret your data. Doing so will give you the full power of the process behavior chart methodology.

Endnotes

1. Donald J. Wheeler, *Understanding Variation: The Key to Managing Chaos,* 2nd ed. (Knoxville, TN: SPC Press, 2000), Chapter 6.

2. The 2.66 scaling factor used in the formula for the Natural Process Limits converts the Average Moving Range into an estimate of the distance between the central line and the limits on the X Chart. For a description of the origin of the scaling factor see: Donald J. Wheeler, *Making Sense of Data: SPC for the Service Sector* (Knoxville, TN: SPC Press, 2003), 165-166.

3. The scaling factor is 3.268, but it is acceptable to round it to 3.27 as outlined in: Donald J. Wheeler, *Making Sense of Data: SPC for the Service Sector* (Knoxville, TN: SPC Press, 2003), 164.

4. The 3.27 scaling factor used in the formula for the Upper Range Limit converts the Average Moving Range into an estimate of the upper limit for the Moving Range Chart. For a description of the origin of the scaling factor see: Donald J. Wheeler, *Making Sense of Data: SPC for the Service Sector* (Knoxville, TN: SPC Press, 2003), 166.

ACKNOWLEDGMENTS

First and foremost, I am grateful to my wife Jen and my kids Jackson, Allie, and William for their support as I spent many early mornings consumed by the writing process. Thank you for believing in me. To my parents John and Beth, thank you for a lifetime of love and support that gave me the confidence to take on a book project.

Over the years, I've frequently remarked that I'm still waiting to come up with an original thought of my own. *Win-Win* is no different in that the ideas herein have been built upon the writing and teaching of many that have been applying W. Edwards Deming's System of Profound Knowledge for far longer than me. Of course, I have to start by acknowledging the impact that W. Edwards Deming himself has had on my life and work, which I hope is readily apparent in this book. Similarly, I have been fortunate to speak with many people throughout my own learning journey, many of whom had direct contact with Dr. Deming. In alphabetical order those people include Kelly Allan, Dr. Bill Bellows, Dr. Donald Berwick, Andrei Cojoaca, Mark Graban, David Langford, James Leonard, Skip Steward, Dr. Doug Stilwell, Andrew Stotz, Travis Timmons, Dr. Frony Ward, Dr. Donald Wheeler, and Fran Wheeler. Among this group, I'd like to especially thank Kelly Allan and David Langford for their willingness to patiently share their Deming wisdom with me through many conversations and emails.

Loyal friends and thought partners who have helped encourage and shape this book in numerous ways over the years include: Kathryn Anstaett, Joe Baszynski, Sue Brennan, Matthew Brunell, Andrew Boy, Jennifer Felbaum, Chris Gibbons, Jeffrey Greenley, Justin Jones (illustrations), Matthew King, Jim Mahoney, Trevor Manendo, Jessica McAdoo, Trisha Meier, Ben Pacht, Henry Seton, Laura Steinmaus, Diana Wakim, Kimberly Williams, and many more.

I'm also grateful to the many students, teachers, and school leaders at the United Schools Network who trusted me enough to participate in the network's Continual Improvement Fellowship, improvement projects, and Deming book studies. It is through these relationships and activities that many of the applications of the System of Profound Knowledge in schools portrayed in this book occurred.

ABOUT THE AUTHOR

John A. Dues is an accomplished education systems leader and improvement science scholar-practitioner with more than two decades of experience in the sector. He is the Chief Learning Officer of the United Schools Network (USN), where he directs the network's Continual Improvement Fellowship and serves as an improvement advisor. In this role, he provides education, coaching, and mentoring on continual improvement methods, data collection and analysis methods, and project management and change management techniques with the purpose of enabling teams across the organization to become experts at guiding their own improvement. He draws heavily on the work of W. Edwards Deming and his System of Profound Knowledge (SoPK) to equip him with the theory and statistical tools by which to perform this role.

Previously, he served as a school director and dean of academics at USN as well as in school leadership and teaching positions in Atlanta, Denver, and Cleveland. Under John's leadership, USN schools have regularly been among the state and nation's highest performing urban schools. In 2013, John was recognized as the Ohio School Leader of the Year by the Ohio Alliance for Public Charter Schools.

Over the course of his career, John has served on the start-up teams of seven school and nonprofit organizations. He has been engaged as a consultant to a variety of education organizations including public charter, private, and traditional public schools and is a regular presenter at conferences and workshops. His internal and external improvement work is focused on developing organizational capability and long-term constancy of purpose through the application of Deming's methods, principles, and theories.

John graduated with Honors from Miami (OH) University, holds a Master of Education degree from the University of Cincinnati, and is an alumnus of Teach For America. He is currently continuing his education through the Improvement Advisor program at the Institute for Healthcare Improvement in Boston, Massachusetts.

INDEX

NOTE: numbers appearing in *italics* indicate index entry in captions

#plotthedots, 141
10 Key Lessons for Data Analysis, 114, 139–40, 140–43, 144–53
14 Principles for Educational Systems Transformation, 42–43, 45–69, 98–99, 108, 198–99
14 Points for Management, 42

A

abandon, 180
accountability
    myth of, 35–36
    systems, 131
Ackoff, R., 8, *59*, 79, 80, 180
adapt, 180
aim, 75–79, 215
aim statement, 75–76, 78
American Institutes for Research (AIR), 6
analytic study, 14
Anstaett, K., 73
Appreciation for a System, 4–8, 73, 106, 110, 180, 215
    definition, *5*
arbitrary numerical targets, 62–64
Atlanta Public Schools, 36
average moving range, 142
average values, 58

B

Baker, E.M., 106, 192
barriers
    as impediment to innovation, 60
    long-term constancy of purpose, 55
    removal of, 48, 59
baseline period X-chart, *151*
Bell Labs, 9, 14
Berwick, D., 141
best practices, myth of, 29–30
Bill & Melinda Gates Foundation, 172
burlesque, 64, 121

C

Carnegie Foundation for the Advancement of Teaching, 171
charts, plotting data on, 9–10
classroom assessments, 50
color-coded scales, 137–38
Columbus Collegiate Academy-West (CCAW), 73
common cause variation, 8, 10, 12, 52, 114, 121, 122, 126, 138, 142, 150, 160, 215
competition, 35
constancy of purpose, 46, 102
continual improvement, 14, 46, 47–48, 49, 52, 68–69, 159–60, 204
control charts, 9
controlled variation, 10, 115
cooperation, 35
core system, 82
Crawford-Mason, C., xvi
cut score, 130
Cutler, J., 207

D

data
    arithmetic means and, 148
    in context, 118–21, 140
    insight and, 143
    predicting the future, 142
    previous levels of variation and, 142
    shortage of, 141
    table of values and, 119
    temporal spread and, 119, 123–25
    time order and, 119, 141
    viewing, 15
    writing fiction and, 127–31
data boards, 138–39
deductive learning, 13, 164, 215
Deming Dimension, The, 58, 198
Deming Prize, xvi
Deming, W. Edwards, xv
    abolishment of grading in schools, 195–97, 199–200
    as business consultant, 97

definition of quality, 159
early life of, 192
education of employees, 67
fear and, 58
forces of destruction and, 29, 183
grading and, 50
History's Hidden Turning Point and, 2–3
individual transformation and, 185–86
in Japan, xv, 42
limited testing of initial theories, 168
measurement and, 29
merit pay and, 33
New York University and, 42
stable systems and, 91
suboptimization of systems, 192–93
training, education and, 47
understanding of variation, 9
Win-Win philosophy, 59, 107
working with CEOs or presidents, 97–98
Also see System of Profound Knowledge
Department of Energy, 24
distorting the data, 35–36, 134, 159
distorting the system, 35–36, 134, 159

E
education, 47, 48, 53
    as a system, 85–88
    vigorous program of, 67–68
education reform battles, 25
effects heterogeneity, 164, 215
elements, 79, 216
empathy interviews, 174
enumerative study, 14
Escalante, J., 30
Every Child Succeeds Act, 43, 44
extrinsic incentives, 17
extrinsic motivation, 18–19, 35, 184, 192, 193, 195, 216
    myth of, 37

F
facts of life, 64

feedback, 80, 87
feedback delays, 88
feedback loops, 87–88
fishbone diagram, 210, 216
Five Whys, 174–76
flow diagram, 68–69
forces of destruction, 29, 183
foundational skills, 91
Frank, R., xvi
function, 79, 216
Fundamental Attribution Error, 18–19, 216

G
Garfield High School, 30–31
Glasser, W., 95
Goals 2000, 24, 41, 44
grading, 49, 65, 66
    abolishment of, 50, 194, 195–97, 199–200

H
Hardin, G., 106–7
Hawthorne Works, 115, 191, 192
hierarchical organizational structures, 190
hierarchy of embedded systems, 82
hero educator, myth of, 30–31
hero leaders, 55
History's Hidden Turning Point, 2–3
hypothesis, 12

I
If Japan Can, Why Can't We?, xvi
improvement
    case study for, 207–13
    definition of, xvi–xvii, 121, 216
    percentage of responsibility for, 7
    three dimensions of, 145
    three parts of definition of, 127
    timely data and, 143
incentive systems, 192
individual transformation, 185–88
individuals chart, 139
Individuals with Moving Range Chart, 148
inductive learning, 13, 164, 217
innovation, 48

INDEX

243

instant pudding, 49, 98
Institute for Healthcare Improvement
    (IHI), 165
interconnections, 79, 217
interventions, 143
intrinsic motivation, 18, 35, 37, 193,
    217
IQ tests, 65

J
Japan
        industrial output post-WW2,
        xv–xvi
        as a system, 6
job-related training, 53–55
Joiner, B., 34
Joy in Learning, 45, 46, 56, 77, 183,
    217
        definition for case study, 208
        removing barriers to, 64–67
Joy in Teaching, 45
Joy in Work, 35, 46, 56, 77, 183,
    189–93, 217
        removing barriers to, 64–67

K
knowledge, 162
        purpose of, 161
        temporal spread and, 163
Knowledge about Variation, 8–12, 31,
    44, 57, 106, 114, 116, 118, 135,
    137–39
        definition of, 8, 217
Kohn, A., 50

L
Langford, D., 42–43, 189
leader, attributes of, 56–57
Leonard, J., 42–43, 96, 199
Lewis, C.I., 161
Lower Natural Process Limit (LNPL),
    11, 126, 140, 150, 155, 156,
    209
lowest bidder, 51–52, 60
lowest qualified bidder, 51–52, 60

M
Making Sense of Data, 140
Management by Objective (MBO), 35,
    43, 55, 58
management mythology, 26, 43, 44, 55
        education reform and, 28
        origins of, 28–29
management philosophy, 188–89
Meadows, D., 85, 87
Measures of Success, 140
median moving range, 142
merit pay, myth of, 32–35, 65
merit rating, 65
Mind and the World Order, 161
mission statement, 77–78
Mistake 1, 11–12, 114, 115, 121, 122,
    126, 217
Mistake 2, 11–12, 114, 115, 121, 122,
    126–27, 218
motivation, 18, 193–200
Moving Range Chart, 139, 218
mR charts, 139

N
Nation at Risk, A, 23, 41
National Commission on Excellence in
    Education, 23
National Health Service (England), 141
Natural Process Limits, 12, 122, 126,
    127, 129, 131, 132, 133, 139,
    142, 147, 148, 150, 153, 162,
    218
Neave, H., 42, 58, 198, 203
Nelson, L., 44
*New Economics for Industry, Govern-
    ment, Education, The*, 58, 110,
    185, 193
New York University, 42
No Child Left Behind (NCLB), 24, 36,
    41, 43, 44, 82
noise, 10, 11, 125–27, 135, 144, 147,
    149, 160
normal distributions, 124
numerical naiveté, 114, 116–18, 134

O
Ohio Achievement Assessment, 130
Ohio Achievement Test (PAT), 130
Ohio State Test, 130, 132

on-track indicator systems, 173
operational definitions, 15–16, 53, 218
Out of the Crisis, 33, 42, 58, 68
outlier, 30
optimization, 218
organizational chart, 190
organizations
    actual behavior of, 81
    stated purpose of, 81
    systems view of, 76
outcomes, 113

P

Partnership for Assessment of Readiness
    for College and Careers, 130
performance appraisals, 58, 65
    five factors of, 32
    myth of, 31–32, 65
Performance Index (PI), 66
piece-rate payment, 192
Plan-Do-Study-Act cycles, 12–13, 53,
    69, 160, 164–65
    Change Idea Scorecard, 19–20
    deductive and inductive learning,
    13
    definition of, 161, 218
    template for, 165–72
plot twist, 154
poverty, 81
prediction, 12, 162, 164, 168
probably wrong, definitely incomplete,
    172
problem statement, 208
process behavior charts, 9, 11, 14, 61,
    101, 122–23, 125, 130, 139,
    141, 142, 208
    case study using, 147–53
    definition of, 219
    different types of, 147–48
    how to create, 227–36
    interventions and, 143
    methodology of, 139–40
    shifting the limits of, 153–57
process improvement teams, 54
professional development, 5–6
Profound Knowledge, xvii–xviii, 26,
    100, 101, 141, 185
    definition of, xvii, 219
    four components of, xviii
    Also see System of Profound
    Knowledge

psychology, 16–20, 106, 183–84,
    188–89
    definition of, 17, 219
    motivation and, 193–200
    organizational improvement and,
    185–88
purpose/aim, 79
Pygmalion Effect, 65

Q

quality, defining, 121, 219
quality improvement, defining, 121, 219
quotas, 63

R

Race to the Top, 24, 32, 43, 186, 205
randomized controlled trial (RCT),
    13–14
rating and ranking, 29, 58, 66, 93, 185,
    186–87, 194
    myth of, 31–32, 32–35
research, 48
Rothstein, J., 33–34
run chart, 101, 129–31, 132, 139, 140,
    142, *146*, *147*, *149*, 208, *209*,
    219

S

Sandia National Laboratories, 24, 44
Sandia Report, 24
Scherkenbach, W., 196
Scholtes, P., 32, 86, 92
school district report cards, 35
school systems
    bidding and, 51–52, 60
    importance of business and
    financial managers in, 60
    purpose of, 59
self-improvement, 67–68
Shewhart charts, 9
Shewhart, W.A., 9, 10, 14, 115, 116,
    118
signals, 126, 133, 138, 144, 147, 149,
    150, 160, 212
    baseline data and, 150–52
    Rule 1, 126, 133, 143, 149, 150,
    151, 154, 155, 211, 212, 236
    Rule 2, 126, 143, 149, 211, 212
    Rule 3, 133, 143, 211

INDEX

rules for finding, 127, 143
Simpson's Paradox, 24
slogans, 61
Some Attributes of a Leader, 56–57
special cause variation, 8, 10, 12, 52,
114, 121, 122, 126, 138, 142,
160, 219
stable but incapable processes, 52
stable process, 10
stable systems, 61, 91, 142
Stand and Deliver, 30
standardized testing, 49
subject-matter knowledge, xvii, 219
subsystem, 82
supra system, 82
*Symphony of Profound Knowledge,
The*, 106
System of Profound Knowledge, xv, xvi,
27, 43–44, 48, 56, 68, 69, 74, 92,
98, 100, 106, 110, 116, 118, 141,
157, 159, 161, 183, 184, 188,
189, 193, 198, 200, 203, 205
Appreciation for a System and,
4–8
definition of, 3–4, 219
description of, 1–3
four components of, 3
Knowledge about Variation, 8–12
Psychology and, 16–20
Theory of Knowledge and,
12–16
systems
basics of, 73–74
definition of, 75, 79, 219
four components of, 76–77
need to have aim, 75–79
optimization of, 218
reason for failure, 5
structure of, 83–85
thinking in, 79–82, 83
underappreciation for, 6
working in, 94
working on, 94
Also see Theory of Variation
systems leadership
basic orientation of, 17–18
definition of, 219
systems thinking, 66, 91–92, 160, 196
definition of, 92
individuals, interactions and,
93–95

obstacles to, 101–5
roles of school boards and administration, 97–99
roles of students and teachers,
95–97
secret weapons in, 100–1
whole systems thinking, 105–10

T

tampering, 43, 122, 126, 138, 220
Taylor, F., 191, 192
Taylorism, 191
teacher base salary levels, 33
teacher evaluation systems, 31
temporal spread, 15, 119, 123–25, 163
theory, definition of, 12, 220
Theory of Knowledge, 12–16, 106,
159–60,
core ideas of, 161–63
definition of, 12, 161, 220
Theory of Variation, 10, 14, 113–14
definition of, 115
goal setting as desperation,
131–33
numerical naiveté and, 114,
116–18
understanding, 121–25
understanding system capacity,
132–33
understanding system stability,
133
understanding system variation,
133
Thinking in Systems: A Primer, 87
three-sigma, 14, 122, 220
time order, 119
TNTP, 6
tracking, 194
training, 47, 53
formula for, 54
transformation, 23–26
definition of, 26, 220
discontinuous, 186
individual, 184–86
new philosophy for, 37–38
state of change and, 68
what and how of, 68–69
Also see 14 Principles for Educational Systems Transformation

U
uncontrolled variation, 10, 115
Understanding Variation, 116, 118, 140
Union of Japanese Scientists and Engineers (JUSE), xv–xvi
United Schools Network
    2018-19 organizational chart, 5
    about, xx
    case study to improve science class, 207–13
    as a core system, 84
    development of, 50–51
    organizational history, 83
    PDSA cycles and, 19, 172–80
    process improvement teams at, 54
    remote learning at, 9–12, 15
    supra system at, 84
    system aim at, 77–79
    system and subsystem at, 78
    systems view of, 6–7, 205
    vigorous training of new teachers, 67
University of California Berkeley, 33
unknown and unknowable figures, 44–45, 55
unstable process, 11, 52
Upper Natural Process Limit (UNPL), 11, 126, 140, 150, 156, 209
U.S. News & World Report, 2

V
Value-Added Models (VAMs), 33
variation, 34, 57, 58
    case study of, 144–53
    Also see Knowledge of Variation, Theory of Variation
vicious cycle, 55–56
virtuous cycle, 55–56
vision statement, 77
Voice of the Customer, 150, 220, 232
Voice of the Process, 125, 141, 150, 220

W
W. Edwards Deming Institute, xvi
Wheeler, D., 114, 117, 118, 126, 137, 143, 153, 159
whole systems thinking, 74, 105–10
Win-Lose, 204
Win-Win philosophy, 65, 107, 203
    definition of, 204
    transformation and, 204–6
work standards, 62–64
writing fiction, 127–31, 134, 145
wrong figures, 58

X
X-charts, 139, *154*, *156*
XmR chart, 148